# The Presidency in the Era of 24-Hour News

# The Presidency in the Era of 24-Hour News

*Jeffrey E. Cohen*

PRINCETON UNIVERSITY PRESS

PRINCETON AND OXFORD

Cohen, Jeffrey E.
The presidency in the era of 24-hour news / Jeffrey E. Cohen.
p.   cm.
Includes bibliographical references and index.
ISBN: 978-0-691-13306-5 (hardcover : alk. paper)
ISBN 978-0-691-13717-9 (paperback : alk. paper)
1. Presidents—United States. 2. Mass media—Political aspects—United States. 3. Press and
politics—United States. 4. Presidents—press coverage—United States. 5. United States—Politics
and government—Press coverage. I. Title.
JK516.C5299 2008
352.230973—dc22        2007037176

British Library Cataloging-in-Publication Data is available

This book has been composed in Adobe Caslon

Printed on acid-free paper. ∞

press.princeton.edu

Printed in the United States of America

10  9  8  7  6  5  4  3  2  1

# CONTENTS

# ILLUSTRATIONS

# TABLES

Several years ago, I wrote a book, *Presidential Responsiveness and Public Policy Making*, which looked at how the president and the public affect each other's policy preferences. Nowhere in that study did I ask whether the news media affects the relationship between the president and the public. Noting the absence of the news media in my earlier work, but continuing to be interested in the relationship between the president and the mass public, I embarked on this study by asking whether the news media affect the relationship between the president and the public.

Numerous studies have contended that the news media of the late twentieth and early twenty-first centuries are a far cry from what they were like a quarter century ago. The news media of the mid 1960s to about 1980, an era of broadcast television dominance, what some call the "golden age of television" (Baum and Kernell 1999), has given way to, for want of a better term, the "age of new media." This transformation raises a question: How has the change in the news media from the broadcast to new media age affected the relationship between the president and the mass public?

To answer this question requires delimiting the transformation from the broadcast to new media age. Chapter 2 deals with this in more detail, but for now let me briefly outline the major changes in the structure of the news media. First, the degree of competition among news organizations has increased, a function in part of the proliferation of 24/7 channels on cable television in the early 1980s and the internet in the late 1990s, leading to what West (2001) describes as a highly fragmented news sector. Second, the style of news reporting has changed. Soft news increased its share of the news hole, with a corresponding decline in hard news (Patterson 2001). Most news about the president is by definition hard news. News about the president also became increasingly negative and cynical (Ragsdale 1997, 1998).

Also, the tenor of relations between presidents and reporters frayed (Kurtz 1998). Clayman et al. (2002, 2006) demonstrate that questions posed to presidents at news conferences increasingly have become challenging, adversarial, and less deferential. Question style at press conferences may be a useful indicator of general relationship patterns between presidents and journalists, especially Washington press corps journalists.

Public attention to news and attitudes toward the news media also evolved from the golden age to the new media age. In particular, public attention to the news declined over the past four decades. This is evident from analyses of public opinion surveys (Cohen 2004) as well as network news broadcast ratings (West

2001, 132), all of which is detailed later in this book. As a corollary, the audience for presidential addresses has also contracted (Baum and Kernell 1999).

Finally, public regard for the news media has eroded over the past three decades. The decline of trust in almost all major social, economic, and political institutions accounts for some of the erosion in public trust and regard for the news media. But the erosion in regard for the news media is steeper than that for other societal institutions (Cook and Gronke 2001).

The import of these changes on the presidency lies in the fact that presidents must use the news media for most of their communications efforts with the mass public. Thus the decline in news coverage of the presidency means that presidents have a harder time reaching the public through their public activities, which are designed in part to stimulate news reporting on the presidency. Moreover, the change in tone of news coverage undermines the message that the president is trying to communicate to the public through news. No longer can presidents assume that the bulk of news reporting about them will be supportive, positive, uncritical, or at least neutral. Moreover, the decline in the size of the attentive news audience affects presidential access to the broad mass public through news, and even major presidential addresses (Baum and Kernell 1999).

These changes in the structure of the news media, the tone of news coverage, public attention to the news, and public regard for the news media have implications for presidential leadership. In response to these changes in the presidential news environment, presidents have altered their leadership style. Where presidents once built a public leadership strategy that placed considerable weight on leading the broad mass public, they now place marginally less emphasis on leading the broad mass public and more on mobilizing narrower segments of the populace. This shift in leadership style has important implications for the relationship between the president and the mass public, as for democracy as well.

To organize my thinking on this topic, I rely on a concept, the *presidential news system*, which is discussed in greater detail in chapter 2. Briefly, the presidential news system is composed of the president, the mass public, the news media, and their interrelationships. The major insight of the concept is that changes in one element of this system can reverberate to affect the other elements. In this sense, this system is not static but highly dynamic. A second insight of this concept is that when studying the presidency, it is quite important to study the relationship that the president has with others in the political system, in this case the news media and the mass public.

To understand the presidency in the age of new media using the presidential news system concept requires a variety of data reflecting the interactions and relationships of the components of the system. In this study, some data are used to describe the transformation of the news media, public opinion, and presidential behavior from the golden age of broadcasting to the new media age. Other data are used to understand the linkages among the news media, public opinion, and the president, including various content analyses of news, surveys of the mass public, and indicators of presidential activities. I collected some of the data used here, but I also borrowed data from other scholars. Three people, Adam Lawrence, Thomas Patterson, and Lyn Ragsdale, allowed me to use data that they collected. I could not have conducted this research without their data. I also extensively use publicly available survey data from the American National Election Study and the General Social Survey, among other sources described in more detail in the pages that follow.

Much of the analysis presented in this book relies on highly complex and arcane statistical techniques. To avoid unduly burdening the reader, many of the more technical issues of statistical analysis have been placed in appendices that are posted on the web. Princeton University Press has provided a web link to those appendices (http://press.princeton.edu/titles/8592.html). In other instances, I have placed some of this type of material in footnotes and chapter appendices, where the interested reader may easily gain access to my design and analytic decisions, but without interrupting the basic flow of the argument and findings for readers less interested in these types of details.

## Acknowledgments

Writing a book is a collective enterprise, even if only one author's name appears on the title page. I presented pieces of the research reported in this book at seminars to the political science departments at the University of Minnesota and the University of Pittsburgh; to the American Politics Research Group, cosponsored by the Political Science Departments of the University of North Carolina and Duke University; to the Conference on researching the Public Presidency, Texas A & M University; and Joan Shorenstein Center on the Press, Politics and Public Policy, John F. Kennedy School of Government, Harvard University. I want to thank all the seminar and conference participants for their comments, many of which found their way into these pages.

A number of people either read selections and/or discussed aspects of this project with me. I thank them for my imposition on their time. They include Scott Althaus, Matthew Baum, Brandice Canes-Wrone, Jamie Druckman, George Edwards, Mathew Eshbaugh-Soha, Tim Groeling, Will Howell, Sam Kernell, and David Lewis.

I also want to thank Fordham University for providing me with a Faculty Fellowship during spring 2004 that released me from my teaching responsibilities that term and for a variety of other support and assistance. As ever, thanks to the Political Science Department of Fordham University, in particular Bruce Berg, chair of the department, for providing a congenial place to work, and Rich Fleisher, for his collegiality and interest in this project.

I also want to thank the readers for Princeton University Press, David Barker and Scott Althaus, who offered numerous constructive suggestions that improved this book, including its argument, analysis, and presentation. The editorial and production team at Princeton University Press deserves a special thank you, especially my editor Chuck Myers. Chuck has been very patient with me, guiding me through the various stages of preparing this research for publication. He is a true scholar's editor, and his sound advice is always worth listening to.

And as ever, Phyllis deserves special mention for putting up with me and my moods while working on this book.

The Presidency in the Era of 24-Hour News

# CHAPTER 1

# The Growing Disconnect between Presidential News Coverage and Public Opinion

The news media are no longer as consequential in helping to frame public opinion toward the president as they were a generation ago. This decline in the impact of news media on public opinion about the president is puzzling given the increasing access to news because of such developments as the 24/7 cable news networks and the internet. The aims of this book are to address this puzzle—the declining impact of news on public evaluations of the president—and to provide an explanation that accounts for it.

This initial chapter serves two purposes. First, I demonstrate that news coverage of the president over the past quarter century or so does not affect public attitudes toward the president as much as it did during the previous twenty years. To demonstrate this point, I first turn to the three great scandals of the modern presidency, Clinton-Lewinsky, Iran-Contra, and Watergate. Each episode produced large volumes of negative news, but for a variety of reasons, negative news seemed not to touch Bill Clinton as deeply as Richard Nixon or Ronald Reagan.

Then, using more systematic data, I show that for the period beginning roughly in the mid to late 1970s, no correlation exists between the negativity of presidential news and public approval of the president. This stands in sharp contrast to the twenty-five years prior, roughly the late 1940s until the mid 1970s, when there was a strong correlation between the tone of presidential news and presidential approval—a negative tone is associated with lower approval. Why did the correlation between news coverage and public approval seemingly vanish?

The second task of this chapter is to introduce an explanation to account for this disconnect between the tonality of news and presidential approval. My argument, briefly, is that the presidential news system—the web of relationships among the president, the news media, and the mass public—has evolved in such a way that news coverage about the president no longer resonates so strongly with the mass public. Moreover, these changes in the presidential news system also affect the nature of presidential leadership, which has consequences for the larger political system. The chapters that follow document the evolution of the presidential news system and detail the implications of this evolution for American politics and governing in the late twentieth and early twenty-first century.

## Three Scandals and the Public Response

### *The Clinton–Lewinsky Scandal*

By almost any standard of presidential scandal, 1998 was a horrible year for the sitting president. On January 19, 1998, the internet site, the Drudge Report, mentioned that *Newsweek* magazine was sitting on a story that President Clinton had an affair with former White House intern Monica Lewinsky.[1] In the ensuing days, the mainstream news media began to run stories on the allegations. This set off the political firestorm that was to become the Monica Lewinsky scandal, which led to the impeachment of President Clinton.

Impeachment proceedings began formally on December 11, 1998, when, after many months of investigation and hearings, the House Judiciary Committee voted on several impeachment resolutions and sent four articles of impeachment to the House.[2] The House voted to proceed with impeachment on December 19, and the impeachment trial began in the Senate on January 7, 1999. It continued until February 12, when votes on the articles of impeachment were taken, with the president acquitted. On all counts, the vote broke narrowly in Clinton's favor, as Democrats stood steadfast behind him, while from five to ten Republicans also supported his acquittal on the various votes.[3]

From January 1998 until his acquittal, Clinton received a steady stream of bad press. Clinton was known for having bad relations with the press (Kurtz 1998), but the degree of press negativity escalated to new heights during 1998 and early 1999. Thomas Patterson (2000) has collected some data that gives us a sense of the tone or valence of news in 1998 compared to other years. Patterson randomly sampled five thousand news stories from Lexus-Nexus from 1980 through 1998. These data cast a wide net beyond stories on the presidency, and the number of presidential stories per year is modest, which precludes making definitive statements about news coverage of the presidency. Yet because of the long time span and the random selection of stories, we can gather a sense of the comparative tone of news reporting on the presidency across these nearly two decades.

Figure 1.1 traces the percentage of news stories about the president and various administrations from 1980 that Patterson coded "clearly negative" or "more negative than positive." As the figure demonstrates, 1998 stood out in the degree of negative news reports. Only 1987, the year of the Iran-Contra scandal, produced a higher percentage of negative stories. Even 1994, the year of Clinton's ill-fated health care initiative, itself a bad press year for Clinton at 58 percent, is still less negative than 1998 by nearly 10 percent.

What is so remarkable about these figures is not that Clinton received so much bad press in 1998, but that his job approval polls rose that year. As figure 1.2 shows, Clinton's polls spiked upward in early 1998, as the scandal became public, reaching a high note in February 1998 at 67 percent (based on averaging the Gallup polls of that month). His polls deteriorated somewhat thereafter,

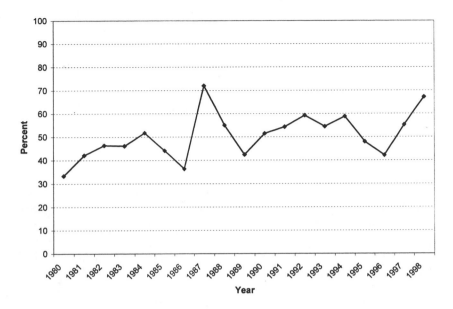

Figure 1.1 Percentage of negative news stories about the president, 1980–98. Source: Patterson (2000).

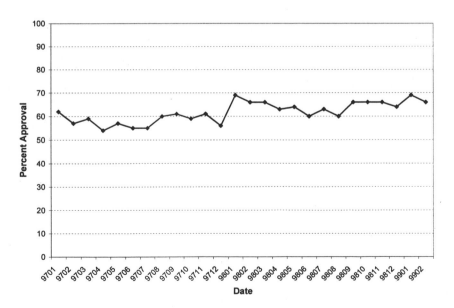

Figure 1.2 President Clinton's monthly approval, 1997–98 (Gallup polls).

sliding to 60 percent by June 1998, but recovered to 65 by the end of the year, reaching a peak of 73 percent in Gallup's December 19–20, 1998, reading. According to Gallup, on February 12, 1999, the day of the Senate vote, Clinton's poll ratings stood at a lofty 68 percent.

We must be careful not to conclude that the scandal helped the president's polls. In a careful analysis, Brian Newman (2002) finds that the scandal depressed Clinton's polls. He estimates (796) that in February 1998, Clinton lost 1.2 points due to the scandal and that poll losses accumulated over the year, cumulating in a 7 percent loss by February 1999. Shah et al. (2002) also find that news about the scandal hurt the president, with the type of scandal news making a difference. While scandal stories that mentioned the president drove Clinton's poll numbers down, stories about his opponents, for instance, Ken Starr, and stories framed as strategic moves by conservatives against the president had the opposite effect, uplifting his polls. Despite the volume of negative press that he received, Clinton was helped during the scandal by the even greater share of negative news about his adversaries, such as Ken Starr.[4] Other aspects of public opinion, in particular likes and dislikes, also sometimes called favorability, also declined across 1998 (Cohen 1999a, 1999b, 2000).

Overall, Clinton's polls weathered the storms of 1998 and early 1999 quite successfully. Despite the depressing effects that bad news seems to have had (Newman 2002, Shah 2002), Clinton's aggregate poll ratings remained quite high throughout the year. That Clinton's ratings hovered in the 60–70 percent band through the year in a relatively steady pattern suggests that other factors, such as economic performance (Newman 2002) and countervailing news stories that cast the president's antagonists in a poor light offset the negative effects of the scandal on the president's polls. In other words, it appears that scandal news did not dominate thinking about the president (Popkin 1998) despite its volume and tone.

## Watergate

The public response to the Clinton scandal and news about the president during 1998 differs considerably from the public response to the other two major scandals of the modern era, Watergate and Iran-Contra.[5] The Watergate scandal, which led to Richard Nixon resigning from the presidency on August 9, 1974, began nearly three years earlier, in September 1971, when Daniel Ellsberg's doctor's office was broken into. Several months later, on January 17, 1972, Washington police were called when the Democratic National Committee (DNC) headquarters at the Watergate complex was burglarized. Yet, the scandal did not become a public concern until August 1, 1972, when Bob Woodward and Carl Bernstein published their first article in the *Washington Post* tying the break-ins to the administration. We can mark August 1972 as the beginning of the public phase of the Watergate scandal, which ended two years later with Nixon's resignation.

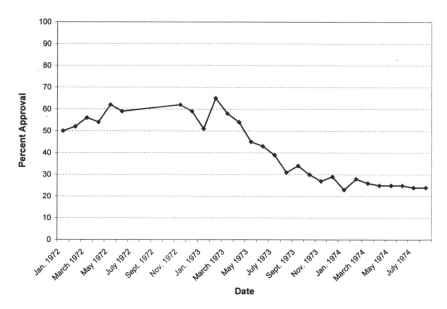

Figure 1.3 President Nixon's monthly approval, January 1972–August 1974 (Gallup polls).

Figure 1.3 plots Nixon's approval polls by month, beginning with January 1972 and ending with his resignation in August 1974. Consistent with the idea that little bad news about the scandal was aired during the remainder of 1972, we see in figure 1.3 that the president's polls remained essentially flat, hovering in the 60 percent range.

However, negative news began to accumulate as events related to the scandal became more common and as Watergate became a major news story. In a content analysis of presidential news in the *New York Times* from 1949 to 1992, Lyn Ragsdale found that in 1973 and 1974 more than 50 percent of the news that the president received could be coded as negative. This was 20 percent more bad news than any president had received up to that time.[6] Moreover, the volume of Watergate news was quite heavy. Ostrom and Simon (1989, 365) estimate that the *New York Times* ran Watergate-related front page stories on 74.6 percent of days between March 23, 1973, and August 9, 1974, the day Nixon resigned. The effects of the bad news are easily apparent in figure 1.3. After reaching a poll reading of 65 percent in January 1973, Nixon's polls slid steadily over the next twelve months, touching 25 percent by January 1974. His polls never broke 30 percent thereafter. In contrast to Clinton, whose polls rose during his scandal-ridden year, Nixon's sank, and sank deeply, as one would naturally expect.[7]

## Iran–Contra

Ronald Reagan's travails in 1986 and 1987, during the Iran-Contra scandal, also seemed to follow the classic story of a major scandal harming presidential approval ratings.[8] On November 21, 1986, the Justice Department began an investigation of the National Security Council (NSC) over charges that money from an arms sale to Iran were diverted to the Nicaraguan Contras, in violation of federal law. Unlike Nixon, who stonewalled the Watergate investigators, Reagan took swift action once the Justice Department revealed that it held documentary evidence of the Iran-Contra connection, which consisted of a memo by NSC staffer Oliver North.

On November 26, President Reagan convened an independent commission, to be headed by former Senator John Tower (R-Texas), to investigate the allegations, and in mid December the Senate set its own committee to investigate the Iran-Contra affair. The Tower commission submitted its report to the president in late February 1987, criticizing the president for not controlling his NSC staff. In July, the major Iran-Contra participants, Oliver North and John Poindexter, testified before Congress, and in November, Congress issued a report critical of the president. Unlike Watergate and Lewinsky, Congress declined to take further action against the president. Although this ended Iran-Contra as a major news story, its effects on presidential approval persisted for some time afterward.

Figure 1.4 plots Reagan's polls from his second inaugural (January 1985) through the end of his second term. The plot shows a sharp decline in Reagan's approval from 63 percent in October 1986 to 45 percent by March 1987. Ostrom and Simon (1989, 377) estimate that Iran-Contra depressed Reagan's polls by about 12.5 percentage points and that the effects of Iran-Contra persisted well into 1987. Reagan's polls stayed flat, ranging between 40 and 50 percent until late 1988, and only began to rise to the upper 50 percents near the end of his term.

Despite Reagan's label, the "Teflon president," to whom no bad news would stick, news seemed quite negative toward Reagan during this two-year span. Patterson's Lexis-Nexis data (figure 1.1) indicate a bad news spike in 1987 that rivals 1998. Ragsdale's data also indicate a high volume of negative news (figure 1.5). By her count, about 52 percent of news stories in the *New York Times* were negative in 1987 compared to 26 percent the year before and 29 percent the year after. Ostrom and Simon (1989, 365) report that the *Times* ran front page stories about Iran-Contra on 76 percent of days from November 8, 1986, and August 31, 1987, a volume similar to that for Watergate. Again we have some circumstantial evidence that a scandal led to bad news, which seemed to affect presidential polls.

This presents us with a puzzle: Why didn't the Lewinsky scandal and impeachment hurt Bill Clinton's standing with the public more than it did? Al-

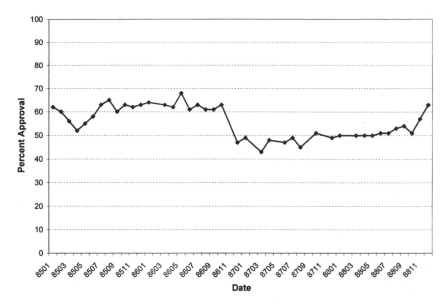

Figure 1.4  President Reagan's monthly approval, January 1985–December 1988 (Gallup polls).

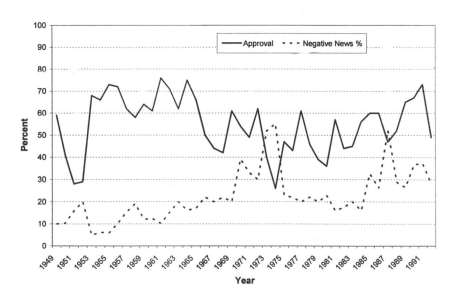

Figure 1.5  Trends in presidential approval and news tone, *New York Times*, 1949–92.

though one may argue that Reagan defused the Iran-Contra scandal by admitting responsibility and taking action, Reagan's poll loss of 12.5 points (Ostrom-Simon 1989 estimate) resembles Nixon's poll loss from Watergate (16–17 percent, Newman 2002) more than the 6–7 percent loss that Newman (2002) estimates Clinton suffered.[9] One may even claim that Clinton's stonewalling resembled Nixon's behavior in the face of scandal. Another distinguishing factor is that Congress refused to take any action against Reagan, unlike the impeachment processes that targeted Nixon and Clinton. By refusing to act against Reagan, Congress may have minimized the damage done to Reagan in the public's eyes. Still, it is puzzling that Clinton did not suffer more with the public than he did.

This book is not an attempt to understand public reactions to these three scandals. They serve merely as illustrations of the larger point that I will try to make, that the structure of the relationships between the president, the news media, and the public fundamentally changed during the years from the mid to late 1970s to the present. News during this period may not have had as big of an impact on public thinking toward the president as it had during the two decades or so before.

First let us review some of the more common explanations for the relatively mild public reaction to the Clinton-Lewinsky scandal. As I will show, while each makes a useful point, none can account for the differing public reaction across these three major scandals.

## The Lewinsky Scandal: Explanations of the Public Reaction

The Monica Lewinsky scandal and impeachment of Bill Clinton stand in sharp contrast to the Watergate and Iran-Contra scandals. Where presidential approval fell during the two earlier scandals, Bill Clinton's polls rose in the aggregate. And even if we prefer Newman's (2002) finding that the scandal depressed Clinton's polls, it did so less severely than Nixon's and Reagan's poll losses as a result of Watergate and Iran-Contra.

Many theories have been offered to account for Clinton's ability to weather the storm of scandal and congressional attack in 1998. As the literature is voluminous, here I only address the major explanations, which can be roughly categorized into accounts that look at presidential character and the public response, the policy success of the Clinton administration, and public disdain for the news media's reporting of the Lewinsky scandal and impeachment.[10]

First, some argue that the public distinguishes between the public performance of president and the person in office and that the public does not care much about personal character. As Kagay argues, "The American public made an immediate distinction between Clinton the man on the one hand, and Clinton the president, on the other hand. People could be sharply critical of the man and his behavior even at the same time they thought that as president he was doing a pretty good job" (1999, 450–51). Zaller makes the point even more forcefully, "The public is, within broad limits, functionally indifferent to presidential character" (1998a, 188), and goes on to point out that the public elected Richard Nixon despite concerns that the public had with Nixon's character.

There are limitations to this perspective. One, proponents of this perspective spend little time discussing what they mean by presidential character. Character is complex and multidimensional. Pfiffner (2004), for instance, sees three different, although related, aspects of character—lies, keeping promises, and sexual probity. It is possible that the public cares about some character traits more than others: for example, that lying may matter more than sexual probity. Then why did the public disregard the numerous instances of Clinton's lies (assuming that he in fact lied), as Renshon (2002a, 2002b) asserts? Moreover, if Nixon's character mattered so little to the public, why did his polls fall in the wake of Watergate? Last, several studies, using survey evidence, find that character affects approval of the president even when controlling for a variety of other factors (Greene 2001, Newman 2003), results that contradict the position that character does not matter.

This leads to a related argument—when it comes to personal behavior or character, the public distinguishes between public and private matters. Thus the public could have viewed Watergate as a public matter but the Clinton scandal as a private matter, which could account for the different public reactions to the two scandals. Kagay (1999, 454–55) presents evidence that the public viewed the Lewinsky scandal as a private matter and that the public tolerated Clinton's lying about the affair, even to a grand jury, as what one might expect of any man caught in a similar circumstance. No comparable evidence exists on whether the public viewed Watergate as a public matter, leaving us unable to test this hypothesis.

Another character-related hypothesis contends that the public was used to scandal stories about Clinton, that it knew that Clinton had character issues, and thus the revelations about Lewinsky were old hat, adding nothing new to people's assessment of the president (Kagay 1999; Kulkarni, Stough, and Haynes 1999). But if the public had character issues with Nixon, as Zaller (1998) argues, why should the Watergate revelations have had such a deep impact? By Zaller's reckoning, the public should have discounted Watergate, basing its support for Nixon on his policy performance.

A second set of arguments, which are not inconsistent with the above, is that the public cares more about performance than character. Several studies point to the high marks that the public gave to Clinton for the state of the economy and other policies (Andolina and Wilcox 2000, Kagay 1999, Miller 1999, Newman 2002, Zaller 1998a). While this might explain why Clinton's polls were higher than Nixon's, it fails to account for the plunge that Reagan's polls took during Iran-Contra, a period when the economy was also riding relatively high and the public thought well of Reagan as president.

Nor does this performance perspective answer why the Clinton scandals hurt so little compared to Nixon and Reagan. Recall that Newman's (2002) analysis controlled for the state of the economy and still found that Clinton's scandal had less impact on his poll ratings than Watergate and Iran-Contra had on Nixon's and Reagan's. Perhaps, as some suggest (Kagay 1999), the public did not want to lose Clinton's leadership and thus rallied to his side. But the same could be said of Reagan, yet Reagan's polls took a deep slide.

Another set of ideas looks to the public reaction to news reports on the scandal. Polls during the period indicate that the public disliked the way that the media reported on the scandal, which the public thought was overly critical of and unfair to the president (Kagay 1999, Miller 1999). In contrast, during the Watergate period, the public gave the press relatively high marks. For instance, a Roper poll of June 1974 found 47 percent saying that the news media were properly balanced in their treatment of Nixon, 14 percent thought them to be considerate to the president, and only 30 percent saw the news media as unfair.

The media perspective may help us address why the public reacted less sharply to the Lewinsky scandal than Watergate, but in making this point, we need to ask what accounts for the shift in public reactions to the news from Watergate to Clinton-Lewinsky? Is there something different about the two scandals or about the way that the news media reported on the two scandals that led to these differing public reactions? Studies, reviewed in more detail below (e.g., Bennett et al. 1998; Cook and Gronke 2001, 2002; Cook, Gronke, and Ratliff 2000; Robinson and Kohut 1988), show that public regard for the news media drastically declined from the 1970s to the 1990s. Perhaps the explanation for the changing public reaction resides more in factors that affect public evaluations of the news media than any differences in the Watergate, Iran-Contra, and Lewinsky scandals.

None of the above explanations provides a totally satisfying answer to the question of why the public reaction to the Lewinsky scandal pales in comparison to its reaction to Watergate or Iran-Contra. For the most part, analyses of public reactions to the Lewinsky scandal are case studies of that event and not comparative analyses across the scandals. An answer to the question of differences in public reactions to Watergate, Iran-Contra, and the Lewinsky scandal requires a comparative analysis, but few such studies exist.[11]

There is a second and, for my purposes, perhaps more important limitation of analyses of the public reaction to the Clinton-Lewinsky scandal. The puzzle that I seek to address is why bad news about that scandal did not greatly affect public evaluations of the president. Analyses of public reactions to the Clinton-Lewinsky scandal assume that there is something unique about that scandal, the time period, and possibly other factors that somewhat immunized the public from the bad news. But as demonstrated in the next section, for the past twenty years or so, bad news *in general* does not seem to affect public evaluations of the president very strongly, at least compared to its effects on public thinking two decades ago. In fact, there does not seem to be a correlation between bad news and lower approval. The analyses of the public reaction to the Clinton-Lewinsky scandal, inasmuch as they view that event as unique, cannot explain this more general tendency of the last several decades.

## The Disjuncture between News and Presidential Approval: The Puzzle Generalized

My argument is that structural changes have occurred in the president-press-public sector of the political system, what I will call the *presidential news system*. These structural changes began to emerge in the mid to late 1970s, fully embedding into the body politic by the 1990s. Because of these changes, news and public opinion about the president decoupled. In other words, news reporting about the president lost some of its ability to shape public opinion toward the president. If this structural argument is correct, then Bill Clinton's experience in 1998 is not an isolated case, but merely an extreme example of the nature of the relationship among the president, the press, and the public in the 1990s.

Figure 1.5, already noted, plots two series that will help sort out the relationship between presidential news and public opinion. The first series plots the percentage of negative news stories about the president as reported in the *New York Times* from 1949 to 1992.[12] The second series plots the president's annual approval level from the Gallup poll. There are important limitations in using these data. First, the news tone data end with 1992. Thus we cannot say much about the years following 1992. But it appears safe to assume that the processes that changed the relationship between news and approval, which began in the 1970s, are likely still present, and perhaps more firmly embedded in the political system after 1992 than before. Second, and perhaps more important, the data are highly aggregated. Thus we cannot be very precise about the relationship between news tone and presidential approval. But still these data allow us to see if the two series are related as one would expect.

Our simple expectation is that the higher the volume of negative news, the lower the president's approval (Brody 1991). Visual inspection of the two series reveal that the two tend to diverge for the first half of the series, but sometime in the mid to late 1970s, negative news and approval began to track together. Across the 1950s and 1960s and into the 1970s, when presidential approval is high, negative news is low, and visa versa. After the mid 1970s, except for a few time points, like 1987 (Iran-Contra), when presidential approval moves up, so does the percentage of negative news.

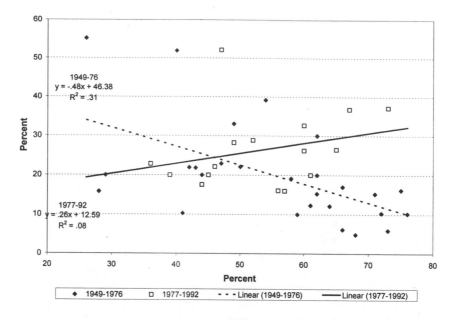

Figure 1.6 Scatter plot of presidential approval and news tone, *New York Times*, 1949–92. Source: News Tone, Ragsdale (1997); Approval, Gallup poll.

Visual inspection is fraught with all sorts of problems, although it is useful in providing a feel or sense of the data. Regression analysis reveals that the two series are, as one would expect, negatively related.[13] Based on the regression analysis, each 1 percentage increase in negative news will lower the president's approval rating by about 0.4 percent. This result is statistically significant and indicates that approval is highly responsive to news tone. But when we bisect the series into two subperiods, 1949–76 and 1977–92, the relationship between news tone and approval differs. Figure 1.6 plots presidential news tone and approval, separating the two periods. Filled diamonds represent the 1949–76 years, while white boxes represent the 1977–92 years.[14] Separate regression lines for each time segment are overlaid in the figure.

From 1949 through 1976, negative news clearly depresses presidential approval. The two series are correlated at −0.56 (p = .00) and the regression line slopes downward sharply. Regression analysis indicates that each 1 percentage point increase in negative news leads to a 0.66 percentage point loss in presidential approval. This simple relationship accounts for nearly one-third of the variance in presidential approval. News tone for these years varies from a low of about 5 to a high of 55. This fifty-point range in negative news tone can account for as much as a 33 percentage point shift in presidential approval (50 * 0.66 = 33). A change of one standard deviation in negative news tone (9.6) translates into about a 6.4 percentage point shift in presidential approval. The average yearly shift, however, is quite small at 0.4 percentage points. Still there are some large year-to-year shifts in news tone (1972–73, 1974–75). Thus while year-to-year shifts in presidential news tone tend to be small in this early period, occasionally massive changes in news tone do occur. By all accounts, presidential approval, even highly aggregated into annual units, appears quite sensitive to the tone of presidential news, again highly aggregated.

The relationship between approval and news tone for 1977–92 differs. Figure 1.6 indicates relatively little impact of news tone on approval. The regression line is flat (b = 0.31, t = 1.10). Moreover the two series correlate at 0.28, which is not significant (p = 0.28), and only a small amount of the variance is accounted for when regressing approval on news tone.[15] In contrast to the strong impact of news tone on presidential approval in the pre-1977 era, from 1977 to 1992 news tone appears to have no impact on presidential approval. Strangely, if we remove 1987 from the analysis, the year that the Iran-Contra scandal became public and began to affect public opinion toward Ronald Reagan, we find a strong *positive* relationship between the amount of negative news and presidential approval, just the opposite of what one would expect. The regression slope is 0.90 without 1987 included, which is statistically significant (p = 0.02) despite the small n (15) and accounts for about one-third of the variance in approval (equation F = 6.65, probability of F = 0.02). It makes little sense to argue that bad news about the president lifts his approval. Instead, it appears that bad news during the years since about 1977 has little impact on presidential approval, except under certain circumstances.[16]

Other evidence also points to the decoupling of news tone on presidential approval. In a recent paper, Gaines and Roberts (2005) construct a weekly measure of presidential approval for George W. Bush from January 21, 2001, to February 27, 2005, 215 weeks. Their analysis includes a weekly news tone measure based on *Newsweek*'s reporting of the president, as well as controls for events, major presidential addresses, the honeymoon effect, and the economy. They find, consistent with the analysis of annual data presented above, that news tone has no effect on George W. Bush's approval during his first four years in office.

This book is an attempt to understand why news has lost its ability to affect public attitudes toward the presidency. Clinton's experience in 1998 is not an isolated incident. Rather, it is but an extreme example of processes at work beginning in the last quarter of the twentieth century and seemingly present as we enter the twenty-first century.

## The Argument

The decoupling between the tone of the news and presidential approval from approximately the mid to late 1970s to the present challenges many widely held assumptions about the role of news in shaping opinions. Brody's (1991) seminal study, *Assessing the President*, argues that the balance of positive and negative news about the president will affect public attitudes toward the president. When the news leans in a negative direction, presidential approval should dip (also Erikson, MacKuen, and Stimson 2002). The Brody approach suggests that Clinton's approval should have declined in 1998, yet it rose! Our existing theories and understandings of the relationship among the news, the presidency, and public opinion cannot explain why Bill Clinton's approval rose in 1998 or apparently did not suffer very much (Newman 2002).

The world has changed considerably over the past twenty to twenty-five years. In this book I will discuss several interrelated changes that have implications for the role of news in politics, opportunities for presidential leadership, and public opinion, especially with regard to the presidency. These changes are (1) the structure of the news industry, (2) the content of news about the president, (3) the audience for news, and (4) public regard toward the news media.

The news industry is now more competitive than it was two decades ago. Competition has accelerated the trend away from objective reporting toward a more interpretative and cynical news style (West 2001). Political commentary, which is often disguised as news, is now also more prevalent than was once the case. The public has reacted to these changes, too. The audience for news shrank.[17] West, for instance, reports that the percentage of households that watched the ABC, CBS, and/or NBC evening news declined from about 60 percent across the 1960s to 30 percent by the late 1990s (2001).[18] Availability of entertainment programming on cable has peeled away a large segment of the broadcast news audience (Baum and Kernell 1999). Partially as a reaction to the new style of news, public regard for the news media has plummeted.

During the "golden age" of presidential television, roughly the 1960s through mid to late 1970s, the press tended to be deferential to the president (Clayman et al. 2002, 2006).[19] Thus, when the press reported news to the public that was critical of the president or indicated a problem associated with the president, what we might consider negative news, the public paid heed and began the process of reevaluating its views of the president. In other words, because the media tended to be deferential to the president, negative news, which was rare or unexpected, was also credible to the public. Patterson's Lexis-Nexis data, discussed above (figure 1.1), and Ragsdale's 1949–92 time series (figure 1.5), indicate that presidential news has gotten more negative from the 1980s through the 1990s.

Furthermore, the news media was highly concentrated, with the three major networks not only dominating people's news, but providing essentially the same news and same tone as their competitors. Last, the news audience was abnormally large during the precable television era because of the limited viewing choices. Thus the negative news signal reached a large audience. The combination of strong credible news signal and the large audience meant that negative news could affect public support for the president.

All of this changed with the advent of cable television and other communication media, including VCRs and the internet. The news audience shrank as other viewing choices became available. The news media, because of greater competition and declining audience shares, as well as other factors, became increasingly negative toward the president (see the data on figures 1.1 and 1.5, also Patterson 2000). Rather than being deferential, cynicism, and sometimes outright hostility, became the norm of the media toward the president (Clayman et al. 2002, 2006; West, 2001). The norm of negative or critical news had important implications for the public. It meant that the public could no longer tell, when faced with negative news, if that news was truly bad or if it was just typical journalistic reporting. In other words, the news signal to the public became noisy and unreliable. This noisiness, coupled with the smaller news audience, meant that news in general will have a smaller impact on public opinion.

In the "new media" era that began sometime in the mid to late 1970s, one last process also transpired.[20] The variety of news choices allowed viewers to find news and other programming that fit their tastes. Talk radio, which emerged as an important forum in the mid 1980s, seemed to attract conservative listeners. Some cable networks became known for a brand of news, like Fox, which began broadcasting only in 1996, with its reputation for conservatively slanted news.[21] Moreover, entertainment values entered into some news formats, such as *Crossfire* and other programs, where political pundits of obvious ideological and partisan leanings presented their opinions. People tuned into programs with compatible political leanings. These shows often merely reinforced preexisting political values.

Pure entertainment programs also began to present some political content, whether the comedy routines of the late night talk shows or daytime talk shows. Political information in typically nonpolitical, nonnews shows may have high credibility among some viewers. Thus where traditional news may have lost its impact on public opinion, these other niches in broadcasting may be able to influence their audiences' political attitudes (Baum 2003a).

Thus the declining news impact on public thinking about the president resulted because the news media provided less news about the president than it once did, the audience for news is smaller, the public is less trusting of the news media than it once was, and the regularity of negative news makes it hard for the public to tell if the bad news reflects truly bad conditions that it should pay attention to or if it merely reflects the agenda of journalists. As detailed below, some of these same factors also limit the president's ability to lead the public writ broadly. As their ability to lead the mass public has eroded, presidents have altered their leadership style, increasing the amount of effort used to mobilize special interests, narrower publics, and/or their own partisan base, while decreasing their engagement with the broad mass public. These changes in presidential leadership style have important implications for our democracy.

## Plan of the Book

The presidential news system—the interrelationships among the president, the press, and the public—serves as the organizing concept for this research. In chapter 2 I present and discuss the presidential news system concept, and then trace the evolution of the presidential news system from the golden age of presidential television of the 1950s through the mid 1970s to the new media age of the mid 1970s to the present.

In the next four chapters I look at trends in news coverage of the presidency, one of the major changes that occurred from the golden age to the new media age. In chapter 3 I chart the decline in the amount of news coverage of politics and the presidency using a variety of indicators across different news media.

In chapter 4 I present and analyze a new data series on presidential news coverage in the *New York Times* that stretches back to the mid nineteenth century. That series not only documents the drop off in the amount of presidential news over the past quarter century but puts this decline into context of trends in presidential news coverage across a century and a half, in which, up to the mid 1970s, the amount of presidential news steadily climbed. The analysis presented in this chapter indicates that something unique to the new media age seems to account for this relatively recent decline in the amount of presidential news.

In chapter 5 I document the increasing negativity in the tone of presidential news from the golden age to the new media age, using a variety of data sources, including the Patterson and Ragsdale series presented in figures 1.1 and 1.5 in this chapter. In chapters 5 and 6 I assess why presidential news has turned so negative in the age of new media. In chapter 5 I analyze the Ragsdale series, based on the *New York Times* from 1949 through 1992. Again we find that something about the rise of the new media age accounts for this trend in presidential news.

In chapter 6 I analyze the Patterson data, which is based on a sample of five thousand news stories from 1980 to 1999. All of these years are in the new media age, obviating any attempt at comparison between the golden age and the new media age. But here we have data on individual news stories, not aggregates of stories, like the Ragsdale series. This allows us to paint a more refined picture of the content of presidential news in the new media age.

In the next two chapters I shift gears and look at the mass public. In chapter 7, relying heavily on American National Election Studies data, but also reporting the results of other data collections, I outline and analyze the decline in news consumption in the mass public, another important trend. As other analyses reveal, something intrinsic to the new media age seems to help explain the decline in the size of the audience for news, at least of the traditional and major news media.

The public's regard for the news media has also eroded. In chapter 8 I document this erosion by presenting data from a number of sources while also analyzing the sources of the decline in regard for the news media. That analysis uses General Social Survey data from the mid 1970s to the late 1990s, as well as more recent American National Election Study data. Again something about the new media age seems implicated as a source of this trend.

In chapter 9 I look at the impact of these changes on the presidency. Due to the changes in news coverage of the presidency and public use of the news, the style of presidential leadership of the public has changed. In the new media age, presidents devote more time to mobilizing specialized constituencies and less time to engaging the broad mass public than they did in the broadcasting age. I test this notion in this chapter.

Finally, in chapter 10 I conclude by assessing the impact of this new media system on the democratic linkage role of the news media, the style of presidential leadership, and the quality of American democracy in the late twentieth and early twenty-first centuries.

# CHAPTER 2

# The Presidential News System during the Golden Age of Presidential Television

## Introduction

The previous chapter raised this puzzle: beginning around the late 1970s and continuing until the present, the tone of presidential news no longer appears to affect public evaluations of the president. During this period, it matters little to the public whether news about the president is good or bad for assessing the president. This differs starkly from the previous several decades (e.g., the 1950s through the 1970s), when public approval of the president covaried strongly with the tone of presidential news. The aim of this book is to provide an explanation for this disconnect between the tone of the news and public support of the president. My argument is that we have entered an age of new media, a process that began in the mid to late 1970s and that we are still in that age of new media. The changes associated with the rise of the new media age have led to this disconnect between news and approval of the president.

For analytic purposes it is useful to distinguish two eras, the golden age of television, approximately from the 1950s through the mid to late 1970s (Baum and Kernell 1999), and the age of new media, spanning approximately from the mid to late 1970s to the present. These two eras roughly correspond to Blumler and Kavanagh's (1999) second and third ages of political communication. To make sense of how the transformation from the age of broadcasting to the new media age affects the president, the public, and the press, I develop a new concept, termed the *presidential news system*. The bulk of the research presented in this book shows how the transformation from the broadcasting to the new media age affected this presidential news system.

## The Evolution of Political Communication Systems across the Twentieth and Early Twenty-first Centuries

Blumler and Kavanagh (1999) provide a useful starting point for understanding the evolution from the broadcasting or television age of roughly the early 1950s through the mid to late 1970s, into the new media age, which began in the mid to late 1970s and persists to this day. Blumler and Kavanagh employ less descriptive labels for these two eras, which they call the *second* and *third* eras of political communications.

Blumler and Kavanagh (1999) describe a first age of communication, which lasted roughly for the two decades after the end of World War II (211), an era they describe as dominated by parties. In the second era television emerged as a major factor in political communication. The arrival of cable television, the internet, and other technologies ushered in the third age. Blumler and Kavanagh do not provide specific time periods for the three ages, suggesting a secular change from one era to the next, meaning that the different eras overlap for a time, as the early era gives way slowly to the new era.

Further, as British scholars, their discussion focuses heavily on events taking place in Great Britain, and secondarily in the United States. Although the trends they identify in general seem to apply equally well across the two nations, and perhaps others, there are some differences in terms of specific factors associated with the several ages, the relative weight of factors in defining the ages of political communication, and the timing of the emergence of new eras and dissipation of old eras. For instance, the second age may have arrived earlier in the United States than Great Britain because of the faster diffusion of television, which had become commonplace in American homes by the late 1950s, somewhat earlier than for Great Britain. Still, their broad outline of what distinguishes the three eras is applicable to the United States and helps inform my discussion that follows, even if I use the terms *golden* or *broadcasting* or *television age* and *new media age* rather than second and third age.

Several characteristics mark the second age of political communication in Blumler and Kavanagh's scheme. These include (1) the diminished importance of political-party-based messages and communications, (2) the rise of limited channel or network broadcast television for political communications, (3) the growth in the size of the audience for political communication because of the diffusion of television, and (4) the replacement of long-term influences on politics, like party identification, with short-term influences, like current events, because of television. This replacement of long-term by short-term influences boosted the importance of personalized aspects of politics, such as candidate traits, over long-standing political organizations, like political parties (1999, 212–13).

The rise of the third era is associated with five major changes. These include the rising professionalization of political advocacy, as seen in the growing importance of professional political advisers, pollsters, speechwriters, and the like. Also important is an increased competitive pressure on journalists, in part a consequence of the greater exposure of newsrooms to market forces and the financial concerns of their larger parent organizations. A third characteristic of the third age is the rise of anti-elitism and populism in communications and journalism, which we see for instance in the rise of populist forums such as talk shows on television and especially radio; interviews with average people about their reactions to major events that sprinkle many news reports; increasing use of poll results as news; and blogs, among other publishing forms on the internet. This populist emergence has undermined the authority of hierarchical organizations in society, such as the establishment press (e.g., *New York Times*). Fourth, a diversification of news media and communications media character- izes the third age. Unlike the second age, where centripetal or centralizing forces held greater sway over the political communications system, this diversi- fication fosters centrifugal forces within society and politics. Finally, Blumler and Kavanagh identify a change in the structure of the audience for political content, noting, for instance, the fragmentation of the audience and its exposure to "bits and pieces of information" that it picks up "here and there," which may lead to a less integrated, less contextualized understanding of political affairs.

Blumler and Kavanagh's discussion helps to organized and make sense of many changes in political communications and will help guide the research that follows, but it provides little direct guidance for understanding the puzzle that motivates this research. Such guidance will come from a new concept, the presidential news system.

## The Presidential News System

Our puzzle, the decreasing impact of news tone on public evaluations of the president, requires that we understand the relationships among three actors— the news media, the mass public, and the president—and how the transforma- tion of the broadcasting age to the new media age affected those relationships. Thus rather than speak of changes in the mass public or the news media or presidential behavior in isolation from each other, it is useful to understand how changes in one actor affect the others. The web of interrelationships among the president, the news media, and the mass public is what I will call the *presidential news system*.[1] The notion of a presidential news system is analyt- ically useful, in part, because it calls attention to the mutual needs of one actor in the system for the others.

### Presidential Needs

To lead the public, the president requires access to the public. Beyond access, his message must also be persuasive. To be persuasive, the president must be able to capture public attention, focus the public's attention on the issue at hand, and convince the public to follow his (or her) lead, either by agreeing with him on what should be done or by allowing him to do what he deems best.

Presidents may gain access by addressing the nation with a prime-time speech. Major, prime-time addresses are useful in capturing public attention and focusing that attention. That a president would spend the time and energy to prepare a major speech and deliver it to the nation when he could be doing something else signals to the public that the topic of the address is important. Moreover, that the networks allow the president's speech to preempt normal entertainment programming signals to the public that the networks consider the president's speech important enough to supersede regular programming. With the public tuned in and attentive to what the president says, the quality of the president's speech, the types of arguments that he offers, as well as the public's preexisting attitudes on the issue at hand will affect whether or not the president is persuasive (Edwards 2003).

Not only do presidents want to lead the public on issues; presidents also want to promote an image before the public. Presidents aim to present their best qualities to the public, but also to symbolically link themselves as the person in office to the office and all that the office means to the public—its constitutional authority, its prestige, its history, and its past occupants. By instilling in the public such an image, the president may enhance his ability to lead the public.

Major, prime-time addresses can be useful in such image building. Presidents speak to the public alone or before an audience, usually of dignitaries, such as members of Congress. They present themselves as the president of the nation, often with symbols of the office and the nation, like the presidential seal and the flag in the fore- and/or background. The audience, if in attendance, is respectful, applauding when required, and opposition leaders refrain from interrupting or intruding into the president's speech.

But presidents can use this method of communicating with the public only occasionally. If a president addresses the public too frequently, he may wear out his welcome, overloading the public, testing its patience with matters political, and perhaps making it difficult for citizens to distinguish important from less important issues. Presidents, thus, can only use major, prime-time addresses on those rare occasions, lest they undermine the power and effect of such speeches.

Still presidents want to generate public support for many more issues than they can promote with major, prime-time addresses. Leading the public requires a more constant and regularized effort than major addresses allow. News organizations provide an alternate access route to the public that the president can employ on a regular and frequent basis. The advantage of news coverage to the president is that it not only allows him frequent access to the public but allows him to convey his message to the public across a wider range of topics than is possible with major, prime-time addresses.

News coverage may also help in presidential image building. The White House works hard to provide a setting that will enhance the president's image and that the news media will cover, especially in pictures and film. For instance, the president may be filmed in ceremonial or emotional settings such as on the White House lawn or at Ground Zero, a site that George W. Bush appeared

at just days after the 9/11 terrorist attacks. A president may be shown inter-
acting with constituents. News clips may also show the accoutrements of presidential and national power, such as the helicopter that takes the president to
Air Force One or onboard an American warship. Recall the image of George
W. Bush, who flew an airplane onto an American aircraft carrier once the first
phase of the war in Iraq had ended with the capture of Baghdad. These types
of settings are meant to associate the president with the power of the office
and the nation.

The downside of using the news to lead the public is that presidents lose
some control over the content of their message to journalists.[2] As a result news
stories may not emphasize the issues or arguments that the president wants.
Thus the news media may help a president as he tries to lead the public, which
entails both gaining access to the public and persuading the public to follow
the president's lead. Given the limitations of using major, prime-time addresses, news coverage is indispensable to presidential leadership, although it
has its limitations as well.

## News Media Needs

News about the president also serves the needs of the news media. Consider
first that most news organizations in the United States are profit-making businesses. Thus they require news stories that will attract readers (viewers) to
generate revenue from subscriptions and advertising, both of which are based
to a large measure on circulation size. But also consider that modern journalists
are trained professionals. Since the early twentieth century, academic training
has been important as an entry into a reporting or other journalistic job. As
professionals, journalists want to exercise their professional judgment over
what constitutes news. From these twin motivations, it is easy to see why news
stories should contain some combination of these characteristics as pointed out
by Groeling and Lichter (2004)—novelty, negativity or conflict, balance, and
authority. A fifth characteristic of news is that it be about important matters,
and Graber (2002, 108–9) offers another characteristic of news with relevance
to the president, familiarity.[3] She argues that people are attracted to news about
the familiar, which in part drives news about celebrities. The president is perhaps the most familiar personality to the largest number of people.

These characteristics meet journalist definitions of news, while also producing stories that they think will be of interest to readers and viewers. Presidential
news, by its very nature, contains some of these characteristics; journalists may
be able to inject other characteristics into presidential news stories under some
circumstances.

Authority and importance are the two primary characteristics of presidential
news. Journalists, in writing their news stories, are more prone to report on
people who hold authoritative positions or who can speak authoritatively (Page

1996a). Presidents are authoritative in the sense that they occupy a constitutional office. Presidents are also important. This importance derives from the constitutional position of the office, the powers and responsibilities granted to the office. Presidents are also important in that they are elected by a national constituency and that they speak for the nation or can be thought of as a national representative. The actions and policies that presidents take tend to have nationwide implications or impacts, which is another source of importance. And as noted above, presidents are familiar, easily the most recognizable political figure to most people.[4] In sum, the president is the most important, authoritative, and familiar figure in the nation. This makes the president and his actions newsworthy.

News organizations also require a steady stream of stories, enough to fill their newspaper and broadcasts everyday. News by definition, however, can occur at any time in any place. Not only can it be expensive to cover news defined this way, but the volume of news may be erratic; some days there may be too much news, and other days not enough. Thus news organizations seek to make the flow of news more predictable. For instance, they identify certain types of people and organizations, such as the presidency, as being newsworthy. The president helps by generating a steady flow of activities for journalists to report on and by providing reporters with services that make their news gathering task more predictable and manageable. These services may include announcing the president's schedule, logistical support, and physical space to work in. By helping to serve the needs of journalists, presidents may also satisfy their own need for access to the public through the news (Grossman and Kumar 1981, Cook and Ragsdale 1998).[5]

## Public's Needs

As discussed thus far, the president needs public support, and the news media, through reporting on the president, can help the president generate and/or maintain that support. The news media need consumers of its product for economic reasons but also want to define the news for professional reasons. News about the president helps the news media attract consumers, assuming that the public wants news about the president.

From an accountability perspective, the public has a need for news about the president. The president is an important political actor. The decisions that presidents make and the policies that they pursue can affect quality of life of the nation's citizens. Thus the public needs to know something about what the president did and the results or impact of those actions and decisions if they are to hold the president accountable for his actions. Only with such knowledge and understanding can the public make an informed decision about whether to continue to support and reelect the president or his party to another term of office.

Average citizens do not, except under the rarest of circumstances, possess firsthand knowledge about presidential actions and decisions (Brody 1991). The public learns of the president's actions primarily through news reports on the president. Beyond mere knowledge of what the president did, the public also needs to make sense of his actions, whether they approve or disapprove of those actions and decisions. News reports may also help citizens make sense of the president's actions.

A final point about the mass public is that most people rarely want to spend much time following the details of political debates. But the public does want to be clued in when consequential events occur (Zaller 2003). The public uses the news media to scan the political (and other) environments for information about important and consequential events from the vast array of decisions and actions that presidents take.

### Sources of Conflict within the Presidential News System

The three actors in the presidential news system derive some benefit, have some needs met, from the others. But the three actors in the system may find themselves at odds with the other system participants, and the presidential news system is relatively permeable to the outer environment, the rest of the political system, the economy, and the society. These two factors—conflict among the system actors and penetration from factors besides these three actors—create dynamism within the presidential news system.

As to the first point, the needs (or goals) of the press and the president may diverge (Grossman and Kumar 1981). For instance the press and the president may disagree over the definition of news and the way that stories on the president are reported (Cook 1998, Cook and Ragsdale 1998, Zeidenstein 1983). Consider the themes of conflict, balance, and novelty (Groeling and Lichter 2004). Journalists want such themes in their stories, but presidents do not.

Often when presidents make policy decisions or take policy positions, conflict may emerge as a characteristic of a news story. Some people, for instance, might disagree with the president. Policies confer benefits on some and costs on others. In this sense we can think of policies creating winners and losers. Conflict may become a theme in presidential news stories when opponents and losers voice their complaints and criticisms of the president's policy. Naturally presidents try to make the case that their policy choice is best for the nation overall.

The debate between the president and his critics not only reveals a conflict theme but may allow journalists to write balanced stories. Balance in this sense refers to presenting both sides of the conflict. Instead of applying their own perspective on an event or action, journalists can remain "objective" observers by allowing the antagonists in the conflict to speak for themselves. Both conflict and balance potentially undermine a president's authority when other people, especially those who occupy authoritative positions of their own, such as members of congress, criticize the president. While presidents like to be portrayed in the news as authoritative and important, a point of convergence between presidential and journalistic needs, presidents do not want stories filled with conflict or balance. A news story containing conflict and balance may become a source of tension between presidents and journalists.

Presidential news may be novel when a president takes a position on a policy that he has not previously addressed or even when he shifts course. The vast array of policy topics on which the president takes action also provides novelty as presidents shift their attention from one issue to another. By taking positions or actions across an array of issues, presidents can build as image of activity and responsibility, that he is actively addressing the nation's concerns.

But novelty has its costs to the president. Presidents may look unfocused if they skip from one issue to another too frequently. Second, a difficult problem for presidents is to gain sustained public attention to a topic. Without sustained public attention, it may be hard to apply public pressure on Congress to take legislative or other action. As presidents shift their own attention from one topic to another, they may undercut public attention to the first topic. Thus presidents have to manage their activity across policies, but journalists may try to push the president to be novel, to move on to another topic or issue.

Furthermore, presidents may not receive as much access to the public or news coverage as they prefer. Foote (1988) contends that in the early 1970s the networks began to balk at allowing the president unconstrained access to prime-time audiences because of the large number of such requests from President Nixon. In more recent years, the networks have rotated coverage of some prime-time presidential addresses (Baum and Kernell 1999, Edwards 2003). Obviously presidents prefer that all major networks broadcast the speech, which would help maintain audience size. Furthermore, not all presidential activities receive news coverage. Barrett (2003) calculates that between 1977 and 1992, only about one-quarter of presidential remarks about policy were covered in either the *New York Times* or *Washington Post*, and only about 15 percent were reported by both newspapers. Presidential remarks were more likely to be covered if they were extensive and if the president made the remark in a televised speech. Presidents, it seems, have to work for their policy remarks to make it into the major, national news media.[6]

The press and the public may also hold divergent needs. Professionalism may lead journalists to prefer stories that fail to capture the public's interest, such as stories about major issues and international events. The public, however, may prefer stories about topics other than politics or that focus on personalities, sports, life style concerns, and crime, among other topics. King, Cooley, and Curtis (1999, 18) in their analysis of the Pew News Interest Index conclude that "politics seems to be over-covered, relative to consumer demand."[7] And despite the obvious need for the president, as an elected politician, to be responsive to public opinion, it is not unheard of for presidents and the public to disagree to some extent over the agenda (Cohen 1997). Perhaps the greatest gulf between the president and the public is the public's general distaste and/or apathy for politics, which erects a barrier to presidential leadership (Edwards 2003).

Thus the actors within the presidential news system need the others but at times find themselves at odds with them. As one actor changes, the others may respond to that change; such adaptive interaction makes the presidential news system highly dynamic and protean.

## Impact of Outer Environmental Forces

Second, the presidential news system is highly permeable to external forces. Many external factors may enter the presidential news system and alter the relationships among the president, the press, and the mass public. Technological change in mass communications at times has profound effects. For instance, the introduction of cable television altered the competitive stance of news organizations (Hamilton 2003) and offered television viewers a wider range of program offerings (Baum and Kernell 1999); consequently fewer people watched news programs (Baum and Kernell 1999). The internet may be having similar impacts on people's use of time, providing them with more alternatives than previously existed and diverting some of their time away from activities they once engaged in for activity on the internet. Some contend that the internet may be eroding social capital and reducing civic and political engagement (for a review of this literature and a test, see Moy et al. 2005). Reporting styles have also changed, with soft news replacing hard news. Some argue that this change in reporting style undermined public trust in the news media (Patterson 2000).

Besides technology, market forces, telecommunications policies, the public's political attitudes and behavior, the behavior and professional orientation of journalists, and the structure of political and party competition are other external factors that may alter the presidential news system. The permeability of the presidential news system to these many external forces will make it difficult at times to isolate the factors that stimulate changes in the system. Moreover, changes within the system at times will affect the outer political world too. I will have more to say about the effects of these outside forces in the analysis presented in this book.

## The Presidential News System and the Study of the Presidency

This system perspective alters how we study the presidency. Many studies of the presidency focus on the person in office, asking, for instance, whether this or that incumbent was a good president, or how a certain personality trait affected presidential behavior in office. The system perspective leads us away from an exclusive focus on individual presidents and their character traits to the relationships among presidents, the mass public, and the press. Not wanting to suggest that individual presidential traits are unimportant to the study of the presidency and presidential behavior, personal traits in this context only become important if they affect or alter the system. Presidential traits are only likely to alter the presidential news system if they have lasting impact on the system. If, however, a personal trait vanishes because a new president assumes office, that trait probably can have at best a fleeting impact on the system. Only if the political system selects for a particular trait in presidents will that trait become important for understanding the nature of the presidential news system. Thus this study sits closer to the perspective of the "presidency" as opposed to the "president" (e.g., Hager and Sullivan 1994, Krause and Cohen 2000).

This system focus becomes theoretically useful because it alters our expectations about presidential leadership. One would expect that as a presidential administration acquired more resources, skill, and experience with the news media and public activities, that president would become increasingly able and successful in leading the public and in influencing the news. Recent research (Edwards 2003) suggests otherwise, that late-twentieth-century presidents find it difficult to lead the public, and they may have a harder time leading the public than presidents of the 1960 and 1970s (Baum and Kernell 1999, Young and Perkins 2005). While many factors, as Edwards (2003) reviews, contribute to this difficulty, the structure of the presidential news system in the late twentieth century, a structure quite different from that during the 1960s and 1970s, is one factor.

Finally, the presidential news system is important because of the centrality of the presidency, the mass public, and the news media to modern American politics and governance. Many of the most urgent issues in American politics are played out in this system. Controlling the presidency ranks as one of the highest priorities of both political parties, and presidents deem it important that they possess public support while in office (Edwards 1997). As noted above and throughout, the news media are critical in building and maintaining support for the presidency. Through this connection, the presidential news system takes on importance for politics and governance.

## The Presidential News System in the Golden Age of Television

During the golden age of television, roughly from the mid 1950s through the mid to late 1970s, the news media were highly concentrated and produced a comparatively high volume of news about the president. News about the president tended to be favorable during this era, and the relationship between presidents and journalists was generally civil and respectful. The mass public, while not notably interested in politics, tuned in to television news broadcasts in relatively large numbers and held the news media in relatively high regard. Presidents, during this age, spoke to the public directly on nationally televised addresses but also provided the news media, especially television, with material to use in their news stories. Through these direct and indirect routes of access to the mass public, presidents enjoyed an ability to lead the public as never before.

However, while this system appeared beneficial to presidents, it also posed great danger to them. When the news media turned against a president, his leadership capability and even tenure in office were threatened. The combination of the press's credibility with the public and the large audience for news often resulted in startling declines in approval and support for the president. Still, because of the nature of the presidential news system of this era, news would generally only turn negative if events warranted it—such as Vietnam for Johnson and Watergate for Nixon. Bad news in the golden age of broadcasting was rooted in real world events. This changed in the age of new media, when bad news became a routine of news production.

## The Structure of the News Media in the Golden Age

For present purposes, the defining characteristics of the news media during the golden age include (1) the dominance of television as a provider of news to the public, (2) the highly stratified hierarchy among news organizations, (3) the relative insulation of news organizations from economic competition and pressures, and (4) the concentration of the news industry.

### TELEVISION'S DOMINANCE AS A NEWS PROVIDER

Although the Second World War delayed its commercial introduction, television proved remarkably popular, diffusing more widely and quickly throughout American society than almost any other innovation (Rogers 2003). Television was introduced commercially in 1949; by 1954 one-half of households owned televisions and 90 percent did so by 1960. By the early 1970s, household ownership of televisions in the United States was nearly universal and Americans spent many of their waking hours watching television. Time-use studies estimated that Americans watched 10.5 hours of television per week in 1965, growing to 15.1 in 1985 (reported in Mayer 1993, 606). Television also altered the structure of the news industry, increasing the degree of news industry concentration and nationalization, a process that began with the invention of the telegraph in the nineteenth century and was spurred on by radio in the first third of twentieth century. Because of television, national news organizations emerged as significant, and perhaps dominant, news providers.

### PRESTIGE HIERARCHY

By the mid 1960s, national network television news organizations entered the ranks of the prestige press. According to Grossman and Kumar (1981), the prestige news organizations of the golden age included several newspapers of national repute, led by the *New York Times* and the *Washington Post*; the weekly newsmagazines, *Time* and *Newsweek*; and the three national news networks,

CBS, NBC, and ABC. This small cadre of news organizations defined the news, set the agenda of most other news providers, and through the nightly television news broadcast, provided the public with the bulk of its national news.

INSULATION FROM MARKET FORCES

During the golden age of broadcasting, several factors partially insulated segments of the news industry from market forces, despite the fact that most news organizations were profit seekers who competed in a market economy. Federal regulations, such as the fairness doctrine and federal licensing of broadcasts, required television and radio broadcasters to offer news and public service programming. The great profitability of television entertainment programming allowed the television networks to cross-subsidize their news operations, which were often kept organizationally separate from the entertainment divisions. Moreover, the heads of the major networks, like David Sarnoff at NBC and William Paley at CBS, were supportive of their news divisions. These corporate leaders felt that the independence of the news divisions increased their and their news organizations' power and prestige, protecting the networks and local affiliates from excessive regulation. And as Hamilton (2003, 163) argues, the three major networks held an oligopoly in the provision of television broadcasting, which further reduced competitive pressures.

The newspaper sector, while subject to stronger market forces than television during this era, also saw some easing of competitive pressures because of the local consolidation of competitive papers. Newspapers underwent major consolidation during this era, a process that had actually begun long before, with two waves of consolidation hitting newspapers in the early 1900s and again in the 1920s (Adams 1995). The growth of national newspaper chains, like Gannett and Knight-Ridder, was one factor in the consolidation of newspapers. The national newspaper chains could realize economies of scale in news production, an economic condition that pushed newspaper consolidation. In this consolidation process, the number of newspapers serving cities declined. By the late 1990s, only a small number of cities could boast competitive daily newspapers. This partial insulation from market forces in both the broadcasting and newspaper sectors would have implications for the content and style of news reporting, a point that I turn to below.

CONCENTRATION

The news industry in the golden age was highly concentrated. Television clearly dominated all other technology and news delivery systems in terms of public popularity and use. A small number of news firms stood out from the others as to their power, prestige, and ability to define the news. Economically the news industry saw increasing concentration, with an oligopoly of three networks in the television sector and the emergence of several national chains in the newspaper sector. Such concentration would unravel in the new media age.

*The Impact of News Organization Structures on the News Product*

The structure of the news industry during the golden age had important implications for news as a product. Economic concentration, the dominance of television, and the influence of the prestige press over the definition of news led to a relatively uniform news product; West (2001) uses the term *homogenous* to describe news in this era.[8] Communications scholars find high degrees of overlap in news across local as well as national media, what they term *consonance* (Comstock and Scharrer 2005, 180–81; also Fowler and Showalter 1974, Lemert 1974, Stempel 1985, Riffe et al. 1986, and Foote and Steele 1986). News looked quite similar from one news provider to the next, at least among the major national news media. The limited degree of economic competition among news providers also meant that they did not have to engage in product differentiation strategies to protect themselves from competitors.

These same factors also led to relatively high levels of "hard" as opposed to "soft" news about politics and government. The distinction between hard and soft news becomes important later in this analysis; hence this becomes a good place to define these terms as I will use them. Moreover, the terms have been used in different ways, leading to some confusion over what is meant by hard and soft news.

One definition of hard and soft news refers to the types of programs. Used this way, hard news refers to news programs dedicated to news, such as the network nightly news, while soft news refers to entertainment and talk shows that sometimes deal with important public events, such as *Entertainment Tonight* or the *Oprah Winfrey Show* (Baum 2003a, 2003b; Prior 2003). A second definition of hard versus soft news refers to the content of particular news stories, no matter who broadcasts or writes them. From this perspective, hard news consists of stories about government, its leaders, public issues, and significant disruptions in daily life, such as weather and other disasters (Patterson 2000, 3). In contrast, soft news concerns celebrities, sports, entertainment, fashion, lifestyle. Throughout this book, I use the terms *hard news* and *soft news* in this second way, as an aspect of the content of the news, unless noted otherwise.

Returning to the point that the structure of the news media in the golden age produced relatively high levels of hard news, Zaller (1999) presents some evidence that "news quality declines as competition increases" (44). While there are several ways of defining news quality, one would probably look at the amount of hard news. Due to the lower degree of competition in the golden age, we are thus likely to see comparatively more hard news in this era than the new media age, with its higher levels of competition among news organizations.

Patterson (2000) also suggests that news over the past two decades had gotten softer than news of early times, directly pointing to the increase in competition among news organizations for this trend. Hamilton (2003) offers an economic logic that also suggests that market competition may lead news organizations to deemphasize hard news for other types of news stories that consumers seem to prefer. Other studies also argue that market competition among news organizations altered news content decisions in similar ways (McManus 1994, Underwood 1998).[9]

Without excessive economic pressure, news providers were somewhat insulated from consumer definitions of news. News producers and journalists could substitute their own definitions of news without much economic effect. This journalist definition of news would offer somewhat more "hard" and less "soft" news than a consumer definition of their preferred news mix of soft and hard news. Television viewers would not stop watching because they had no place to go if they wanted to watch television. In localities served by only one newspaper, a similar situation occurred. Newspaper subscribers in one-newspaper cities would not stop subscribing if the paper heavily emphasized hard news, as long as the paper still satisfied peoples' desire for information about the weather, sports, entertainment, and other soft-news topics. Hard news could still dominate the front page.[10]

National news also rose in prominence during this period. Television had a national audience it wanted to reach. Television news producers presumed that national news would be more appealing to the television viewing audience than local or regional news for its nightly news broadcasts. As Iyengar and Kinder (1987) write: "Network news is national news." Similarly, the prestige press was national in outlook, promoting a definition of news that emphasized the national. Important to this study is the great overlap between national and presidential news. Presidents perform on a national stage and the president is the most important national political figure. Paraphrasing Iyengar and Kinder, "Network news is presidential news."

## NEWS COVERAGE OF THE PRESIDENT

Estimating the amount of hard news and presidential news is difficult because of the numerous news outlets and the sheer volume of news. Consequently, most studies of presidential news look at only the number of presidential news stories and perhaps collect similar figures for news about Congress. Rarely do such studies attempt to calculate the percentage of news about the president as a proportion of the total amount of news. Frank Baumgartner and Bryan Jones's Policy Agendas Project (www.policyagendas.org) provides one data source that can give us a glimpse at the comparative volume of presidential news.

The Policy Agendas Project randomly sampled news stories from the index of the *New York Times* from 1946 into the mid 1990s. They identify from the index description whether the president was an actor in the story and give other actors (Congress, the Supreme Court, among others). Figure 2.1 traces two trends lines using these data, presidential mentions as a percentage of all news stories and presidential mentions as a percentage of news stories about

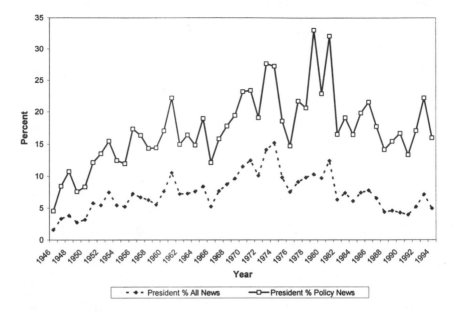

Figure 2.1 Presidential news volume, *New York Times*, 1946–94. Source: Baumgartner and Jones, Policy Agendas Project (www.policyagendas.org).

government. This second indicator is useful in that it provides us with a sense of how often the president appears in governmental news stories. Conventional wisdom suggests that the president is a leading, if not the leading, actor in governmental news stories (Graber 2002). The agendas' data allow us to test this conventional perspective.

Both trend lines display an unmistakable and similar pattern, a growth of presidential news from the 1940s into the 1970s. The two are highly correlated in spite of their differing bases.[11] From 1946 to 1959, presidents received on average about 5 percent of all news and 12 percent of government/policy news. These figures jumped to 8 and 17 percent for the 1960s, growth rates of 60 and 42 percent. The growth in presidential news continued into the 1970s, with the president receiving 11 percent of all news and 23 percent of governmental and policy news during that decade. Considering the scope of the governmental news category, that we find presidents in nearly one-quarter of such news stories testifies to the importance of the president in governmental news.

It is difficult to collect comparable data on presidential coverage for the network evening news broadcasts. First, such data have only been archived since 1968, when the Vanderbilt University Television Archives began operations. Broadcasts prior have been lost to history. And the Vanderbilt TV Archives have their limitations for online searches. One, the Vanderbilt TV Ar-

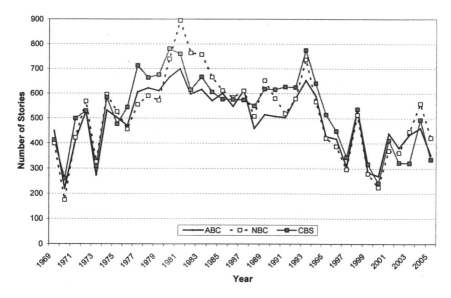

Figure 2.2 Annual number of news stories on the ABC, CBS, and NBC evening news broadcasts that mention the president's name, 1969–2005. Source: Vanderbilt Television News Archives.

chive only allows a search of an abstract. If the president is mentioned in the news story but not the abstract, one will miss that story. Two, the Vanderbilt search engine does not offer Boolean searches. Boolean searches allow flexible combinations, such as search for words that appear near each other or when one word appears but only if another is absent. With the Vanderbilt Archive search engine one can search for an exact phrase, such as "President Clinton," or one can search for the appearance of a word or words, such as *president* and *Clinton*, but more complex search queries that would allow for more precise retrieval of stories is not possible.[12]

With these limitations in mind, I ran a search asking the Vanderbilt archive to retrieve all stories that contained the words *president* and *name of the president* (e.g., Clinton, Bush) in the abstract by year. Such a query may include stories that are not primarily about the president and may overlook stories in which a top-level administration spokesperson or official is the primary actor but where the president is not named in the abstract. Still, this simple search query does provide us with one comparable indicator of the number of presidential news stories on the three major networks.

Figure 2.2 produces the annual time path for the three major network (ABC, NBC, CBS) evening news broadcasts from 1969 through 2005.[13] These figures do not weight the stories by length; thus we cannot say how much of the broadcast is devoted to the president. Several patterns, however, are evident in these data. First, all three networks display the same basic trend over time.[14] Second, each network shows an increase in the volume of news about the president until about 1980 or 1981, after which the volume of presidential news begins to recede. Third, each network on average aired more than one news story on the president per evening from 1969 through 1980. Across those twelve years, ABC averaged 1.34 stories, NBC 1.35, and CBS 1.41. The president is a consistent presence on network news broadcasts across this period, and a growing presence through the early 1980s, although these data in this form cannot tell us how much of the news broadcast presidential news occupies. Moreover, as the search fails to pick up others news stories that one may consider presidential or administration news, these figures likely undercount the amount of presidential news.

These television data also seem to indicate that the networks pay some attention to what the other networks report. They may do so as a reality check, to insure that their reporters are not being scooped by the reporters of other news organizations, and to insure that their reporters are not promoting their own personal news agendas. The high correlation across the networks in the amount of presidential news also is consistent with the consonance hypothesis. Last, in an age of common definitions of what was newsworthy, the credibility of any major news outlet depended in part on presenting news that resembled the news of major news providers.

## THE TONE OF PRESIDENTIAL NEWS

The structure of the news industry in the golden age also affected the style and tone of the news. News reporting during this era tended to be "objective" or "balanced" and relatively positive toward the president. Although objectivity in news reporting is impossible, journalists have termed a certain style of news reporting "objective." Objective reporting requires that reporters refrain from taking a side or advocating a position in their story. Instead they should present facts and allow partisans from opposing sides of an issue speak for themselves in the story. Several factors led to this objective reporting style. These include the commercialization of the press, in which the press would aim to appeal to a broad cross-section of potential consumers, rather than those of a particular political perspective (Baldasty 1992, Hamilton 2003). Growing press professionalism and reactions to the criticism of "yellow journalism" in the late 1800s also stimulated a movement toward this "objective" reporting style (Mindich 1998).

Some have claimed that objective reporting tends to be supportive of the existing political and power structure (e.g., Fishman 1980). Being cited or quoted in a news story lends a degree of legitimacy and authority to that person. This enhances the position of the existing political and power structure because the news media rely so heavily on official sources for news. In contrast, opposition voices, especially from people who do not hold positions of authority, rarely are used as news sources (Page 1996a).

This produces news that on average is supportive of establishment figures, such as the president. Surely tension exists between reporters and political figures, such as the president, even in such a climate (e.g., Grossman and Kumar 1981). Presidents and reporters may differ over definitions of the news. When establishment competitors to the president are willing to speak out publicly against the president, the news may become critical of the president. The argument is not that news about the president during the golden age was entirely positive or uncritical of the president, but compared to the current new media age, the tendency was for presidential news to lean in a positive direction.

The best data on the tone or valence of presidential news during this age comes from Grossman and Kumar's study, *Portraying the President* (1981). Grossman and Kumar ambitiously content analyzed news stories about the president from three news sources, *Time* magazine, the *New York Times*, and CBS News. For *Time* and the *Times*, their data span from 1953 through August 1978. The CBS data begins with August 1968, when the Vanderbilt Television Archives began collecting tapes of the broadcasts, and like *Time* and the *Times*, ends with August 1978. In all, they coded 5,270 stories from the *Time*, 2,550 from *Time*, and 922 from CBS (254).

They find that all three news organization provided the president with more favorable than unfavorable news stories. Approximately 60 percent of *Time*'s stories were favorable, with about 11.8 percent neutral and 28.2 percent negative. The *New York Times*' breakdown resembles *Time*, with 48.7 percent of stories being positive, 24.1 percent neutral, and 27.2 percent negative. CBS, which spans a shorter time frame, displays a balance between positive (38.5) and negative (38.6) news, with 22.9 percent neutral.

The greater representation of the Watergate years in CBS's totals account for the difference between CBS and the other media. From 1953 through 1965, both *Time* and the *New York Times* gave the president favorable to unfavorable news at a rate of approximately 5 to 1. In the next decade, from 1966 to 1974, news from both *Time* and the *Times* was more negative than positive, as was the case for CBS. In the post-Watergate years, 1975–78, however, news for all three news organizations shifted back; again positive news outweighed negative news about the president, often by hefty margins (Grossman and Kumar 1981, 255–56). Thus other than when extraordinary events led the press (and the public) to view the president in a negative light, presidents during the golden age could count on favorable news. It may not be too far-fetched to argue that during the golden age, the operational code of journalists was to presume that political leaders, such as the president, were doing a good job, were trying to serve in the public's interest, and thus deserved the benefit of the doubt, unless evidence proved otherwise.

Despite studies that claim or emphasize tension in the relationship between the president and the press in this era (Grossman and Kumar 1981), evidence from the questioning style of journalists at presidential press conferences suggests a respectful, civil tone on the part of journalists toward the president from Eisenhower through the pre-Watergate Nixon years (Clayman and Heritage. 2002, Clayman et al. 2006). Press conferences, by Eisenhower's time, were institutionalized, formal, and public settings, which prescribed certain norms of behavior. The style of reporters' questions gives us one view of how these norms exhibit themselves as behaviors. From these data, we can suggest that reporters generally held to a norm of civility and respect toward the president in this era. The questioning style turned more adversarial in the new media age, suggesting a change in reporters' norms of behavior toward the president. This leads us to a discussion of other aspects of the relationship between the president and the press in the golden age.

## *The Relationship between the President and the Press in the Golden Age*

In the late 1800s, news reporters began to increase the attention that they paid to the presidency. This increased attention derived from several sources, including the growing importance of the presidency as a policy leadership office. But presidents also aimed to increase their news coverage. To this end, they provided journalists with physical resources that made their job easier, such as space, typewriters, and telephone access in the White House. Press releases and interviews with the president and White House personnel were offered to journalists. By the turn of the century, a White House beat had become recognizable (Kumar 1997).

The institutionalization of the press conference was the most important aspect of the press-president relationship. During the first third of the twentieth century, press conferences became regularized both in format and frequency (Cornwell 1966, Ponder 1998, Ryfe 1999). Press conferences provided journalists with direct access to the president and material for their reports. Their regularity insured that reporters who attended would continue to have a presidential story to file. Moreover, some material was presented off the record. Journalists would know something that the public would not, in effect making them into insiders. By feeding journalists with such inside information, presidents could bring them into their confidence, sometimes converting journalists into presidential allies. Franklin Roosevelt used press conferences this way to great effect, building support among White House reporters for him to counterbalance the antipathy of their editors to the New Deal (White 1979, Winfield 1990).

This system remained intact until the advent of television. While Truman and Eisenhower (Allen 1993) made some tentative steps to adapt to television, their news management styles more closely resembled their predecessors, who emphasized the importance of the print media, than their successors, who would upgrade their relationship with television journalists (Kernell 1993). The relationship between reporters and the president fundamentally altered when John F. Kennedy became president, as Kennedy adapted to and aimed to exploit television.

Kennedy saw television as a way of reaching the entire nation without the mediation of reporters. He innovated by having his press conferences broadcast live to the nation. From a relatively intimate and special relationship between reporters and presidents, the press conference evolved into a staged media event. In time, press conferences would fall into disuse, as presidents preferred to deliver a prepared speech on television and print reporters lost interest in press conferences. The transformation of the press conference, however, is but one example of presidents altering their interactions with the press to serve television, sometimes at the expense of print journalism.

Presidents also offered services and aids to electronic journalists, much like they did for print journalists in earlier times. They designed their public appearances for filming and often in settings that would appear visually attractive. They timed their announcements to allow television to prepare film for broadcast for that evening's news. Transportation was provided for journalists when presidents traveled around the nation and abroad, and White House facilities were constructed to aid television journalists in their type of reporting.

The White House also became more skillful at news management. To that end, the number of staff devoted to news and publicity operations in the White House increased. As these staffs grew, personnel duties became more specialized and differentiated, which added to White House expertise. New organization units within the White House were created and rationalized, for example, the Office of Communications created in 1970 (Maltese 1992).

Print journalists, unable to compete with the timeliness of the television nightly news broadcast, felt increasingly marginalized. Still, print journalism could provide more detail than television, and newspaper articles grew increasingly long (Barnhurst and Mutz 1997). Perhaps more important, print journalists carved out a new role for themselves, that of interpreter or news analyst (West 2001). In time, this interpretive or analytic role would pave the way for increasingly negative news under the guise of analysis, but such a development was not to arrive in full force until the age of new media.

Generally, this system worked well for presidents and television journalists. As noted above, presidents enjoyed favorable news coverage during this era. Such a portrait may seem at odds with historical understandings of president-press relations during this era. For instance, in 1966 the phrase "credibility gap" was coined to characterize the Johnson administration's public relations problems over the Vietnam War. This phrase intimated that the administration was either not forthcoming or that it lied about the war (Deakin 1968).[15] However, a search of the *New York Times* on Lexis-Nexis found that it was used only forty-three times in that paper from 1966 through the end of 1968. Similarly, Watergate affects much of what we think about president-press relations during the Nixon years. But as Grossman and Kumar's data indicate, 1973 and 1974, the Watergate years, stand out in their negativity.[16] Otherwise, Nixon did not receive inordinately negative news.

How can we square this portrait of this era as one of generally positive presidential news and comparative harmony between presidents and the press? First, historians and others who study president-press relations during this time period, especially the Johnson and Nixon years, focus on the major events in their relationship, which are often events of conflict and discord (e.g., Liebovich 2003). Rarely do such studies look at routine or normal affairs, the bulk of interactions between the president and the press. Notice too the term *credibility gap*. In the new media age, journalists would be less restrained in saying that the administration lied. The "credibility gap" was a polite or indirect way of saying that the administration was lying or withholding information. Its use indicates a reticence among journalists to saying outright or directly that the administration and president had lied.

Yet, in the new media age, not only would presidential news turn increasingly negative, but relations between the president and the press would become increasingly strained and hostile (e.g., Kurtz 1998). Moreover, negative news about the president in the golden age was rooted in real world events, like administration handling of the Vietnam War or Watergate. In the new media age, while disconcerting real world events would stimulate much negative news,[17] coverage of scandals and press feeding frenzies (Sabato 1991) would also produce high levels of negative and critical news reporting. Scandal was not reported as often or as deeply in the golden age as the age of new media, and sex scandals, such as Clinton's, were rare in the golden age. Still we can see some of the seeds of the presidential news system of the new media age being planted in the golden age.

### The Public as News Consumers in the Golden Age

Finally, in describing the presidential news system in the golden age, we turn to the mass public. Two attributes define the role of the mass public in the presidential news system of the golden age. First, average people were relatively well exposed to news, mostly by watching the nightly news broadcast. Second, the public held the news media in relatively high regard. This produced a large audience that was receptive to the news. Inasmuch as the president could get his message across to the public in this age, he was presented with an opportunity to lead the public.

As noted above, in the 1950s, television emerged as the most popular entertainment and news medium for American citizens. West (2001, 132) reports ratings data that indicates that across the 1950s, 1960s, and into the mid 1970s, about 60 percent of households with televisions tuned into one of the "Big

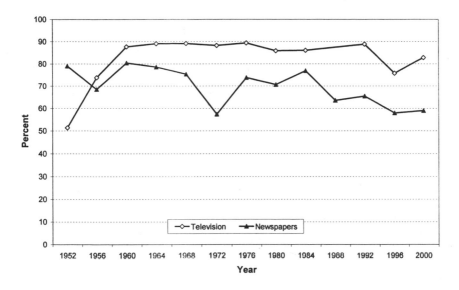

Figure 2.3 Percentage of respondents who watch TV and read the newspaper for presidential campaign news, 1952–2000. Source: ANES, 1948–2000. No data for TV watching in 1988.

Three" (ABC, CBS, NBC) evening news broadcasts.[18] Just as television entertainment programming captured much of the filmgoing audience, television supplanted newspapers as the source that Americans relied on for their news.

American National Election Study (ANES) data allow us to compare television and newspaper use patterns, but only for information about presidential election campaigns.[19] For instance in 1952, 79 percent of respondents claimed to have read something about the presidential campaign in the newspapers, where only 51 percent said that they watched a television program about the campaign, a 28 percentage differential between newspaper reading and television watching.[20] By 1956, according to ANES figures, the pattern had shifted. Newspaper reading declined to 68 percent, while TV watching rose to 73 percent. From then on, more people would claim to have received news about the campaign from TV than from newspapers (see figure 2.3).

Moreover, the percentage of people who only relied on TV for news increased from about 8 percent in 1952 to 18 percent in 1956, ranging between 14 and 19 percent through 1968 (figure 2.4). From one-sixth to one-fifth of the public claimed that television was its sole source of news. At the same time, the percentage of the public that only used newspapers dwindled precipitously from more than 35 percent in 1952 to 12 percent four years later. Thereafter it never rose above 10 percent. As figure 2.3 indicates, the public basically had bifurcated into two segments by the late 1950s, those who only watched TV for news about the campaign, and those who used both TV and newspapers.

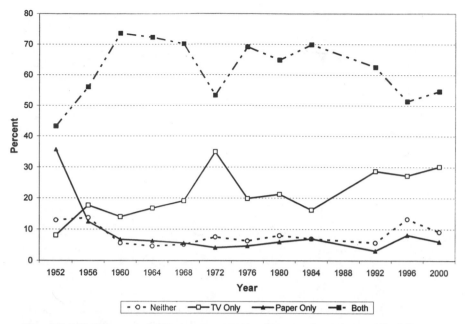

Figure 2.4 Reliance on television and newspapers for news about the presidential campaign, 1952–2000. Source: ANES, 1952–2000. No data for 1988.

Sketchier evidence exists on public attitudes toward the news media during these years. For instance, Gallup polls report that about 70 percent of their respondents had either "a great deal" or "a fair amount" of trust and confidence that the news was reported "fully, accurately, and fairly."[21] Seven Harris surveys conducted in the 1970s count that on average 23 and 32 percent of the public had a great deal of confidence in the press and television, respectively. Finally, in a series of six polls across the 1970s, the General Social Survey found that 75.5 and 82.5 percent of respondents held either "a great deal" or "only some" confidence in the people running the press and television, respectively. These surveys point to a relatively high level of public confidence and trust in the news media in the 1970s.

## Implications of the Golden Age News System on Presidential Leadership

What does the structure of the presidential news system mean for the president in the golden age of broadcasting? First, presidents tried to lead the broad mass public. They did so using a "going public" strategy that entails directly addressing the nation on television during prime time (Kernell 1993). Such a strategy, which allowed presidents to go over the heads of the news media, became highly attractive. Nixon made it a centerpiece of his public activities, making increasingly frequent demands on the networks for air time until the networks began to deny some of his requests (Foote 1990).

However, during this age, presidents did not rely solely on major national address to lead public opinion. They could also use the news in their public opinion campaigns because the volume of presidential news was high and generally favorable and the news audience was large and positively disposed toward the news media. This combination made it likely that the public, on average, would be receptive to news accounts of the president. As those news accounts tended to be favorable to the president, presidents could expect some degree of success in leading the public. Thus presidential leadership of public opinion, or at least a presidential strategy of trying to lead public opinion, characterizes this age.

But the structure of the presidential news system during the golden age also posed a threat to the president. If the news media turned on the president, attacking him and/or transmitting consistently negative news to the public, the president's standing with the public could be undermined. Although presidential news was generally positive in this era, journalists were not administration patsies. The canons of objectivity required that news be firmly rooted in reality or at least in objective indicators.

For example, journalists began to question the Johnson administration's handling of the Vietnam War as body counts mounted but administration spokespeople continued to pronounce progress on the war, leading to the "credibility gap." Similarly, mounting evidence as to the scale of the Watergate scandals led the media to also attack the Nixon administration. In both instances, objective indicators (e.g., body counts and illegal activities) provided the foundation for unfavorable news reports about the administrations. Moreover, the concentration in the news industry and the importance of elite news organizations in defining the news produced relative uniformity in news reporting on these administrations. The press spoke with basically one voice during this age. Not only did this news climate undercut presidential leadership of public opinion during these two episodes, but one can argue that negative news so damaged these presidencies that the incumbents were forced to leave office. Thus while the golden age presented presidents with opportunities to lead the public, the structure of the presidential news system in that age also contained grave threats to presidents under certain conditions.

Much would change as the presidential news system evolved from the golden age to the new media age. To preview, the amount of news coverage of the president declined in the new media age compared to the golden age. Further, the tone of presidential news became increasingly negative and critical. Mass behavior and attitudes about the news media changed as well. In the new media age, the level of news consumption decreased, despite the increased opportunities to get news. Moreover, public trust of the news media eroded. The combination of these factors created barriers to presidential leadership of the mass public. During the age of new media, presidents would shift their style of public leadership from one that tried to lead the broad mass public to one that focused relatively more on targeting special interests and segments of the public, under some circumstances, the president's partisan base. This change in presidential leadership style has important implications for democracy in the new media age. I describe and analyze trends in the amount of presidential news in the next chapter. Before turning to those questions, the next section presents a short history of the rise of the new media, which provides a context from which to understand the other changes that rippled through the presidential news system.

## The Emergence of the New Media: A Short History

Although the new media is not the only factor that altered the presidential news system, its emergence had profound effects that rippled throughout that system. This section presents a short history of the new media, focusing on three major forms that have received the most attention and had the greatest implications for the presidential news system: cable television, talk radio, and the internet. Two other forms of new media are also notable, satellite television and VCRs. Despite growth in subscriptions to satellite since the early 1990s, the number is still small and VCR's primary impact seems closely associated with cable. Technological innovations, federal policies, the adaptation of older communication media to a changing environment, and changes in the political climate all stimulated and helped shape the new media.[22]

### Cable Television

Cable television is a primary component of the new media. Cable television technology dates to the late 1940s. An FCC decision in 1948 to freeze broadcast licensing spurred the delivery of cable television services, especially in smaller- and medium-sized communities not yet served by broadcast television. In 1952 an estimated fourteen thousand households subscribed to cable television.

Initially, the FCC did not see cable as within its regulatory scope. A 1954 decision by the FCC, *Frontier Broadcasting Company v. Collier*, determined that cable companies were not common carriers and thus the commission could not regulate them. In such an open regulatory environment the cable industry grew, although not swiftly, owing in part to the high cost of building cable infrastructure compared to broadcasting. Still, by 1963 cable services existed in twelve hundred communities with more than 1 million subscribers.

Under pressure from broadcasters, the FCC's cable policies began shifting in the early 1960s. In its 1963 decision, *Carter Mountain Transmission Corp. v. FCC*, the FCC determined that cable posed negative economic effects on broadcasting and common carriers and thus could be regulated. Resultant FCC policies began to restrict cable's growth. By 1966, the FCC extended it regulatory powers over all cable systems, requiring a license for their operation. Finally in the late 1960s, the FCC froze cable licensing in the largest one hundred media markets.

The new deregulatory climate of the 1970s pressured the FCC to change its policies toward cable. Home Box Office (HBO) and TelePrompTer, the first pay cable services, began in 1972. A federal appeals court decision in 1976 struck down FCC rules on pay television, thus opening the way for greater cable expansion. As a result, other cable channels and services began to proliferate in the mid to late 1970s, including Christian Broadcasting Network and Warner Cable in 1977 and Viacom-Showtime in 1978. In 1979 the so-called superstations, WGN-Chicago and WOR-New York, began national distribution through satellite signals to cable stations. That same year cable coverage of the House of Representatives began with C-SPAN; C-SPAN coverage of the Senate began in 1985. Other decisions by the FCC in the late 1970s further eased restrictions on cable, resulting in more expansion of the industry.

By the early 1980s a wave of corporate mergers occurred in the cable industry and many new cable channels were founded. For our purposes, perhaps the most critical event during this wave of cable expansion was the launching of Cable News Network (CNN) in April 1982, the first 24/7 news service. By the mid 1980s more than 40 million homes subscribed to cable. Furthermore, in 1984 Congress passed the Cable Act, which deregulated pricing and systematized the franchise renewal process. Not surprisingly, cable corporate profits rose as a result of pricing deregulation. Cable was further strengthened in 1985 when the U.S. Court of Appeals struck down FCC rules requiring cable operators to carry all local broadcast signals. A backlash against deregulation ensued, as the public, facing steeply rising cable rates, began to cry out for relief. In 1992, over a presidential veto in the midst of the presidential election season, Congress passed the 1992 Cable Act, regranting the FCC the power to regulate cable rates. The 1992 regulations also stimulated direct or satellite TV services, which as a result began to compete more effectively with cable.

Cable as a news source received a lift from the 1991 Gulf War. CNN, the major player, saw its audience increase by providing live, around-the-clock coverage, something the major broadcast networks did not do. CNN's financial and journalistic success led to imitators and competitors. In October 1996, Fox News Channel began operations in the United States, while MSNBC, a joint venture of NBC and MSN began the same year, providing cable viewers with three 24/7 cable news channels. On the regulatory front, in 1996 Congress passed the sweeping Telecommunications Act, which among other things, deregulated rates for small cable carriers. A major goal of the Telecommunications Act was to increase competition across the entire economic sector in the hopes of stimulating development. The commercial promise of the internet began to be realized as a result, and computers and the internet finally began to appear in households in large numbers.

The three cable news networks saw audience growth, although they never approached the size of the three broadcast networks, even though the audience of the broadcast networks had steadily declined over the past two decades (West 2001, and figure 7.1 of chapter 7). Figure 2.5 plots the monthly number of households that tuned into the evening news broadcasts of the three cable news networks from October 1997, about a year after Fox and MSNBC went online, through December 2004. Combined audience size fluctuates, often rising with important events, like 9/11, the war with Iraq, and presidential elections. The viewership of the three cable networks peaked in March and April 2003, as the U.S. invasion and war with Iraq commenced, at about 7 million, but typical audiences in the late 1990s to 2000s hovered in the 2.5–3 million range, some 10–15 percent of the combined audience for the three broadcast networks at that time. In the 1980s and early 1990s cable audiences were an even smaller fraction of the broadcast audience.[23]

Although CNN was the early ratings leader, Fox News began to poll larger audiences than CNN by early 2002. Still CNN is more profitable than Fox, despite having higher news costs. CNN has been steadily profitable in the $250–$400 million range since 1997. Fox only achieved profitability in 2001, but its 2004 profits almost matched CNN's ($274 million for Fox to $337 for CNN). MSNBC first achieved a profit in 2003; its 2004 profit stood at a paltry $32 million, compared to Fox and CNN. CNN's costs in 2004 were nearly double of those of Fox ($550 million to $265 million) because CNN supports a larger infrastructure, which includes twenty-six foreign bureaus, compared to five for Fox, plus a larger stable of reporters. Higher advertising rates, in part a function of the greater public credibility at this time of CNN over Fox, the more attractive demographic of the CNN viewer, plus CNN's selling of its product to other outlets, some within the AOL Time Warner corporation, of which it is a part (e.g., Headline News, the CNN international networks) account for CNN's relative profitability in the face of its higher cost structure than Fox.

## Talk Radio

Talk radio, another important form of new media, is often characterized as the adaptation of an old media form to a new context (e.g., Davis and Owen 1998). The rise of political talk radio is more complex however. While the political context obviously affected the rise of talk radio, so did technological innovation

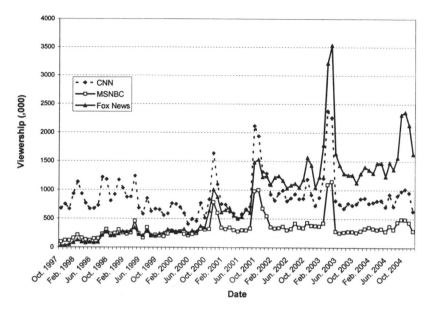

Figure 2.5 Monthly number of households (in 000s) that watch the evening news broadcasts of the three cable news networks, October 1997–December 2004.
Source: Journalism.org, http://www.stateofthemedia.org/2005, based upon Nielsen media research data.

and federal policies (much of the following discussion comes from Cappella et al. 1996)

Broadcast television in the 1950s pushed radio to the sidelines as a source of entertainment and news. Radio programming shifted to the all-music format, which people listened to on their commutes to work, but rarely outside of their cars. In the 1970s, because of its superior sound quality and greater geographic reach, FM displaced AM radio. AM radio needed a new program niche that would attract listeners or its days would likely come to an end. Talk radio offered one alternative. It was cheap to produce, but not viable until satellite broadcasting in the 1980s allowed local AM radio stations to tap into high-quality signals. In 1985 the FCC dispensed with the Fairness Doctrine, which opened up the possibility of airing politically oriented programming on radio. No longer did political or public affairs broadcasting have to allow opponents or alternative voices access to the airwaves. Radio hosts with avowed political positions and agendas could now build a program dedicated to that point of view. By the mid 1980s several conservative political radio talk show hosts became quite popular, notably Rush Limbaugh. The ability of a listener to call in and voice his or her opinion anonymously increased the popularity of talk radio, especially among those who felt disenfranchised or disaffected from traditional mainstream politics.

In the 1990s conservative political talk radio became increasingly popular; the number of stations offering such programs grew, the number of such hosts multiplied, the audience expanded, as did the profits derived from such programs. Few of the conservative hosts or programs were able to build an audience the size of Limbaugh's, who remained the dominant political radio voice into the 2000s. Reacting to the success and supposed political influence of conservative talk radio, liberals began talk radio broadcasting efforts but to date have not been nearly as successful in attracting a large audience.

## *The Internet*

The internet as a mass public phenomenon comes relatively late in the development of the new media age. The new media age was already relatively mature, at least with regard to the presidential news system, by the time the internet became a mass phenomenon. For the most part, the internet either reinforced or accelerated some of the trends that had been developing for the previous two decades. As a consequence, the internet plays a small part in this study, and it is as yet unclear what implications the internet will hold for the future.[24]

Prior to the passage of the 1996 Telecommunications Act, the internet primarily served some federal government agencies, the scientific and research and development centers of some technologically oriented corporations, some "do-it-yourselfers," and the higher education establishment (Chadwick 2006, 38–48). Although many people had home computers by 1996, few, other than those noted above, accessed the internet. With the passage of the 1996 act, the internet became a commercial and popular phenomenon. The number of households with access to the internet exploded, and time spent on the internet increased, especially as broadband became more available and affordable.

We can see the relatively late arrival of the internet in the new media age by inspecting diffusion patterns within the mass public from public opinion surveys. For instance, the National Science Foundation–sponsored "Surveys of Public Understanding of Science and Technology" (PUST) found that 8.5 percent of respondents had home computers in 1983. That number grew steadily, reaching 38.1 percent by 1995, the year prior to the passage of the Telecommunications Act and 56.2 percent by 1999.[25] People seem to have somewhat greater access to computers at work. In 1983, 43.2 percent of those asked by the PUST said that they had access to a computer at work. The number grew to 63.3 percent in 1995 and 70.2 percent in 1999. More recent survey data, collected by Pew Internet and American Life Project, reports that in April 2006, 75 percent of respondents say that they use a computer.[26] The Pew question is not perfectly comparable with the PUST question, because people may use a computer at either home or work.

Access to a computer is a precondition to access to the internet. The PUST surveys found only 7.3 percent of respondents with access to the internet at home in 1995. This is already arguably fifteen or more years into the new media age. In 1997, the year after the passage of the Telecommunications Act, the percentage had risen to 18.0 percent, while their 2001 survey found 64.7 percent with home access to the internet. Pew surveys indicate further growth in internet access, reaching 73 percent by 2006, but again the Pew question does not distinguish between home and work access. All data indicate increasing access to the internet, but prior to the 1996 Telecommunications Act, few had access. By 1996, when access to the internet began to grow noticeably, the new media age was already reasonably mature.

More important for present purposes than mere access to the internet is the use that people make of the internet, especially with regard to news acquisition. In the first decade of the twenty-first century, small fractions use the internet as their primary source of news. The 2001 PUST survey found 8.1 percent claiming that the internet as their primary news source, compared to 47.8 percent who mostly rely on television and 30.8 percent on newspapers. In an April 2006 survey, Pew found that 13 percent primarily look to the internet for news about political figures and events in Washington, while 58 percent used television and 23 percent newspapers. Comparable figures do not exist for earlier dates.

Larger percentages, however, do use the internet *sometimes* for news. In 2001 Pew found that 37 percent of all respondents "ever go online for news," with 46 percent doing so in their in 2005 survey. Pew also found that 39 percent used the internet for news about the 2004 presidential election campaign.[27] That few use the internet as a primary news source, but many sometimes use the internet for news, is consistent with the idea that people use the internet to supplement rather than to substitute for other news media (Althaus and Tewksbury 2000).

The internet first made its political presence felt in late 1997, when Matt Drudge published in his *Drudge Report* a story concerning the affair between Monica Lewinsky and President Clinton. This report set of a classic feeding frenzy (Sabato 1991), and it is easy to imagine that a noninternet-based publication could have stimulated this feeding frenzy and what was to transpire afterward. We can think of Matt Drudge as a journalist common in the new media age, someone who just happened to be among the first to exploit the internet as his medium of communication.

Subsequently, the internet was adapted for a variety of political purposes. As a factor in elections, the internet began to emerge in the 2000 presidential election, but its presence was felt more strongly in the 2004 campaign. For instance, Howard Dean made great use of the internet for campaign contributions, something that other politicians copied. Notably, Dean did not win the Democratic nomination. Weblogs, which existed sometime earlier, became a notable presence in the 2004 campaign as well (Williams and Tedesco 2006). Politicians and their press secretaries have been feeding press releases to reporters for some time, but that phenomenon only became common in the late 1990s and early 2000s, again late in the new media age. The same can be said of other political uses of the internet.

In contrast, talk radio and cable television, as forms of the new media, were to have major implications for the presidential news system. Cable especially allowed people to find alternatives to the television programs that the three national networks offered, which resulted in declining audience shares for broadcast entertainment and news programs alike. Talk radio and the 24/7 cable news networks also attracted people with a thirst for political news and information, people already motivated to acquire political information. The internet would reinforce and accelerate these tendencies. Introducing and developing these new media would affect the amount of hard news, the tone of that news, public attention to the news, and perhaps even public regard for the news media. The next chapter begins the analysis of one major change from the broadcasting age to the new media age relevant to this study, the decline in presidential news.

# CHAPTER 3

# The New Media Age and
# the Decline in Presidential News

## Introduction

As noted in the previous chapters, the new media age differs from the earlier broadcasting era in several regards, one being the lower levels of governmental and public affairs news, or "hard news," reported in the traditional news media. Thus we find that over the past several decades the news has softened and the amount of coverage in the traditional news media devoted to public affairs, including the presidency, has declined. For instance, the Project for Excellence in Journalism (1998) reports that between 1977 and 1997 governmental affairs on network evening news broadcasts declined from two-thirds of all news to 40 percent. Others report similar declines (Hess 1994, 2000; Patterson 2000; Slattery et al. 2001), while journalists and news scholars bemoan these trends (Feder 1997, McCartney 1997).

The president occupies a key position in governmental and public affairs news. Just as the new media age offers less governmental and public affairs news than the broadcasting age, it also offers less news about the president. In the new media age, the president occupies less news space than he did in the broadcasting age.

Why should the amount of presidential news matter? First, the amount of news on the president affects the public's ability to hold the president accountable. As the quantity of presidential news diminishes, the amount of information that the public possesses about the president may also decline. The public may not possess all of the relevant information that it would like to have in holding the president accountable for his leadership and actions in office. As Leighley (2004, 100) remarks with regard to the decline in hard news reporting, "Without [hard news] . . . it may be impossible for a citizen to judge his or her own interests, or to evaluate government officials accordingly."

Second, the quantity of presidential news affects the president's ability to lead (Edwards 2003). Although presidents may try to lead the public by addressing it directly in major national speeches, they can do so only occasionally. To reach the public, presidents must also rely on the news. Visibility in the news does not guarantee that presidents can build public support, but a president invisible to the public forecloses any opportunity to mobilize public support. Moreover, since the news hole is limited in size, the more news there is about the president the less news there is about his competitors, such as members of Congress, opposition party spokespeople, prospective candidates for the presidency from the presidential and opposition party, and interest group leaders. As the president occupies a greater proportion of the news hole, not only does the volume of opposition and competitor voices diminish, but the president appears to occupy a larger and more important presence in public and governmental affairs. As Miroff (1982) reminds us, part of the power of the modern presidency derives from its ability to monopolize the public space. The public space includes news coverage.

Some commentators argue that changes in the structure of competition in the age of new media may in part account for the decline in public affairs and presidential news reporting. In the age of new media, economic competition across news organizations increased. The relaxing of federal regulations and the introduction of new technologies such as cable television spurred this competition, sensitizing news organizations to consumer tastes about the news product. News organizations increasingly employed and relied on market research in designing their news product. That market research found many consumers preferring entertainment to news (McManus 1994, Underwood 1998). As a result, the amount of hard news declined, replaced by softer news and features (Hamilton 2003, Patterson 2000).

These trends—changes in the structure of the news media and less hard news—may have important implications for our understanding of presidential news. Commonly presidential scholars contend that presidents stimulate much of their news coverage. By engaging in public activities, presidents give reporters something to write about, and by providing services and supports for journalists, presidents make it easier for reporters to do their job (Cornwell 1966, Grossman and Kumar 1981, Lammers 1982, Maltese 1992). Presidential public activities have been on the upswing, especially in recent years (Powell 1999), and Maltese (2003, 16) argues that presidents have increased their volume of "newsworthy" public activities in reaction to changes in the structure and behavior of the news media.

This presents us with a puzzle. The level of presidential activities designed to generate news coverage has increased, but the amount of presidential news in the age of new media has declined. Do presidential activities have as much impact on presidential news as commonly supposed? To date, the connection between presidential public activities and news coverage has been assumed but not tested. Moreover, no one has compared the relative effectiveness of different presidential activities in generating news about the president. Nor has anyone directly compared the impact of the structure of the news industry and presidential activities on presidential news coverage. This chapter and the next address these questions.

The next section develops a market theory of the provision of presidential news, followed by a review of the evidence that the amount of presidential news has declined during the age of new media. The market model is useful in that it helps organize a number of factors within a single framework. It also focuses attention on dynamics, that is, trends over time in the amount of presidential news, our primary concern here. And the market model allows us to test whether the change in the economic structure of the news media from the broadcasting age to the new media age affected the production of presidential news. Other factors that might affect the provision of presidential news are also incorporated into the analysis in the next chapter, which in combination with the market model provide a more complete explanation of trends in presidential news. The remainder of this chapter presents empirical evidence that the level of presidential news has declined from the broadcasting to the new media age.

Chapter 4 presents and analyzes a new data series on the amount of presidential news over a long time span. That series, the percentage of front page news stories on the president in the *New York Times* from 1857 to 1998, can be viewed as an indicator of the national news agenda. Results suggest that the rise of the new media may indeed have depressed the amount of news about the president, although presidential public activities also seem to affect the level of presidential news. This presents us with a much more complex and subtle understanding of the provision of presidential news than currently exists in the literature on the topic.

## Constant and Variable Components in the Provision of Presidential News

News organizations are often pulled in two opposing directions. On the one hand, they want to fulfill what we can call their public service mission. This public service mission entails informing the public about government and public affairs, much of which involves the president. On the other hand, news organizations are also businesses that need to turn a profit in order to survive. The public service mission will lead news organizations to present their readers (viewers) with a certain amount of news about the president. News organizations believe they have an obligation to do so and that their credibility as a news provider hinges on this service. Once this minimal level of presidential news is attained, however, then news organizations will begin to calculate the profit implications of producing additional news about the president.

For instance, the three major networks (ABC, CBS, NBC) will allow the president to use their broadcasting systems for making major, prime-time addresses to the nation, even though such broadcasts preempt regularly scheduled programming. Yet when Richard Nixon began to make numerous requests for such airtime, the three networks balked and refused some of his requests. It became too expensive for them to allow the president to preempt their profitable programs as often as he wanted (Foote 1990).

Thus we can think of the amount of president news as having constant and variable components. The constant component is the amount of space given to news about the president no matter what. This constant component derives from the public service mission of news organizations. The variable component is governed more by the economic needs of news organizations and the effects of increased levels of presidential news on the news organization's bottom line. The research below focuses on explaining the variable component in the provision of presidential news.

## The Market for Presidential News

Most news organizations in the United States operate in the private sector. Their ability to survive depends on turning a profit. The major product that news organizations produce is news. Thus it is useful to think of news as a commodity produced in a competitive market and presidential news is but one type of news. Hence we can say that there is a market for presidential news. This section outlines the market for presidential news, which will serve as the foundation for understanding the factors associated with the production of presidential news.[1]

The profit that a news product generates is a function of the revenues that news organizations collect minus the costs of production. Revenues come from two sources, consumer purchases of the news product and advertising. Free media such as network television generate all of their revenue through advertising, and advertising revenue depends on the number and characteristics of consumers. As consumers either directly, or indirectly through advertising, affect revenue totals, news organizations will to some degree be sensitive to consumer tastes in news, that is, will produce news that consumers want to know about.

The costs of producing news are also well understood. All else being equal, a news organization may increase its profits by reducing its costs of production. These production costs have fixed and variable components, composed of the physical facilities necessary to produce the newspaper or broadcast; personnel, such as reporters, editors, and other production staff (e.g., compositors); and the delivery or distribution system. News organizations can employ standard techniques of costs control to lessen their production costs, such as increasing efficiency and productivity, subcontracting parts of the production process, and shifting the costs of production to others. Government sometimes subsidizes the costs of news production by providing journalists with a place to work, by holding regular press conferences and making other types of news announcements, and by hiring press secretaries and information offices, who provide journalists with information conveniently packaged for use as a news story.

Consider two types of news media content, presidential news and nonpresidential content.[2] In equilibrium, the profit derived from a presidential news story will be equal to the profit from a nonpresidential media content story. (Recall, we are only speaking of the variable component to presidential news here.) If the profit associated with one type of news story increases, we expect news organizations to increase their provision of that type of news and decrease their provision of the other type of news.

As the equilibrium model suggests, factors associated with nonpresidential news production may affect the production of presidential news, even if the factors associated with presidential news do not change. Under some conditions, even if presidential news becomes more profitable, the amount of presidential news produced may decline because nonpresidential news may be relatively more profitable than presidential news. For instance, assume that the cost of producing presidential news declines. Everything being equal, we would expect an increase in presidential news production, because such news has become more profitable. But if the cost of producing nonpresidential news declines by an even greater rate, the amount of presidential news will decline, while the production of nonpresidential news will increase. The same dynamic holds if revenue associated with presidential news increases, but revenue from nonpresidential news increases at a higher rate. Under this condition, we should see a decrease in the amount of presidential news and an increase in nonpresidential media content.

This model has important implications for understanding the provision of presidential news. Theories of presidential news that only look at revenue and cost factors associated with presidential activities overlook the market dynamics that the market model of the presidential news reveals. This will sometimes lead to incorrect predictions about the provision or level of presidential news. Decisions to run a story on the president are not made independent from decisions to run nonpresidential news stories. The comparative profit potential of both types of stories affects how many of each type appear in newspaper pages and news broadcasts. To understand more completely the provision of presidential news requires that we take into account the factors that affect the profitability of presidential news *as well as nonpresidential news*, as the market model outlined above does. Thus the market model directs our attention to production costs, opportunity costs, and consumer demand as factors that account for the provision of the variable component of presidential news.

## News Organization Routines and Presidential News

Modern news organizations also exhibit many of the characteristics of industrial organizations. They are formally and often bureaucratically organized. Production processes, due to high initial costs but declining marginal costs for each successive unit of production, tend to be rationalized and routinized. We see this in the "beat system," which characterizes news production in most news organizations (Becker et al. 2000, Fishman 1980, Tuchman 1973). The beat system is a prominent characteristic of presidential news production. One implication of industrial-scale production is the establishment of organizational routines, which may slow down the organizational response to changes in the market.

Below I statistically model the impact of organization routines in presidential news as the lag of presidential news. In other words, the current amount of presidential news will be a function of the past amount of presidential news plus changes in the news environment and news production practices. These changes temporarily or permanently affect news organization routines. An unexpected event, for example, may lead the news organization to alter its production routines, perhaps by deploying journalists to the event site. But after the newsworthiness of the event has ceased, journalists return to their previous assignments. Such an event leaves but a temporary mark on the news organization. Other events may become incorporated in the organization's news productions routines and thus permanently affect the way that the news organization produces news. A new beat may be established, for example, requiring the permanent deployment of a journalist to cover that beat. Or the invention and adoption of a new technology may permanently alter the news production process.

## *The National News Media and the National News Agenda*

The market model of presidential news pertains primarily to the *national news media*. We can distinguish between national news media and nonnational, or local, news providers. Only the national news media consistently produce enough national (and presidential news) for such news to have major economic consequences on these news organizations. Part of what distinguishes national news organizations from local ones is that national news organizations make it part of their business to cover national news on a routine basis.[3]

The national news media collectively produce the *national news agenda*. Traditionally, several topics have been given a prominent place in this national news agenda. These topics include news about the activities of the national government in Washington, issues that affect the entire nation, and foreign events, especially when they have implications for the United States, its policies, and its citizens. The president is often a major actor in these stories. Hence a major component of the national news agenda consists of news about the president. During the age of broadcasting, the major national news organizations for the most part defined the national news agenda; the ability of these news organizations to define the national news agenda weakened in the new media age.

Cook (1998) argues that the national news media can now be thought of as an institution: "Both the process of news making and the content of the news are so similar across organizations that we can begin to talk of the news media as a single institution" (76). Sparrow (1999) does not go so far as to consider these news organizations as an institution but argues that "given their similar environment, the largest news organizations develop and use the same practices by which to cover national political news."[4]

The seeds of a national news media and its national news agenda can be located prior to the 1920s, even before radio first began broadcasting nationally. Comstock and Scharrer argue that a national news system was in place in the nineteenth century (2005, 184; also Starr 2004). A national news media began to take shape when news organizations possessed the ability to deliver national news across the span of the nation quickly, when they began committing organizational resources to the routine collection of national news, and when they began to define their mission (and product) as the provision of national news. By the turn of the twentieth century, if not before, a national news media that defined the national news agenda was in place.

We see the first stirrings of a national news media in the mid 1800s. The telegraph, invented in the mid 1840s, allowed news to be physically disseminated across the nation speedily. Within several decades, virtually the entire nation was wired and telegraphed news stories became commonplace in most news publications.[5] The Civil War further spurred the development toward a national news media (West 2001, 35–38). With nearly every family directly touched by the war, the nation was hungry for news about the war, especially battle casualties. Major newspapers assigned reporters to cover the movements of the armies and the outcomes of battles; local newspapers routinely printed the names of casualties. Unable to allocate their own reporters around the nation, small local newspapers instead subscribed to the wire services and syndicates, like the Associated Press (AP). Through these syndicates, "it was possible to read the same story by the same writer" anywhere in the nation (West 2001, 37).

An identifiable national news agenda, an outgrowth of the national news media, began to take shape by the 1890s. In 1896, Adolph Ochs purchased the *New York Times*. He instituted an editorial policy for the *Times*—that it be the "newspaper of record." Several factors stimulated Ochs toward this new editorial policy. One was a reaction to the excesses of the yellow press and its sensational news coverage of the preceding two decades. Another was to create a market niche for the *Times* in a highly competitive newspaper environment. Ochs's new editorial policy distinguished the *Times* from the yellow journalism and partisan reporting of that era.[6]

To become the paper of record, the *Times* embarked on an objective style of reporting and began to cover national news, especially from Washington, more systematically. The wire services allowed the *Times* to sell its national news across the nation, making national news economically viable. As early as the 1850s, the *Times* was a major member of AP, providing content for that wire service. This commitment of resources enabled the *Times* quickly to become an influential national newspaper, in short order becoming the most prestigious and influential news provider in the nation.

Other news providers followed the *Times* by increasing their coverage of national news. These would come to include the national newsweeklies, *Time* and *Newsweek*, the radio and television broadcast networks (NBC, CBS, ABC), and other major newspapers, primarily the *Washington Post* (Grossman and Kumar 1981).[7] What these news organizations provided would define the national news agenda, although on occasion other news organizations would uncover a story that would become part of the national news agenda.

While these national news organizations would compete with each other to define the national news agenda, they broadly agreed on the definition and parameters of the national news agenda. Several factors operated to produce this convergence. These national news organizations operated in a similar environment, leading to the same definition of newsworthiness (Sparrow 1999). They deployed reporters to the same national beats and held the same understanding about the nature of news through a shared sense of journalistic professionalism. And despite some differences in their audiences, they all aimed to attract and affect national opinion leaders and the politically knowledgeable and interested public. Furthermore, they would read and watch each others' publications and broadcasts to check the competition, see if they scooped their competitors, and make sure that they did not overlook an important story.[8] Thus the major national news media produced quite similar news products. Media scholars call this imitative process consonance; a large empirical literature has established the similarity in news coverage across news organizations, while the *New York Times* seems the most influential news organization and highly likely to be copied by others (Comstock and Scharrer 2005, 180–81). The market model developed here applies primarily to explaining the provision of presidential news by the national news media.

## Presidential Public Activities and the Production of Presidential News

By the late nineteenth or early twentieth centuries, presidents began to value news coverage. Among other reasons, presidents believed that news coverage would enhance their leadership capability. To garner news coverage, presidents increasingly committed White House resources, such as designated and professional staff, to aid journalists in their task of covering the president. Presidents also provided journalists with services and supports that eased the task of reporting on the chief executive. These included production facilities and a place to work, technical and logistical support, press releases, advance notice of presidential schedules, access to the president and/or White House spokespeople, and the like (Cornwell 1966, Craig 2000, Grossman and Kumar 1981, Kernell 1993, Kumar 1997, Lammers 1982, Ponder 1998, Ryfe 1999).

But perhaps most important, presidents began to engage in a variety of public activities, many designed so that reporters would have something about the president to report on. Some public activities display the president making policy and/or governing decisions. Others are more symbolic or ceremonial, that is, pseudoevents. Many activities combine both substance and symbolism. Typical public activities include major, prime-time speeches, domestic and foreign travel, speeches before groups, and press conferences.

Frequent, common, and regular presidential public activities guarantee that news organizations will have a steady stream of content on the president for their stories; the services that the White House offers to journalists insures that filing stories about the president is easy to do. In effect, these services and activities subsidize the production of presidential news. With some of the cost of production subsidized, the cost to news organizations to cover the president declines, making presidential news marginally more profitable. The market model predicts that the amount of presidential news will consequently rise, everything else held constant. The major hypothesis from this perspective is that news coverage of the president will covary with the level of presidential public activities. As presidential activities increase, so should the amount of presidential news.

## The Age of New Media and the Provision of Presidential News

During the age of new media, the amount of presidential news fell compared to the earlier age of broadcast dominance. The new media age differs from the broadcast age in several regards that may have affected the provision of presidential news. Perhaps most important, competition among news organizations heightened in the new media age, a function of the introduction of new telecommunications technologies, such as cable television and the internet, as well as the relaxation of federal telecommunications regulatory policies. This new competitive environment would affect viewing and news consumption habits, which would profoundly affect the relative profitability of presidential news compared to other types of media content. In other words, due to the changes in the competitive environment of news organizations in the new media age, consumer demand for presidential news was fundamentally altered. Sensitivity to this change in consumer demand by news organizations resulted in less news about the president.

This discussion begins by describing the provision of presidential news in the broadcast age, dating back to the 1920s, with the introduction of the first broadcast technology, radio. The discussion of the new media age focuses on the effects of cable television, noting that the transition to the new media age involves more than merely cable television. But arguably cable television had the deepest and broadest effects on the competitive environment among news organizations and thus on consumer demand for news of any of the changes associated with the new media age.

### Radio, Television, and the Presidency

The introduction of radio in the 1920s and television in the 1950s ushered in the age of broadcasting. These two technologies would affect the market for presidential news in similar ways. They both increased the size of the audience for presidential news by stimulating the demand for news about the president across the broad mass public. As audience size for presidential news grew, so did the revenues that broadcasters and news providers could reap from advertisers. Federal regulatory policies, which erected high barriers to entry into broadcasting, would also play a role in insuring large audiences for presidential news.

Moreover, presidents would notice the impact of radio and television on their access to the mass public and in increasing the level of presidential news. Thus presidents would redirect many of their public activities and relationships with the news media toward the needs of radio and television journalists. Such changes in presidential behavior would in effect subsidize the broadcast production of presidential news, which also increased the marginal profitability of presidential news. Thus through two mechanisms, increasing demand (audience size) and presidential subsidization of news production, presidential news became more profitable and the level of presidential news would rise in the age of broadcasting.

First, radio and television increased the demand for presidential news. Radio created a national audience once the radio networks were established and began to broadcast nationally. Federal Radio Commission (FRC) and later Federal Communications Commission (FCC) regulations required radio broadcasters to offer public affairs programming for licensing purposes. Network radio newscasts, with its national audience, required programming that would appeal to a national audience. News about local figures would not be of interest to listeners in other regions; thus radio networks focused on national politics. After experimenting with coverage of Congress and the national parties, radio news gravitated to the presidency, which possessed a national appeal (Craig 2000). Television copied radio in emphasizing the presidency for this reason as well.

These electronic mass media also personalized the president to the public, which furthered the public's interest in the presidency and presidential news. Eugene McDonald, president of the National Association of Broadcasters, wrote President Coolidge about the virtues of radio shortly after Coolidge assumed office. Not only could radio help save the president's health, a reminder of Harding, who died in office, but radio could also affect the office and the relationship between the president and the people: "The President to most people is rather remote. . . . Radio will draw you closer to the American fireside for you will be speaking to your people as they sit in their living room. . . . Your voice and your personality will become familiar to them and in consequence . . . you will mean more to them than now" (quoted in Craig 2000, 142). Radio would thus make the president more accessible to the public.[9]

Television personalized the president even more by offering visual as well as auditory information about the president to the public. Not only could the public listen to the president speak; with television people could watch the president. Druckman's (2003) experimental evidence suggests that people react differently to radio and television, with television heightening the personal attributes of presidents to viewers. Thus the creation of a national audience and the personalization effects of these media increased public demand for presidential news. A larger audience attracted advertisers, who were wiling to pay more for access to this enlarged audience, making presidential news marginally more profitable to the national news media.

Second, federal regulatory policies also played a part in insuring large news audiences. These policies allowed each locality to have broadcast affiliates of the three major networks; few other broadcasters were allowed into the local market. As television diffused across the 1950s and 1960s, network audiences grew, but mostly as a function of television diffusion rather than the networks capturing the audience of the other networks. In effect, a government-regulated monopoly or cartel existed in this era, which possibly distorted consumer demand. Due to this distortion the networks probably provided the public with more hard news and presidential news than it actually wanted (Prior 2005). Yet because of restricted viewing options, the public consumed more news than it would have if more viewing options existed.

The networks provided more public affairs programming than the public wanted for regulatory protection, among other reasons. By offering public affairs programming, which includes presidential news, network affiliates had an easier time getting their licenses renewed and satisfying government regulators. Further, high levels of news coverage of important politicians, such as presidents, who wanted such coverage, ingratiated the networks with these politicians and reduced the likelihood of onerous regulation. Network executives found that news production enhanced their prestige, and the networks cross-subsidized news operations from the entertainment units in order to ensure the level of public affairs programming (Hamilton 2003).

Yet the structure of program offerings meant that television viewers had little viewing choice. If one wanted to watch television during the dinner hour, when news programs were broadcast, the choice became essentially one of watching the news or turning off the television set. Large numbers decided to watch the news (Baum and Kernell 1999, Prior 2005). Thus despite high levels of presidential and public affairs news, levels probably higher than the public preferred, the networks did not fear that their audiences would decline in the face of such programming decisions. With little prospect of audience attrition, journalists could determine their own definition of newsworthiness; their professionalism and other reasons led them to emphasize hard news and presidential news during this era. In defining the news, this regulatory environment and the high barriers to entry for other broadcasters limited the degree to which national news organizations had to take into account the preferences of consumers.

## The New Media Age, Cable Television, and the Presidency

In the mid 1970s, the news media became increasingly competitive and subject to economic pressures. Nonnews corporations acquired news organizations, often forcing news units to pay for themselves. To control production costs, news staffs were cut back in many news organizations. The federal government also relaxed its regulations, especially of television (Hamilton 2003, 160–63). But perhaps most important was the introduction of cable television, which altered viewer habits, shrank the size of network news audiences, and forced networks to compete with a new form of television. Although it is still too early to tell, the internet may have similar effects.

With cable television, network control of television program offerings ceased. Network audience shares declined as viewers turned to cable entertainment programs. The decline in network entertainment audiences squeezed entertainment division profits, wiping out the cross-subsidy from entertainment to news divisions. Also, the network news audience shrank as viewers substituted entertainment cable programs for network news (Baum and Kernell 1999), an indication of the distortion of consumer demand in the age of broadcasting. The profit potential of news declined because of these lost cross-subsidies and smaller audiences, which lowered advertising rates and revenues. The introduction of 24/7 news on cable (CNN) allowed those with a taste for news to feed it immediately, without having to wait for the evening network news broadcast. This further cut into network news audiences. In efforts to stem the tide and attract viewers, soft news replaced some hard news (Patterson 2000), including news about the president.[10]

In effect, the introduction of cable, and other factors that stimulated competition among national news organizations, broke the monopoly of program offerings that the networks once held. Consumers could now satisfy their true tastes for media content, and as their behavior reveals, they desired less hard news. One sign that the public on average desired less hard news than presented in the age of broadcasting was the drop in the audience for network news.[11] National news organizations, now faced with greater competitive pressures, altered their product mix to more closely match these newly revealed consumer tastes, many using market research to determine what the public wanted in their news (McManus 1994; Underwood 1998). Thus broad-based national news organizations altered their news content away from hard news and presidential news to content that was marginally more profitable.

At the same time, niche outlets increased their provision of hard news to attract the smaller, but often influential, news-demanding segment of the audience. On cable, the 24/7 networks devoted to the exclusive provision of news, such as CNN, MSNBC, and Fox Cable News, began broadcasting. Overall the audience that regularly tuned into these networks was quite small, albeit profitable due to their social and economic desirability among certain advertisers.

In the new media age, almost any news taste could be satisfied, from those who demanded minimal news to those who heavily consumed large doses of hard news. However, the broad-based news media, including most of the major national news organizations, held on to a market model that aimed at the median news consumer. For the reasons noted above, these organizations marginally shifted their content away from hard news and towards softer fare. These news organizations thought that increases in softer fare better reflected the demand for news among their audience in the new media age. Thus, as the market model predicts, we should see a decline in the provision of presidential news in the new media age among the national news media.

## Other Factors Affecting Presidential News Coverage

Besides presidential activities and changes in the structure of the national news media, factors such as government growth, economic distress, war, and the arrival of a new president may also affect the production of presidential news.

### Government Growth

Beginning in the late nineteenth century, the federal government began to grow, becoming a larger presence in society and the economy. By the last third of the twentieth century, the federal government accounted for about 30 percent of the gross national product, a tenfold increase from levels of the last third of the nineteenth century. The presidency acquired a considerable portion of the responsibility for this larger government, from proposing policies to overseeing the bureaucracy. In the eyes of journalists and the public, the presidency grew in importance as the office assumed these new responsibilities and tasks. The political culture transformed over this epoch to one in which the public demanded presidential attention and/or action across a variety of problems and issues. These dynamics should lead to increases in presidential news as government has grown.

## Economic Distress

Economic distress, such as inflationary periods and recessions, may also increase news levels about the president. Several mechanisms may translate economic distress into more presidential news. First, from a mass psychology perspective such as Edelman's (1964, 1971), perceived threats may disquiet the public, who then look to political authorities like the president for reassurance, leadership, and policies to address the source of their disquiet. Presidents often step up to challenge: doing so provides opportunities to enhance their leadership position as well as to implement policies that they prefer. Thus, during times of economic distress, public demand for news about the president, especially with regard to his statements and actions pertaining to the economy, will lead to higher news levels about the president.

## Wars and Presidential News

We are likely to witness increases in the amount of presidential news during wartime. During wartime, public distress is likely to rise. As with economic distress noted above, the public may turn to the president for leadership and to alleviate the fears and insecurities that war induces. Thus during wartime the public demand for presidential news should increase. Presidents also become more important as policymakers during wartime. Through their constitutional role as commander-in-chief, presidents become the central decision maker concerning war policy. Wars also often lead to a centralization of authority and power in the executive, which further enhances the importance of the president as policymaker and government leader. As the president becomes an increasingly important policymaker due to war, we should see increases in public interest in the executive. And as importance is one factor that journalists use to define newsworthiness, we should see more news about the president during wartime because of his increased journalistic newsworthiness.

## New Presidents

Finally, when a new president assumes office, either through election or accession due to the death or resignation of the sitting president, we should see a rise in the amount of news coverage on the presidency. Even in the nineteenth century, when the presidency was institutionally weak, the office and its occupant were important to voters and the parties. The unitary nature of the office allowed people to focus on the person running for and occupying the office, helping to forge a bond between presidents and the average person. Public curiosity may peak during presidential transitions because of lack of knowledge about the new incumbent and their desire to learn the manner of person who will occupy the office. Furthermore, the ceremony and symbolism of the inauguration may heighten public interest. In response to increased public interest during transition periods, press coverage of the president should also rise.

These four factors—government growth, economic performance, war, and a new president—work on the demand for presidential news, that is, the size of the audience, which may affect the marginal profitability of presidential news. As government grows, economic performance erodes, when the nation is at war, and when a new president assumes office demand for presidential news should rise, making presidential news marginally more profitable. During these times, then, we should see an increase in the provision of presidential news.

## Evidence of Declining Presidential News Coverage in the New Media Age

This section reviews some evidence that the amount of presidential news declined with the onset of the new media age, a claim made by several observers (e.g., Hess 1994, 2000; Patterson 2000). It may seem odd to suggest that the amount of presidential news has declined given the creation of dedicated news channels on cable and the 24/7 news cycle, as well as the immediate access to breaking news on the internet. In sorting through this issue, it is useful to distinguish between general news availability from the news sources that most of the public uses. Because of the 24/7 news channels on cable, such as CNN and Fox Cable News, and the internet, news *availability* is greater in the new media age than in the broadcast age. However, the news sources that the largest number of people use for their news, still the network evening news broadcasts and major daily newspapers, have replaced some hard news and presidential news with soft news and features (Patterson 2000). Only a small percentage of the public takes advantage of the greater accessibility of news, a point developed in greater detail in the later chapters. What evidence is there of a decline in presidential news coverage in these major and traditional news media over the past two decades?

### *The Project for Excellence in Journalism*

The Project for Excellence in Journalism (1998) conducted a study that content analyzed the news of seven major media outlets—the three traditional broadcast networks (ABC, CBS, NBC), *Time*, *Newsweek*, and the *New York Times* and the *Los Angeles Times*—for three time points across two decades (March 1977, 1987, and 1997). The project coded entire network broadcasts, the front pages of the newspapers, and cover stories of the news weeklies.[12] Their data reveal a dramatic decline in traditional or hard news across almost all of these news providers (see figure 3.1).

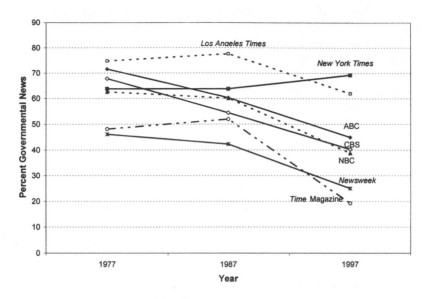

Figure 3.1 Percentage of news stories on government, military, domestic, and/or foreign affairs across major news media outlets, 1977–97. Source: Project for Excellence in Journalism. "Changing Definitions of the News," March 6, 1998. http://www.journalism.org/resources/research/reports/definitions/subjects.asp. The coding period for all years is March, with front page stories coded for the *New York Times* and *Los Angeles Times* and covers coded for *Time* and *Newsweek*.

The project sorted news into several categories. For purposes here, we can consider the project's government, military, domestic policy, and foreign policy categories as hard news. Non–hard news includes entertainment/celebrities, lifestyle, celebrity crime, personal health, other crime, business and commerce, science, technology, arts, religion, sports, weather and disasters, science fiction, and the supernatural.

The decline in hard news among the three networks broadcast is striking. In 1977 about two-thirds or more of broadcast new stories dealt with government and policy, the hard news categories. That dropped to about 40 percent by 1997. This is important because network news remains the major news source for the largest number of people. Similarly, the weekly newsmagazines, *Time* and *Newsweek*, which in the 1970s ran government and policy-related figures and stories on about half of their covers, ran such stories on their covers only about 20–25 percent of the time in 1997, a reduction rate of approximately 50 percent. The *Los Angeles Times* also displayed a minor drop in government and policy news on its front page. In 1977, about three-fourths of its front page stories concerned traditional hard news. That figure dropped to about two-thirds by 1997. Only the *New York Times* seems to have resisted the trend of declining news coverage on its front page according to the project data.

Although useful, these data have their limitations. For instance, these data provide little sense of what news coverage was like in earlier times. For the newsmagazines, exclusive attention to the cover story may overstate the degree of decline in news coverage between the covers, as covers are used primarily to attract newsstand purchases. We also have to assume that the three time points for which the project collected data are representative and do not over- or understate the trend in news presentation.

Moreover, with only three time points, we cannot test which factors account for the trend of decreasing traditional news coverage. The project suggests several causes for the shift in news. One has to do with the decline of the Cold War, arguing that the past emphasis of news reporting is of less relevance to post–Cold War audiences. But the project also notes that declining audience may motivate news organization to shift the mix of news stories in an attempt to attract new audiences. To assess empirically which factors affect the trend in news coverage requires many more data points than collected by the Project for Excellence in Journalism.

### Patterson's Lexis-Nexis Data

Thomas Patterson (2000) selected a random sample of 5,331 news stories from the Lexis-Nexis data base covering the years 1980 through 1998.[13] His sample included stories that appeared in the front page and local sections of newspapers, and during evening news broadcasts. Although Patterson was interested specifically in the rise of "soft news," his content analysis coded a variety of characteristics of news stories. Several of those characteristics are relevant for our purposes, that is, for tracking the trend in presidential and governmental news.

Figure 3.2 presents three trend lines. The "Policy" line presents the trend in stories that were coded as being substantially or somewhat about a public policy. The "Government" trend, which is broader than Policy, counts the percentage of stories that are about government and policy, politics (including elections and campaigns), political scandal, and/or political personalities. Finally, the trend line labeled "President" contains stories primarily about the president and/or the administration. Linear trend regression lines are also displayed on the figure.

All three trend lines indicate a decline over time. The most pronounced decline is for the broadest category, government news. In the early 1980s, the amount of government news varied from 71 to 78 percent. By the late 1990s, the amount of government news occupied from 54 to 66 percent of the news hole. Somewhat closer inspection suggests that the amount of government news was relatively flat from 1980 until 1991. During that time period, the

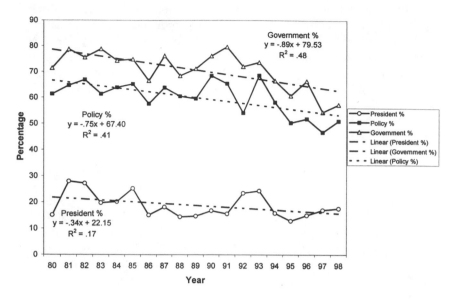

Figure 3.2 Trends in political news coverage, 1980–98. Source: Patterson (2000).

amount of government news rarely fell under 70 percent. The decline in government news appears to have begun in the early 1990s and never topped 66 percent after 1994.[14] The policy trend closely resembles the broader government trend.[15] While the amount of policy news hovered from 61 to 67 percent from 1980 through 1985, it only ranged from 46 to 58 percent from 1994 through 1998. Again, there appears to be a steady decline after 1993, when policy news peaked at 68 percent.[16] The president trend, being the narrowest category, accounts for less news space than the other two series. Presidential news, although it declines overall, does so less steeply than either of the two broader news categories, but the amount of presidential news during these two decades only ranges from about 14 to 28 percent.[17] And there appear to be some cycles in the presidential news series, with peaks occurring early in new administrations.[18]

All three data series indicate less political and presidential news in the late 1990s than early 1980s. Although these data are superior to the project data in that we have nineteen readings instead of only three, they are still somewhat limited for our purposes. First, Patterson's series begins in 1980. Although we cannot pinpoint when the "golden age" of television ended and the "age of new media" begins, some of that transition had probably already begun by 1980. For instance, by 1980, 20 percent of households already had cable television, although about 70 percent would have cable television by the end of the century. Further CNN first began broadcasting in the spring of 1980. The first

VCRs were produced in the late 1970s and quickly diffused through American households by the early to mid 1980s. Last, nineteen data points is a slim number for statistical analysis.[19]

## Baumgartner and Jones's Policy Agendas Project

The Baumgartner and Jones Policy Agendas Project, introduced in chapter 2, gives us another vantage point to look at trends in news coverage.[20] Their data focus exclusively on the *New York Times* but span a much longer time period, from 1946 through 1994. Like Patterson's data, these data record a number of characteristics of the news stories. But unlike Patterson, who coded the actual story, the agendas' data used only the story abstract. Figure 2.1, presented in the previous chapter, displayed two series. The first, labeled "Policy," presents the percentage of news stories coded as having policy content. The "President" series looks only at stories that coded the president as an actor in the story.

Both series suggest a decline in news coverage in the second half of the time frame. Where Patterson's data suggest declines in political and presidential news coverage beginning sometime in the early 1990s, these data suggest that the decline began earlier. The Policy Agendas Project's Policy series peaks in 1974 at 55.7 percent. No year thereafter reaches that level: the last year to break the 50 percent mark is 1976. After 1981, no year tops 40 percent. The President series tells a similar story, reaching a peak of news coverage in 1974 at 15.2 percent, and the last time that presidential news breaks 10 percent is 1981 (12.4).[21]

Unlike the project and Patterson data, which only date from the late 1970s, the Policy Agendas Project series trace back to 1946. These data, with this longer time perspective, reveal something that previous data cannot. Both of the longer series indicate an upward trend in news coverage from the late 1940s until the late 1970s–early 1980s. Although presidential news dips in the 1980s and 1990s, it is a level comparable to that of the late 1960s and very early 1970s. From this perspective, the decline in news coverage of the president in the 1980s and 1990s does not appear so severe or pronounced. Still, the series ends with 1994. If the decline continued through the end of the century, then presidential news coverage might only equal that of presidents in the 1950s.

There is one important difference between the Policy Agendas Project and the Project for Excellence data. Recall that the project data found that hard news reporting did not seem to drop in the *New York Times* from 1977 to 1997. The Policy Agendas Project data, also based on the *New York Times*, in contrast, find a decline in policy reporting. Two factors may account for this difference. One, the project data may have sampled cases that are atypical, that is, that either understate hard news reporting in 1977 or overstate it in 1997. Two, where the Policy Agendas Project sampled news stories across the entire newspaper, the Project for Excellence data only looked at the front page. The

*New York Times*, like most newspapers, added sections, such as technology, science, and health. The addition of these sections may reduce the overall percentage of hard news stories because the size of the newspaper has grown. At the same time, newspaper editors may still think that they should locate important news about government on the front page.

### Television Network News

Last, let's turn to television news. The Project for Excellence and Patterson data include information about television. However, as noted already, the project data are of limited usefulness for present purposes because they provide us with only three data points. Patterson's data includes television broadcasts, but they represent only a small percentage of stories because of the large number of news outlets in the Lexis-Nexis data base. Given that television, especially the evening news broadcasts, remains the public's major source of news, a look at television is warranted.[22]

Two major television databases exist, the Vanderbilt News Archives and the transcripts of broadcasts available on the Lexis-Nexis service. Lexis-Nexis contains full transcripts of ABC News broadcasts since 1980, and other networks afterward, while the Vanderbilt abstracts are available since 1968. But the Vanderbilt archive only allows one to search the story abstract online. Thus the Vanderbilt data may understate the amount of presidential news because the president is not directly named in the abstract. Also recall from our use of the Vanderbilt archive in the previous chapter that the Vanderbilt search engine is quite rigid and does not allow for Boolean or complex searches. This may also affect our ability to locate presidential news stories. A comparison of searches from the two databases found that Lexis-Nexis pulled up more stories about the president than the Vanderbilt abstracts (see below).[23] But since the Vanderbilt archive covers a longer time frame, it is worthwhile to use both series and to compare their results. Our confidence in describing the trend in presidential news will be heightened if both searches identify basically the same temporal patterns.

The procedure for searching the ABC Evening News transcripts on the Lexis-Nexis archive is as follows: using six-month increments, the search engine was asked to retrieve all stories that used the president's last name plus either the term *president* or the president's first name. The search read the transcripts of the ABC Evening News, every day of the week, excluding all other ABC News broadcasts. This search would, for instance, call up an interview with a top administration official who would name the president in response to a question. Creating a list of administration officials to also search is daunting considering the number of them. Figure 3.3 presents these ABC data. And recall the search using the Vanderbilt archive in chapter 2 and dis-

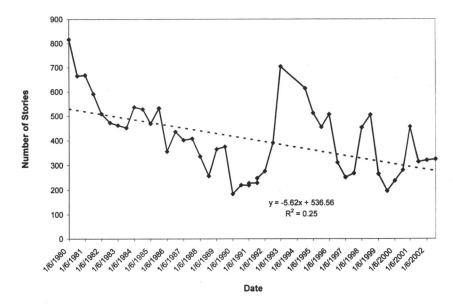

Figure 3.3 Trends in television news coverage of the president, 1980–2002. Source: Lexis-Nexis transcripts, ABC News, evening broadcasts, *World News Tonight*, Sunday–Saturday.

played on figure 2.2, which asked for each story that mentioned the word *president* and the president's last name in the abstract.

A linear time trend is imposed on the ABC data in figure 3.3. The number of stories that refer to the president can be massive, ranging from 816 (January to June 1980) to 180 (January to June 1990). On average there are 404.5 such stories per six months, or about 2.2 such stories per day. These television data also suggest a decline in presidential news coverage across the past two decades. A linear regression indicates a drop of about 5.6 stories each six months.[24] This accumulates to a decline of about 258 stories across the forty-six months recorded here.

Inspection of the series reveals several major spikes, such as the 1998 spike (possible a function of the Lewinsky scandal). But also note that the television data series starts out at a very high level, possibly due to the Iran hostage crisis. This 1980 spike might affect the linear regression trend reported above. Dropping the first two time points to exclude the massive amount of news coverage surrounding the hostage crisis, a regression of a linear counter on the remaining series still detects a downward trend, although it is shallower. Now each six-month increment loses only 4.2 stories.[25]

The major limitation for our purposes to the ABC news data is that the series starts in 1980 and can tell us little about the amount of presidential news in the earlier broadcasting age. The Vanderbilt data in figure 2.2 allow us to compare the amount of televised presidential news from the late 1960s through the early 2000s on all three networks. Those data indicate that the amount of presidential news grew on all three networks across the late 1960s and 1970s until the early 1980s, when the amount of presidential news began to decline. The Vanderbilt data remarkably resemble the trend in the *New York Times* data from the Baumgartner and Jones Policy Agendas Project. No matter which data we inspect, we find declines in presidential news that began sometime in the late 1970s or early 1980s. When we possess data for the broadcasting age, we find growth in presidential news coverage from the 1950s until the mid to late 1970s.

The next chapter presents a new data set that content analyzes the front page of the *New York Times* from the late 1850s through 1998. The very long time frame will allow us to put into long historical perspective the changes of recent decades, something that the series in this chapter do not allow. Although the decline in news coverage of the president looks massive when we compare the coverage totals across the broadcasting and new media age, the drop off in presidential news may not look so consequential if viewed from a longer historical viewpoint. For instance, research on news coverage of the president in earlier times indicates that presidential news was minimal to modest in magnitude throughout most of the nineteenth century, but grew across the twentieth century (Cornwell 1959, 1966; Balutis 1976, 1977; Kernell and Jacobson 1987). Understanding why presidential news grew provides another perspective for understanding the decline in presidential news in the new media age.

# CHAPTER 4

# Change in Presidential News over the Long Haul

## The *New York Times* Historical Series, 1857–1998

The previous chapter presented the market model of the provision of presidential news and reviewed evidence on the decline in presidential news during the age of new media. Each of the series reviewed in that chapter was limited for our purposes of understanding the reasons for the decline in presidential news in the new media age. This chapter presents a new method of collecting a very long time series on news coverage of the president that uses the front page of the *New York Times* from 1857 to 1998.

The market model of presidential news focuses on the behavior of the national news media; these *New York Times* data are used as an indicator of presidential news coverage in the major national news media. As discussed in chapter 3, the major national news organizations produce similar news products for a variety of reasons, which allows us to use the *New York Times* as an indicator of the major national news media. First, the *New York Times* has been the most influential and prestigious news organization in the United States for a very long time. The news agenda of the *Times*, consequently, affects the news agenda of other national news media (Comstock and Scharrer 2005, 180).[1]

Second, using the *New York Times* as an indicator of the behavior of major national news organizations is not unique to this study. Studies of the major national news media often use the different news outlets interchangeably. For example, in his seminal book, *Assessing the President* (1991), Richard Brody uses *New York Times* data for the Kennedy through Ford years, but CBS News data for the Carter and Reagan years, viewing them as basically interchangeable for discerning the impact of news reporting on public approval of the president.

Third, empirical evidence exists on what Comstock and Scharrer term "consonance" in the media, that is, similarity in news coverage across news outlets (2005, 180). In their review of relations between the president and the news media, Grossman and Kumar (1981) indicate a broad similarity in the reporting coverage of the president across CBS News, the *New York Times*, and *Time* magazine, as well as their interactions with the White House. Neuman (1990) finds broad similarity in news coverage across ten outlets, including the *New York Times*. One reason for this similarity in news coverage is that news organizations emulate the elite or national media, especially the *New York Times*, for coverage of national affairs (Comstock and Scharrer 2005, 180; Mazur 1987; Reese and Danielian 1989).

Fourth, from a conceptual level, Timothy Cook (1998) goes so far as to suggest that the national news media comprise an institution, that the more useful unit of analysis should be news organizations collectively, rather than individual news organizations. Bartholomew Sparrow (1999) too argues that the major national news organizations are broadly similar, because, among other reasons, they share the same news and economic environment, the same organizational structures and decision-making routines and definitions, and similar personnel recruitment systems."[2]

Another advantage of using the *New York Times* for present purposes is the series length—1857 to 1998. Only with a long series can we estimate the effects of changes from the prebroadcast age to the broadcast age to the new media age on the provision of presidential news. Furthermore, a long series allows us to place the decline in presidential news during the new media age into perspective. Compared to levels of presidential news during the broadcast age, levels in the new media age may appear meager. Compared to levels before broadcasting, such levels might not appear so low. But we need data tracing back long before broadcasting began to make these comparisons.[3] Moreover, as we will see, the trend in these *New York Times* data closely track the data on network coverage of the president from 1969 to 2005 that was presented in the previous chapter. The close correspondence in the trends across these various national media outlets suggests their interchangeability for our purposes of tracing temporal patterns in presidential news over time.

## Electronic Coding of Presidential News in the *New York Times*

The procedure described below utilizes electronic coding of newspaper articles from the *New York Times* to generate a long time series on presidential news coverage of the president from that newspaper. Recently, electronic coding of text has become a common data collection technique, but is generally limited to the contemporary age, when electronic text databases exist. Electronic coding is efficient; large amounts of data can be processed quickly. But electronic coding is no better than the retrieval systems used or the quality of the database itself.[4] Furthermore, electronic coding relies on a literal reading of text and may be unable to pick up on nuances in language use, which can greatly affect the meaning of the text. Yet Hart (2000) argues that words have meanings, which justifies literal reading of text. Electronic retrieval of text has its advantages, especially in dealing with mountains of text efficiently.

Recently, the ProQuest service has made the full text of the *New York Times*, from 1857 through 1998, available online. PDF images of every item and article can be retrieved and the search engine is quite flexible.[5] The great sweep of this historical series and its flexibility offer a potential for recovering historical data on presidential news.

Because I believe that front page news stories are likely to garner the most reader and elite opinion attention, I have used only this source of data. Editors tend to reserve the front page for stories that they consider the most important. After experimentation, a simple search request for "president" and "president's last name" (e.g., Carter) worked quite well. Adding other phrases or words did not recover any other relevant news items and a reading of sampled front pages indicates that this search did not miss relevant stories. During transition years in which more than one president serves, the query searched for both presidents (e.g., Buchanan or Lincoln for 1861). The search request did not recover stories that failed to mention the president, but it did recover stories in which the initial presidential mention was several paragraphs into the story and stories in which the president may not be the major subject or actor.[6]

This data collection technique has another advantage over past efforts that use newspapers. Past efforts selectively sampled newspapers because of the large quantity of text to code and the labor and other costs of coding such masses of data (e.g., Cornwell 1966; Balutis 1976, 1977; Kernell and Jacobson 1987). But sampling newspapers for content may be problematic. Without much knowledge of population characteristics, it is hard to determine if previous sampling designs are biased or not. For instance, Cornwell samples just one year in the four-year presidential cycle, acknowledging that his sampled years may differ from nonsampled years. As Tidmarch and Pitney (1985, 465) observe with regard to Congress, but which is also relevant to presidential news, "Over the course of a year or more . . . there is a familiar cyclical quality to it all [the congressional session], one which is shaped by election demands, new Congresses, new Presidential administrations, recesses and district work periods, and end-of-session backlogs. *When* one studies congressional press coverage influences *what* one will find" (italics in original). The same can be said of presidential news. The electronic search procedure used here retrieves the population of stories, thus overcoming the limitations of past efforts that relied on sampling techniques.

## Trends in Presidential News in the *New York Times*, 1857–1998

Figure 4.1 plots the annual number of front page stories that mention the president from 1857 to 1998. Overall, the *Times* published 116,722 such stories, a volume of news stories that would easily overwhelm even a large number of human coders. The trend is unmistakable. Presidential news has risen almost continually from the 1850s to the 1960s or 1970s. During the 1980s and 1990s, presidential news began to drop, a trend that others have noted (Hess 2000) and which the market model of presidential news anticipates.

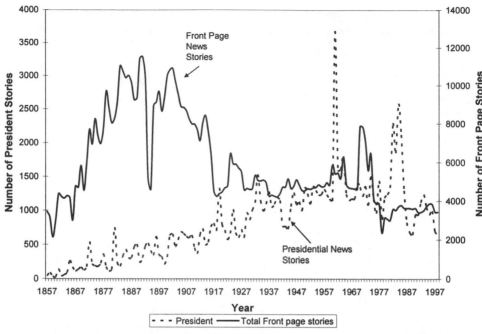

Figure 4.1 Annual number of front-page news stories and presidential news stories, *New York Times*, 1857–1998.

Several notable spikes exist in this series. One occurs in 1961, John F. Kennedy's first year in office. I read many of these stories to see if the search picked up nonpresidential stories. This does not appear to be the case. Several factors account for the spike that year. First, after eight years of Republican control of the White House, liberals inside and outside of the administration saw an opportunity to move their issues and concerns onto the governmental agenda (Sundquist 1968). Some of the increase in presidential news derived from the efforts of these policy entrepreneurs to publicize their issues and mobilize support for them. Second, the administration used family members, such as the president's wife and children, to generate a positive public image. The public also seemed highly interested in the president's young and attractive family. Third, the Kennedy administration possessed a comparatively well organized and sophisticated publicity operation, one that made great strides in using television and in cultivating close relationships with the Washington press (Kernell 1993). Another spike occurs in the early 1980s. Like Kennedy, Reagan brought to office an innovative agenda, this time steering policy in a conservative direction. And like Kennedy, the Reagan administration seemed deft in the arts of political publicity, giving rise to what many call the "Reagan treatment" of the press (DiClerico 1993, Hertsgaard 1989).[7]

Comparison of these two spikes suggests that presidential-press relations and an innovative agenda may promote news coverage of the president. These factors are compatible with the market model of presidential news. An innovative policy agenda may stimulate demand for news about the president and his agenda, which should result in increased news coverage of the president. Presidential-press relations relates to the subsidization of the costs of news production. For instance, while the Reagan treatment aimed to manage the content of news on the president, it did so in part by making it easier for journalists on the White House beat to consistently file stories on the president. And the Kennedy administration's innovations with regard to television made it easier for that emerging medium to produce presidential news. Thus the factors that hypothetically underlie these spikes seem consistent with the market model. The difficulty, however, is developing reliable and valid indicators of policy innovations and presidential-press relations. The analysis presented below uses a dummy variable (1961, 1982–84) to capture these spike effects.[8]

The *New York Times* data in figure 4.1 inform us about the level of presidential news, but not the relative amount of such news. The market model of presidential news suggests a trade-off between presidential and nonpresidential news, once we have taken into account a required or expected minimal level of presidential news. The raw count of presidential news stories tells us little about this trade-off. Moreover, the number of front page stories has varied over time due to shifts in font sizes, use of pictures, the placement of advertising and announcements on the front page, and the trend to longer articles in the latter 1900s (Barnhurst and Mutz 1997, Barnhurst and Nerone 2001). The number of available news "slots" may affect the number of presidential news stories. For instance, figure 4.1 indicates a decline in the number of presidential news stories beginning sometime in the late 1970s or 1980s. During these years, under Max Frankel's editorship, the *Times* altered its marketing plan, attempting to make the paper more competitive with television and more appealing to readers. Anecdotal evidence suggests that the number of front page stories declined as a result (Diamond 1994). Is the decline in the number of presidential front page stories during the 1980s and 1990s a function of the decrease in front page news slots?

A more appropriate measure to test the market model is the percentage of presidential news stories as a function of the total number of front page news stories. Counting the number of front page news stories from the ProQuest database is not straightforward, because the search engine provides no method to directly count articles. In an attempt to create such a base, a search asked for all items that included such common words as "a, an, is, it, of, the, was" that appeared on the front page.[9] This procedure recovered not only news articles, but also advertisements and announcements; the latter two are common on front pages in the late nineteenth century, but nearly nonexistent now. Overlaid on the presidential news series in figure 4.1 is a plot of the average daily number of items on the front page of the *Times* from 1857 to 1998. "Items" is a combination of articles and advertisements that appear on the front page.

The number of front page items ranges from 6 to 31.5 per day. The largest totals occurred in the late 1800s and early 1900s, with about 25 items per day on average. Then the number of items declined steadily, averaging about 13 per day from 1930s through the 1970s, with a daily average of nearly 10 for the 1980s and 1990s.[10] By dividing the count of presidential news stories by the count of these front page items, we obtain the percentage of front page news stories that mention the president. This measure taps the trade-off between presidential and nonpresidential news. As the percentage of presidential news increases, nonpresidential stories must decrease, and visa versa.

Figure 4.2 plots this percentage series, which closely resembles the raw count of stories on figure 4.1.[11] Again we see the 1961 and early 1980s spikes, as well as the slow building in the amount of presidential news from the onset of the series to the early 1900s. Shortly thereafter, the amount of presidential news grows at an accelerating rate, until the 1930s, when it seems to level off at about 30 percent of all front page news. Presidential news begins to increase again in the early to mid 1970s after a dip during the early Nixon years. Then it peaks in the mid 1980s with the Reagan spikes. However, even had the Reagan 1980s spike not been so high, the late 1980s would still show a receding in presidential news broken only by 1992–93, a presidential election year and the first year of the Clinton administration. Across the remainder of the 1990s, presidential news continued to slide, to under 20 percent by 1998.

These data put presidential news into long historical perspective. They indicate the drop off in the amount of presidential news beginning sometime in the late 1970s or early 1980s. Presidential news coverage of the president in the new media age on average looks modest compared to the amount of presidential news during the height of broadcasting age and is about comparable to the coverage of presidents of the early broadcasting age, during the 1950s, while slightly higher than presidents from the previous two decades. From this long historical perspective, the drop off in presidential news in the new media does not look so severe.

How well do these *New York Times* data track with news coverage from other media, especially the networks? The utility of the *New York Times* data is the long time series. However, if the *New York Times* trends differ from the network news trends, then the results of this analysis would speak more to the *New York Times* as a specific news outlet and not to the large national news media, which is our true theoretical interest. We can gain some insight into this question by comparing the trends in the *New York Times* series with the Vanderbilt series on network news coverage of the president presented in chapter 3. Figure 4.3 plots the percentage of presidential stories in the *New York Times* front page from 1969 through 1998 and the total number of presidential

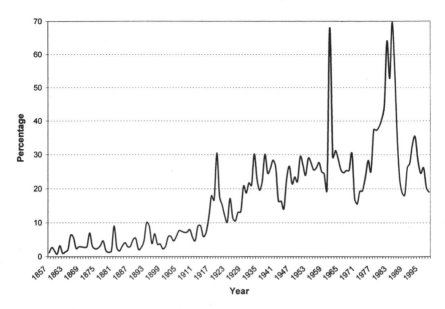

Figure 4.2 Annual percentage of presidential news stories on the front page of the *New York Times*, 1857–1998.

news stories for the three networks for these same years, that is, the year when the two series overlap. Visual inspection suggests a close similarity across the two forms of national news coverage. Both build across the years, peaking in the early 1980s, and then declining. However the "gap" in coverage widens in the late 1980s and 1990s, suggesting that relatively greater importance of the president to the networks than the *Times*. More formally the *New York Times* series correlates quite strongly with the Big Three index on figure 4.3, as well as each of the networks individually, suggesting the great similarity of presidential news coverage across these major national news media.[12] The analysis below uses this percentage series. It captures the trade-off between presidential and nonpresidential news of the market model of presidential news and appears a valid representation of national news coverage in general and not merely news coverage of the president in the *New York Times*.

## Variables and Statistical Estimation Issues in Modeling Presidential News

What accounts for the trends in presidential news, that is, the growth from the late 1800s to the late 1970s, the decline thereafter, and the short-term increases and decreases from year to year? How much do presidential public

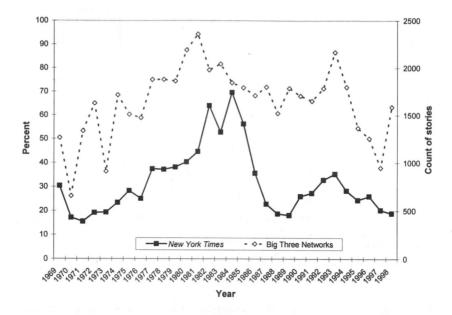

Figure 4.3 Comparison of presidential news coverage in the *New York Times* and big three television networks (ABC, CBS, NBC), 1969–98. Source: Vanderbilt Television Archives for the networks and *New York Times* historical data base from ProQuest.

activities affect the level of presidential news? Did the rise of the new media age lead to a decrease in presidential news? This section and the next address these questions using multiple regression time series. This section discusses the variables used in the analysis. Appendix 4A, located at the end of this chapter, presents details on those variables. The next section presents the results of the analysis. Time series analysis is especially technical. For those interested in the technical details, I have prepared appendices, which are located on the webpage of Princeton University Press at http://press.princeton.edu/titles/8592.html.

The dependent variable here is the percentage of presidential news stories on the front page of the *New York Times*, from figure 4.2. Despite possessing data from 1857, the analysis begins with 1897 because the *Times* only assumed its modern form, evolving into a newspaper of record and a major national news organization, when Adolph Ochs purchased it in 1896.[13] The primary analysis thus uses the years 1897 through 1998.

The primary independent variables of interest concern presidential public activities and the introduction of radio, television, and cable television, the latter keenly relevant to the hypothesis that the new media age drove down presidential news levels. Several control variables, discussed in chapter 3, are also employed. These include growth in the size of government, the inflation rate, growth rate in the gross national product, the first year that a president is in office, war, the spike dummy (to account for the high spikes associated with the early years of Kennedy and Reagan), and a time trend variable.

## Presidential Public Activities

The presidential activity data pose a special complication. Except for one presidential activity, foreign travel, we do not possess a complete nor systematic record of presidential public activities until the late 1920s.[14] Other presidential public activities of interest, such as press conferences and major and minor speeches, have been catalogued systematically only since the late 1920s. This poses a special problem for the analysis. If we want to use the entire 1897–1998 time period, the era of the modern *New York Times*, we will be able to include only one aspect of presidential public activities, foreign travel. But obviously, presidents engage in numerous other forms of public activities, many of them used specifically to drum up news about the president. It would be useful to utilize information about these other public activities in the analysis, and we may understate the effects of presidential public activities on presidential news if we only use foreign travel.

Thus, in addition to foreign travel, the analysis below uses three indicators of public presidential activities, but only since 1929, the first year when reliable counts on these activities exist: (1) an annual index that combines Political Appearances, U.S. (non-D.C.) Appearances, D.C. Appearances, and Minor Speeches (from Ragsdale's [1998] data compendium on the president); (2) the annual number of major presidential speeches; and (3) the annual number of press conferences.[15]

To utilize these other indicators of public presidential activities requires truncating the data series to 1929–98. Thus there will be two sets of analyses. One will cover the entire 1897–1998 period and a second will cover only the years from 1929 through 1998. The 1897–1998 analysis only includes foreign travel as a presidential public activity. For the 1929–98 analysis, we retain foreign travel, but add presidential press conferences, major speeches, and the presidential public activity index as presidential public activity variables.

## Communications Technologies

The discussion above emphasizes the impact of the introduction of radio, television, and cable television on the amount of presidential news. For each medium, I use the percentage of households with access to the specific medium. Years preceding the availability of the medium are coded as "0." One, however, can argue that each communication technology had to reach a certain adoption rate before it would affect the behavior of news organizations. In other words, before journalists would take radio, television, or cable television competition seriously, each had to prove their popularity and staying power. The history of communications is littered with innovations that few people adopted or were discarded shortly after an initial burst of popularity.[16]

To determine these "start" dates, I begin by identifying the date that networks began to broadcast and required one full year of network broadcasting before the start date begins. NBC, the first radio network, began broadcasting in November 1926. Thus the start date for radio is 1928, with 1927 the first full year of radio broadcasting. Prior to 1928, the radio variable is coded "zero." The cable television start date is 1982. CNN, the first cable news network, began broadcasting in May 1980, and 1981 was the first full year of CNN's broadcasts. In contrast, television diffused very rapidly and began broadcasting with networks already in place. Television began broadcasting in 1949, the start date for that medium.[17]

### Control Variables

Presidential public activities and communications technology are the prime variables of interest in this analysis. Yet other factors may also affect the level of presidential news, and we need to take them into account as well. Failure to take into account these other factors may lead us to overestimate the effects of presidential public activities and communications technologies on the level of presidential news.[18]

To measure the effect of government growth on presidential news, I use government expenditures as a percentage of the gross national product. Economic data are only available beginning in 1869 (Balke and Gordon 1989, Lynch 1999).[19] Government expenditure data come from the *Historical Statistics of the United States.* To measure the impact of economic stress, I use Balke and Gordon's (1989) and Lynch's (1999) estimates of GNP and inflation. From the GNP figures, one can calculate GNP growth rates, corrected for inflation.[20] I hypothesize that presidential news levels will rise as growth declines and inflation rises.

To test for impact of a new president on news level, I use a dummy variable, coded "1," for the first year of a new presidency, and "0" otherwise, without distinguishing among the various routes to taking office (election versus succession due to death or resignation of the incumbent). I also include in all specifications a dummy variable coded 1 for 1961 and 1982–85 and zero otherwise, to capture the spikes in presidential news during those years.[21]

The model also includes a time trend counter. Although time is an atheoretical measure, several of our independent variables of interest, such as cable television penetration, are correlated with time. The time counter helps to control for other temporal processes that might affect presidential news coverage but are not picked up in the independent variables and also guards against spurious results. If the independent variables maintain their statistical significance in face of the time control, we can feel more assured of their statistical effects on presidential news coverage. Last, the model employs the lagged form of the dependent variable, which captures organizational routines, the idea that news organizations' level of presidential news might adjust slowly to changes in the environment.[22]

## Results

The discussion below presents two sets of analyses, one for the 1897–1998 years and one for the 1929–98 years. The shorter time frame allows use of more presidential activity variables than the longer period, which only employs the foreign travel activity variable.[23]

### Results for 1897–1998 Period

Table 4.1 presents the results for the 1897–1998 period, which only includes one presidential activity variable, foreign travel. As the dependent variable, presidential news coverage, is expressed in percentages, we can interpret the findings as the percentage impact on presidential news coverage for each unit shift in the independent variables. Several of the independent variables had no impact on presidential news coverage. These include war, change in GNP, inflation, change in television penetration, and change in radio penetration.[24]

Table 4.1 also presents results of a reduced form equation. The reduced form equation excludes the insignificant variables. The remainder of this discussion focuses on the results of the reduced form equation. As to the control variables, the time counter indicates that with each passing year, presidential news increases by about 0.26 percent. Over the 102 years of this time series, there will be about 26.5 percent more presidential news in 1998 than 1897. The spike control variable also had strong effects. In the years of the spike (1961, 1982–85) presidents could expect nearly 39 percent more news than presidents in nonspike years.

Results also show that first-year presidents will garner about 2.3 percent more news than non-first-year presidents. Foreign travel also seems to lead to increased news coverage over this long period. Each day that the president spends outside of the United States per year results in about 0.09 percent more news coverage. During this period, presidents spent on average ten days outside of the United States per year, which converts into just shy of 1 percent in additional news coverage.

Change in the size of the federal government relative to the economy lowers the amount of presidential news coverage, contrary to expectations. I checked to see if this result was a function of another variable that was previously ex-

Table 4.1
Impact of presidential activity, media, and control variables on presidential news, 1897–1998 and 1929–98, AR(2)

| | Years 1897–1998 | | | | Years 1929–98 | | | |
| | Full equation | | Reduced form | | Full equation | | Reduced form | |
| | b | p | b | p | b | p | b | p |
|---|---|---|---|---|---|---|---|---|
| Spike | 38.56 | .00 | 38.72 | .00 | 37.79 | .00 | 37.49 | .00 |
| War | −1.14 | .60* | xxxx | | −2.29 | .36* | −3.46 | .05* |
| First yr. | 2.64 | .00 | 2.28 | .01 | 3.28 | .01 | 2.87 | .03 |
| For. travel | .06 | .02 | .09 | .00 | −.06 | .49* | xxxx | |
| Public activities | xxxx | | xxxx | | −.00 | .89* | xxxx | |
| Press confer. | xxxx | | xxxx | | .08 | .10 | xxxx | |
| Major speeches | xxxx | | xxxx | | .38 | .14 | .52 | .07 |
| GNP-ch. | −11.43 | .12 | xxxx | | −4.49 | .41 | xxxx | |
| Inflation | .22 | .10 | xxxx | | .10 | .37 | xxxx | |
| Fed. spending % | −.11 | .25* | −.25 | .04* | −.20 | .52* | xxxx | |
| TV-ch. | .37 | .18 | xxxx | | .30 | .27 | xxxx | |
| Radio % | −.14 | .84* | xxxx | | −.70 | .45* | xxxx | |
| CATV % ch-1982 | −3.77 | .00 | −3.98 | .00 | −3.06 | .00 | −2.96 | .00 |
| Counter | .26 | .00 | .27 | .00 | .22 | .11 | .16 | .03 |
| AR1 | .49 | .00 | .55 | .00 | .31 | .00 | .37 | .00 |
| AR2 | .26 | .00 | .22 | .01 | .36 | .00 | .25 | .02 |
| Constant | 6.64 | .16* | 6.34 | .18* | 16.42 | .02* | 19.38 | .00* |
| Log likelihood | −294.15 | | −296.54 | | −198.29 | | −201.87 | |
| Wald chi-sq | 461.71 | .00 | 478.48 | .00 | 270.13 | .00 | 212.33 | .00 |
| Q test-Lag 1 | .15 | .70 | .19 | .66 | .28 | .60 | .16 | .69 |
| Q test-Lag 5 | 2.72 | .74 | 3.63 | .60 | 2.44 | .79 | 3.64 | .60 |
| Q test-Lag 10 | 6.92 | .73 | 8.57 | .57 | 12.70 | .24 | 10.41 | .41 |

Source: See appendix 4A for details.

Note: N for 1896–1998 = 102, for 1929–98 = 70.

* Two-tailed t tests used because of wrong sign. One-tail t test used for all other coefficients.

cluded, in particular growth in GNP and inflation, but this did not seem to be the case. It is unclear why a shrinking relative federal establishment should lead to more presidential news. Perhaps when the government pulls back in size, news turns to the effects on citizens of this reduced federal penetration into society. The president, as head of the executive, may receive the bulk of this attention (and blame?) for the effects of these changes in federal policies.

Turning to the media variables, only change in cable television dissemination statistically affects the amount of presidential news coverage. As expected, increases in the percentage of households with cable television depresses presidential news coverage but only after 1982, when CNN began broadcasting and the percentage of households topped 20 percent. The effect is massive. Each

1 percent increase in households with cable television per year erodes presidential news coverage by nearly 4 percent. The average annual change in cable access is 0.4, which translates into an average decline of 1.6 percent per year. But near the end of this time series, the late 1990s, nearly two-thirds of households had cable television. With 65 percent of households having cable television and each 1 percent of households equating with a 0.4 percent decline in news coverage, presidents in the late 1990s can expect a loss of about 26 percent (65 percent * 0.4) in their level of news coverage compared to times when cable did not exist.

Finally, presidential news at lags 1 and 2 affect current levels of presidential news (see the AR(2) statistic on the table), as the organizational routines hypothesis predicts. In other words, news organizations do not immediately respond to changes in their news environment, but they do respond. The coefficient for the first lag is 0.55 and the second is weaker at 0.22. In other words, each 1 percent of news about the president last year resulted in 0.55 percent of news about the president this year, and each 1 percent of presidential news two years ago leads to 0.22 percent this year.[25] These results demonstrate the drag of organizational routines on the definition of news and also the relative speed with which news organizations respond to changes in their news environment.

Overall these results for the 1897–1998 period tell us that, as expected, presidential public activities, here only foreign travel, are statistically associated with marginally higher levels of news coverage, and that the introduction and spread of cable television led to a decline in news coverage. However, we were only able to look at one type of presidential public activity. The next section adds the other presidential public activities into the statistical estimation, but in so doing truncates the analysis to a shorter time period, 1929 through 1998, because we have information on these other forms of public activities only since 1929.

### Results for 1929–98 Period

Table 4.1 also presents the results for the 1929–98 period and follows the presentation format of the longer time period, with both a full model that includes all variables and a reduced-form one that only includes the significant variables. This analysis adds three presidential activities, the presidential activity index, major speeches, and press conferences. Recall that data on these forms of presidential activity do not exist prior to 1929, but as they are substantively important forms of presidential activity, it is useful to add them to the analysis, even if we must delete cases for analysis.

There is much overlap in the findings across the two time periods, although a few notable differences also exist. Again, many of the hypothesized variables failed to produce a statistically significant effect on presidential news. These include both of the economic variables (inflation, growth in GNP), as well as change in the size of the federal government, which was significant for the longer time period.

The advantage of the shorter time period is that we can inspect the impact of a greater variety of presidential public activities. Surprisingly, most of the presidential activity variables failed to have any impact. Of the new presidential activity variables, neither the index of presidential public activities nor press conferences seemed to statistically affect the amount of presidential news. And foreign travel, which was significant for the longer period, is not significant for this truncated period. But major speeches, discussed below, seem to affect news coverage in this more modern age. Also as before, change in the percentage of households with television or radio did not affect presidential news coverage from 1929–98.

With the insignificant variables eliminated from the analysis, a reduced form equation is estimated and presented on table 4.1. From the reduced form equation, we find the time counter to be significant. Each passing year from 1929 to 1998 leads to an increase of 0.16 percent in presidential news. This effect is somewhat weaker than that found for the long period analysis, because news coverage in 1929 is higher than in 1897. Over the seventy-year period, a president in 1998 can expect about 11 percent more news coverage than a president in 1929. Again the spike variable also affects news coverage. Presidents in the spike years will see 37 percent more news than presidents in nonspike years, an amount comparable to the longer period analysis. And, repeating the earlier result, first-year presidents can expect about 2.8 percent more news than non-first-year presidents, an increment slightly larger than the effect for the longer 1897–1998 period.

In this modern period, war now statistically affects presidential news coverage, but opposite to expectations. Wars depress presidential news by about 3.5 percent. This drop in presidential news in wartime may be due to a shift in news attention during wars from government in Washington to the battlefield and the commanders leading American troops. For instance, during World War II, Dwight Eisenhower became a major celebrity and leader of the nation due to his wartime responsibilities, eventually spring-boarding to the presidency. During the Korean conflict, Douglas MacArthur may have played a similar, if more controversial role. Not uncommonly, military leadership during war leads to important political careers and the presidency. Such is the case from George Washington to Andrew Jackson, Ulysses Grant, and Theodore Roosevelt in earlier times.

Our data indicate that of presidential public activities major presidential speeches lead to greater news coverage, but the overall effect may not be substantively large due to the relatively small number of major presidential speeches in any one year. The results indicate that each major presidential speech is associated with increases in presidential news coverage of about 0.5 percent. For a president of average speech-making levels (4.5 speeches), this means an additional 2.25 percent in news coverage. For a president of maximum speech making, 11 speeches, this could translate into about 5.5 percent more coverage. We need to be cautious in assigning significance to major speech effects because the significance value of 0.07 (one-tailed) falls just shy of the conventional 0.05 level.

Assuming major speech effects, how do we reconcile this effect with the lack of effect of other presidential public activities and the lack of effect of foreign travel, which had a significant effect for the longer time period analysis? Novelty is important in attracting news attention. As the presidency's publicity operations developed across the twentieth century, presidential activities designed to attract news attention no longer possessed novelty, but became routine and expected aspects of the presidency. Levels of presidential activity may be forced on the presidency in order to meet these journalistic and mass public expectations and to provide a routine flow of events and activities for the press to report on. Thus, over time, many presidential public activities lost their novelty and became routine.

Major presidential speeches, by their nature, may always contain an element of novelty. Many of these speeches are unexpected, prompted by crises that require presidential attention. Major presidential speeches may also be novel in the sense that they are important, that a president deems the topic of the speech so compelling for the nation that he is willing to preempt normal prime-time television entertainment programming to deliver his speech. For the most part, the networks agree with this presidential assessment by granting him access to their airwaves.

Now let us turn to the other variable of interest, the effects of cable television. Repeating the results of the longer time period analysis, cable television again seems to statistically affect presidential news coverage. Each annual 1 percent increase in households with cable since 1982 reduces presidential news coverage by nearly 3 percent, which is nearly as much as found in the previous analysis. With an average annual change in cable of 0.6 percent, this translates into a 1.8 percent decline on average per year. Comparing a year of maximum penetration of cable (65 percent) with a year without cable at all translates into a decline of 39 percent (65 percent * 0.6) in the amount of presidential news coverage. Again the statistical effects are mighty, and they hold up even when we control for time.

Finally, turning to the lagged terms from the AR(2) analysis, we find that for the years 1929–98, each 1 percent increment of presidential news in the past year leads to 0.37 percent increment in the current year, and each 1 percent increment two years ago, leads to 0.25 percent increment in the current year.[26] The one-year lag effects are weaker for this modern period compared to the longer time period analyzed above, indicating perhaps the increasing ability or speed of modern news organizations to respond to changes in their news environments. Appendix 4F on the webpage discusses a variety of other model estimations, all of which support the general findings reported in the previous pages.

## Conclusion

The amount of news that a president receives affects his ability to lead the mass public. Without a strong presence in the news, the president's ability to lead the public ebbs. Furthermore, without sufficient news coverage of his activities in office, the public may have a more difficult time holding the president accountable. Thus it is important for us to be able to describe trends in presidential news coverage and explain the factors that affect those trends.

One recent trend has become noteworthy: over the past several decades the amount of presidential news has declined. Yet presidential activities designed to stimulate news coverage, like speeches and trips, have increased in volume, while the resources and skills of the White House aimed at generating news coverage have improved. These diverging trends—declines in news coverage while White House efforts and capabilities to generate news coverage have improved—present a puzzle to solve. These divergent trends also undermine conventional views of the effectiveness and utility of White House publicity operations and efforts, which argue that public presidential activities can affect presidential news coverage.

A market model of presidential news, developed in the previous chapter, identifies not only presidential activities, but other factors, such as the changing structure of the news media, as important factors that may affect presidential news. To isolate the effectiveness of White House publicity operations on the ability to generate news coverage requires that we also take into account these other factors, such as the economic implications of presidential news versus other types of content for news organizations. Using newly collected data on presidential news coverage in the *New York Times* that spans from the mid 1800s to the late 1990s, analysis presented in this chapter finds that both presidential activities and changes in news media technology (radio, television, and cable television), among other factors, affect the amount of presidential news. Importantly, changes in technology affected by and affecting the economics of news organizations had major implications for public demand for news about the president. To a large degree, changes in the public's demand for presidential news drives much of the trend over time in the amount of presidential news.

From these findings, we possess a more balanced understanding of the amount of news coverage of the president. Presidential activities clearly have something to do with the amount of news that presidents receive, but the forces of technology and changing structures of competition among news organizations often overwhelm anything that presidents can do to orchestrate their news coverage levels. When presidents want greater levels of news coverage and media factors point in the same direction, such as was the case during the 1960s and 1970s, when the three television networks were so important, presidents can count on high levels of news coverage. But when these factors—presidential activities and media structures—work in opposite directions, presidential activities may make only a marginal difference on news coverage levels.

The findings deepen our understanding of presidential leadership. Recently, George Edwards (2003) has argued that presidents have a harder time leading public opinion than conventional wisdom has led us to believe; he reviews a host of reasons that impede presidential leadership of public opinion. Baum and Kernell (1999) add another piece of the puzzle, at least for the last fifteen to twenty years—fewer people watch presidential speeches. This research adds one more piece to the puzzle—news coverage of the president has also declined. The next chapter turns to another important trend in news coverage of the president over the past several decades, the increase in the negativity or criticism.

## Appendix 4A: Variables Used in the Analysis

Note that further information about statistical methods employed in this book can be found online at http://press.princeton.edu/titles/8592.html.

### Dependent Variable

1. Presidential News: 1897–1998. Front page news stories on the president as a percentage of all front page news stories, *New York Times*. Data source: Proquest. See text.

### Independent Variables

1. Foreign Travel: 1897–1998. Number of days per year the president spent traveling outside of the United States. Source: State Department list of presidential travel abroad: www.state.gov/r/pa/ho/trvl/pres/.
2. Index of Presidential Public Activity: 1929–98. A weighted additive index of the annual number of presidential Political Appearances, U.S. (non-D.C.) plus presidential Appearances, plus presidential D.C. Appearances, and Minor presidential speeches. Source: Ragsdale (1998). See "Constructing the Presidential Public Activity Index" in appendix 4B on the website for details on how the index is constructed.
3. Major Presidential Speeches: 1929–98. Annual number of major presidential speeches. Source: Ragsdale (1998).
4. Press Conferences: 1929–98. Annual number of presidential press conferences. Source: Ragsdale (1998).
5. Radio: 1897–1998. Annual change in the percentage of households with radio, starting in 1928, "0" otherwise. Sources: *Historical Statistics of the United States* and various volumes of the *Statistical Abstract of the United States*.

6. Television: 1897–1998. Annual change in the percentage of households with broadcast television. Sources: *Historical Statistics of the United States* and various volumes of the *Statistical Abstract of the United States*.

7. Cable Television: 1897–1998. Annual change in the percentage of households with cable television, starting in 1982, "0" otherwise. Sources: *Historical Statistics of the United States* and various volumes of the *Statistical Abstract of the United States*.

8. GNP growth rate: 1897–1998. Annual percent change in the gross national product. Sources: Balke and Gordon (1989) and Lynch (1999).

9. Government Size: 1897–1998. Change in government expenditures as a percentage of gross national product. Source for expenditure data, *HistoricalStatistics of the United States* and OMB's webpage: http://www.whitehouse.gov/omb/budget/fy2004/, in particular, table 1.1—Summary of Receipts, Outlays, and Surpluses or Deficits (–): 1789–2008. For GNP data see Balke and Gordon (1989) and Lynch (1999).

10. Inflation: 1897–1998. Average annual inflation rate. Sources: Balke and Gordon (1989) and Lynch (1999).

11. First Year: 1897–1998. Dummy variable for first year that a president is in office, no matter how he came to office, scored 1 = first year, 0 = otherwise.

12. War: 1897–1998. Dummy variable for U.S. involvement in major wars (Spanish-American, 1898; World War I, 1917–18; World War II, 1942–45; Korea, 1950–53; Vietnam, 1965–73; Gulf, 1991), scored 1 = war, 0 = no war.

13. Trend: 1897–1998 and 1929–98. Annual counters with 1897 = 1 to 1998 = 102 and 1929 = 1 to 1998 = 70.

14. Spike: Dummy variable coded.

# CHAPTER 5

# The Increasing Negativity in Presidential News in the Age of New Media

As the last two chapters document, the amount of presidential news declined from the broadcasting age to the age of new media.[1] This lower level of presidential news in the new media age raises the barrier for presidents bent on getting their message to and leading the mass public. When his news coverage declines, the volume of the president's voice fades, making it somewhat harder for the public to hear and heed him. Plus, as the president receives less news coverage, other voices may gain greater access to the news, filling some of the news space once occupied by the president, which makes these other voices more viable competitors with the president for the public's attention. Presidential leadership of the public has always been problematic (Edwards 2003), but leading the public becomes increasingly difficult as the amount of news coverage on the president shrinks. In the age of new media one barrier to effective presidential leadership of the public has been the decline in the amount of presidential news coverage.

But the decline in presidential news coverage levels is not the only barrier to presidential leadership of the public in the new media age. The tone of news on the president has also become increasingly negative. Negative or critical news coverage of the president undermines his persuasiveness and leadership ability. Negativity in news coverage often means that others, whether they are journalists, political competitors to the president, or other important authoritative figures, disagree with the president or refuse to follow his lead. Perhaps the president's best opportunity to lead the public exists when the nation's political elite lines up in support behind him. A unified political elite presents the public, often confused or ill-informed about politics and policy, with a single message and less bewilderment about which direction or politician to follow (Brody 1991, Zaller 1992). There is only one viable policy alternative when the nation's political elite is in agreement. Plus, an elite united behind the president makes the president appear a more commanding, prescient, and/ or wise leader. Negative news undermines the president's ability to lead. Consequently, not only do presidents aim to dominate the news, but they also want to insure that their news coverage is positive and supportive.

## Evidence of Increasingly Negative Presidential News in the New Media Age

Several studies suggest a high and increasing level of negative news about the president in the new media age. For instance, the Project for Excellence in Journalism compared the nightly network news coverage of presidents Bill Clinton and George W. Bush during their first hundred days in office.[2] It found Clinton receiving positive coverage 22 percent of the time, negative news 28 percent, and neutral coverage 49 percent of the time, or 6 percent more negative than positive news. George W. Bush received positive news 27 percent of the time, negative news 28 percent, and neutral news 44 percent, or 1 percent more negative than positive news.

The tallies of the Center for Media and Public Affairs are broadly consistent with those of the Project for Excellence in Journalism. Based on a content analysis of the three major network evening news broadcasts, the center found that of the past four presidents, only George H. W. Bush received a majority of positive broadcast news references in his first hundred days in office (61 percent). In contrast, presidents Reagan, Clinton, and G. W. Bush received positive mentions in only 43, 40, and 29 percent of news broadcasts. As their first years in office progressed, positive news declined for all four, with Reagan receiving 26 percent positive news, G. H. W. Bush, 40 percent, Clinton, 28 percent, and G. W. Bush, 23 percent.[3]

While not extraordinarily negative, that the Project for Excellence figures are not lopsidedly positive is notable given that this is the president's traditional honeymoon period. (The Center for Media and Public Affairs data only provides positive ratings, not negative and neutral, so we cannot make similar tonality comparisons.) If the honeymoon represents a time when presidents can expect their most positive news coverage, these figures do not bode well from the president's perspective for the rest of his time in office.

These figures differ markedly from those that Grossman and Kumar (1981) report for the 1953 to 1977 period; these researchers generally find a high degree of positive news for presidents in the 1950s and early 1960s. One must be cautious, however, in directly comparing the Grossman-Kumar data and Project for Excellence and Center for Media and Public Affairs data. Where Grossman and Kumar look at the entire year, the project data was only for the first hundred days of new presidencies, and as noted, the center data only presents positive news in its public reports.

Fortunately, Lyn Ragsdale (1997) has built on Grossman and Kumar's *New York Times* data, extending the series back to 1949 and up through 1992.[4] Her efforts provide us with a relatively long annual time series, displayed previously in figure 1.5. Figure 5.1 replots the percentage of negative news from her series, but adds to the plot the percentage of positive news stories and superimposes

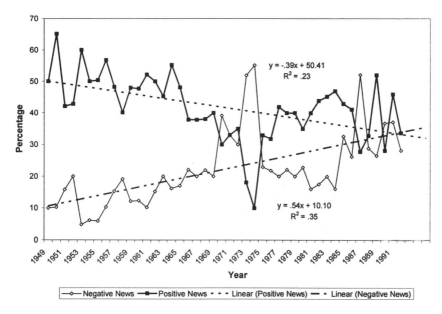

Figure 5.1 Trends in the tonality of presidential news, *New York Times*, 1949–92. Source: Ragsdale (1997).

trend lines over both. (News may also not have a discernable negative or positive tone; thus the amount of positive and negative news does not total to 100 percent.) As the figure shows, negative presidential news clearly trends upward, while positive news slopes downward.[5]

From 1949 through 1959, about 12 percent of presidential news in the *New York Times* was negative. In the 1960s, the percentage of negative news rose to 17.5, climbing to nearly 32 percent in the 1970s and 28 percent in the 1980s. Obviously, Watergate had a huge impact on the average amount of negative news in the 1970s, with more than half of news about the president being negative in 1973 and 1974. If we remove 1973 and 1974, about 26 percent of presidential news is negative in the 1970s. Figures for positive news mirror the pattern for negative news. The key point is that in the 1970s and 1980s, when the era of new media began to replace the golden age of broadcasting, presidential news turned increasingly negative.

Just as the market model developed in the previous chapters helps us understand the trend in the amount of presidential news coverage, the market model provides an insight into why negative news coverage might have increased. Recall, the market model predicts that the relative profitability of a news story affects the probability that it will be reported. News organizations, given two types of news (e.g., presidential versus nonpresidential news) will grant more news space to the more profitable type of news. During the age of new media this meant lower levels of presidential news for the reasons discussed in chapters 3 and 4.

The same motivation, marginal profitability, may explain the rise of negative presidential news. For a variety of reasons, news organizations may have felt that negative news would be more attractive to viewers and readers than positive or even neutral news. Negative news may be more eye-catching, of greater interest, than positive news. Plus the controversy inherent in negative news may stimulate interest, especially among those who generally are disinterested in news about government. Further, negative news, often structured around conflict between two sides, may appear more dramatic, and thereby further stimulate interest. Fourth, the two-sided, conflict-based negative news story may be relatively easy for less well-informed readers to understand and may be conveyed fairly easily in the confines of the short broadcast news spot. This greater attractiveness would increase the relative profitability of negative presidential news, in part, because negative news works to stimulate demand. As news organizations in the new media age feel greater economic pressures, they may turn increasingly to negative news as a way of increasing audience size. Thus we should see a rise in negative presidential news in the new media age. And just as the decline in news coverage may hinder presidential leadership efforts, so may the rise of negative news.[6]

The task of this and the next chapter is to investigate the association between negative news and the era of new media more systematically. This chapter takes a closer look at the Ragsdale *New York Times* data presented on figure 5.1 and asks, What accounts for the rise in negative news in the 1980s and into the 1990s? Did the rise of the new media have anything to do with the increasing amount of negativity in presidential news? Also, I turn to Thomas Patterson's Lexis-Nexis data, which was briefly discussed in chapter 1. With Patterson's data, which covers individual news stories from 1980 through 1999, we will be able to ask whether certain types of news practices characteristic of reporting in the new age of media are associated with negative news coverage of the president. This will provide us with two complementary perspectives on negativity in presidential news.

## Issues in Studying News Tone

There are several issues in studying news tone. First, no absolute standard exists to tell us what constitutes negative news. What is negative for some may be positive for others. To structure this analysis, we will take the president's perspective and ask: Would a president perceive a news story as negative, that is, as harming his public image and thereby undermining his ability to lead the public? When a president's public image is harmed, say through negative news, he may fear that his level of public support will decline, which in turn may make it harder for him to bargain with other politicians and/or lead the public. Thus presidents work hard to maintain a positive public image. Waterman et al. (1999) argue that building a positive public image has become the paramount activity of modern presidents, that it may even be more important than policy leadership and success.

A second issue in the study of news tone relates to the source of the negativity. Negative news may be, for instance, a function of bad events, like rises in unemployment or inflation, a military defeat, or a loss on Capitol Hill (West 1991). However, the decisions of journalists and the routines of news organizations may produce negative news even if no negative event exists. Presidents often decry that the news media report a story negatively when the events do not necessarily warrant such an interpretation, in other words, that the news media are biased against them.

As Groeling and Kernell (1998) observe, it can be hard to distinguish between these two types of negative news. Where Groeling and Kernell are concerned with determining whether news is negative toward the president, whether there is media bias, the task here is somewhat easier—to determine if the amount of negative news has increased and the factors associated with that increase. I am not particularly concerned with whether the news is justifiably negative or not or whether media bias exists. Instead, simpler questions underlie this research: Is there more negative presidential news in the age of new media than before? Is there something about the age of new media that has led to the increase in negative news or is it merely a function of an increasing incidence of bad events?

## The Era of New Media and the Rise of Negative Presidential News

Negative presidential news may arise out of the events that news organizations report as well as from the decisions of journalists in deciding what to report and how to write their news stories. Ragsdale's time series data indicate that negative news is more common in the 1980s and 1990s than it was in the 1950 and 1960s. One possibility to account for the greater frequency of negative news stories in the era of new media is that negative events, the subject matter of much of negative news, were more common in the latter period than the earlier one.

To satisfy ourselves that the new media era had something to do with the rise in negative news, we must control for these other factors that might lead to negative news. From 1949 through 1992, the years of the data series at hand, the nation fought three major wars, two of them highly unpopular. The economy also swung from good times to bad and administrations were embroiled in two major scandals, Watergate and Iran-Contra. Such events are likely to affect news reporting of the president. In fact, it would be astonishing if such scandals as Watergate and Iran-Contra, economic recessions, and/or the Korean and Vietnam wars had no impact on the tone of presidential news.

## War and News Tone

Major wars are momentous events. They command great public attention, in part because of their implications for government and society, but also because of the personal stakes for individuals whose family members and friends may be serving in the armed forces and may be faced with death or injury. Journalists also take great interest in war, motivated in part by the public's interest and by the intrinsic importance of wars, but also because journalistic careers can be built and advanced by war reporting.

Noting that war stimulates the interest of the public and journalists does not tell us if war reporting will be beneficial or not to the president. On the one hand, "rally round the flag" dynamics suggest that wars might stimulate positive news, but war rallies tend to be short-lived or persist only if the war is going well, if the nation appears to be making progress toward victory. Wars that drag out, without an obvious end in sight, with mounting causalities, and with economic sacrifice asked of the populace, may lead to negative news.[7] Controversial wars may stimulate presidential opponents and members of the opposition party to speak out against the president. The public may become activated and agitated, demonstrating against the war, such as we saw during the Vietnam War. Thus not all wars are the same. Some may lead to good news, others to bad news.

From 1949 to 1992, the United States engaged in three major wars: Korea, Vietnam, and the first Gulf War. The first two produced much public outcry, seemed endless, forced both initiating presidents (Truman and Johnson) out of office, and the opposition party assumed the White House. The Gulf War, in contrast, was swift and seemingly decisive, with few American casualties. Thus I stipulate hypotheses that negative news will increase during the Korean and Vietnam wars but decrease during the Gulf War, which are measured with two dummy variables, a Korean-Vietnam dummy (1951–53, 1965–72 = 1, otherwise 0) and a Gulf War dummy (1991 = 1, otherwise = 0).[8] Appendix 5A lists details on all variables used in the analysis in this chapter.

An alterative Gulf War hypothesis should also be entertained. This alternative hypothesis focuses on the short duration of the war itself, the rather lengthy lead up to the war, and the aftermath of the war. Recall that we are dealing with annual time units here. Actual combat lasted from mid January 1991 through nearly the end of February. During this period, we can expect low levels of criticism of the president in the news. Prior to the actual fighting, considerable debate existed among opinion leaders, members of Congress, and the mass public over the wisdom of war with Iraq (Bennett and Paletz 1994;

Mueller 1994). The nation was roughly divided equally over support for the war, which was George H. W. Bush's preferred policy. From this environment, we can expect a significant amount of negative news, or at least news that featured criticism of Bush's war policy.

After the war, despite the swiftness of the war and the low level of U.S. casualties, criticism reemerged as some opinion leaders challenged the president's too-soon cessation of the war. These critics maintained that the United States should have continued to fight until Saddam Hussein was removed from office. This postwar criticism should increase the amount of negative news about the president and lead to the hypothesis that 1991, the year of the Gulf War, should not be associated with positive news for the president. Instead, the positive news of the war coupled with the postwar criticism should cancel out, leaving no effect of the Gulf War on the level of negativity in presidential news. However, inasmuch as the postwar criticism dragged on for an extended period, the amount of negative (critical) news reporting might surpass the amount of positive news coverage received during the period of active hostilities. If this is the case, then we might expect 1991 to be associated with a higher level of negative news.

## The Economy and News Tone

As with wars, the state of the economy can help or hurt presidencies. Rightly or wrongly, given a president's limited economic policy tools, the public holds the president accountable for the economy. When the economy ails, not only does public support for the president falter, but challengers to the president voice their criticisms and the state of the economy becomes a major campaign issue. In good economic times, challengers have a harder time criticizing the president on that issue and presidents tout their economic accomplishments. We should see these dynamics reflected in news too. As the economy falls, the incidence of bad news should rise; when the economy appears healthy, the proportion of bad news should contract (De Boef and Kellstedt 2004). Two variables are used to measure the state of the economy, the annual inflation and unemployment rate.[9]

## Scandals

Scandals, it seems, have become the stuff of news in the new media age. But scandals have been important news stories since the 1830s, when the penny press discovered a public appetite for them. Scandals also come in many varieties, ranging from actions that many think violate the Constitution, to graft and corruption, to sex scandals. And although many scandals touch the White House, only a few have presented major implications for the serving president. Thus the scandal that forced Sherman Adams, Eisenhower's chief of staff, from office, had little impact on the president. Similarly, Bert Lance's problems, which forced him from his post as OMB director under Jimmy Carter, had little lasting impact on news or public opinion about the president.

Across the second half of the twentieth century, three scandals rocked the presidency—Watergate, Iran-Contra, and the Lewinsky affair. What distinguishes these from other scandals is their duration, the amount of news that they generated, and that each raised issues about whether the president should remain in office. Moreover, public opinion research finds that only these three had any impact on public opinion; all other scandals with a White House connection barely registered in the public's consciousness (e.g., Newman 2003, Ostrom and Simon 1989). However, as the *New York Times* data series ends with 1992, we cannot inspect the comparative effects of the Lewinsky scandal. Dummy variables are used to measure the scandals: Watergate (1973–74 = 1, otherwise = 0) and Iran-Contra (1987 = 1, otherwise = 0), which are kept separate as variables because Watergate's effects on public opinion appeared stronger than Iran-Contra (Ostrom and Simon 1989).

### Presidential Honeymoons

Newly elected presidents often receive a honeymoon. During the honeymoon period, criticism of the president is muted, but little scholarly work precisely defines a honeymoon.[10] Some suggest that after an election, the public rallies behind the new incumbent, in effect hoping that the new president will turn out to be a good leader. Others view the honeymoon period as one in which the divisions of the electoral campaign are healed, which is necessary for the legitimacy of the system and for the newly elected government to govern. Elections, by nature, polarize the electorate into two (or more) camps, in support of one candidate and simultaneously in opposition to the other. Such polarization cannot persist without dire consequences for the system's ability to function (Ginsberg and Weissberg 1978). Opposition spokespeople also often limit their criticism of the president during this period.

Whatever the driving force behind honeymoons, we find that early presidential approval tends to be high, usually somewhat higher than the size of the winner's election victory. Being responsive to their market during the honeymoon, when the public feels amicable toward the president, journalists may limit negative news stories so as not to alienate readers. And when opposition voices are quiet, journalists may have a hard time finding a credible and authoritative source willing to criticize the president, which may curb their ability to write negative or critical news stories. Thus our hypothesis is that during honeymoon periods, the amount of negative news on the president will be lower than during nonhoneymoon years. As the data are annual, I measure honeymoon's with an annual dummy variable, 1 = first year of a president's term in office, 0 = otherwise.

## Political Context

The honeymoon effect suggests that political context may affect the amount of negative news. When the political context is hostile, when there are many administration critics publicly voicing their opposition to the president, we can expect the amount of negative news to rise. Authoritative voices are important sources for journalists. Even in the age of interpretive journalism, journalists keep a distance, to appear neutral, balanced, and objective in their reporting. At the same time, journalists like to report news as stories, often ones involving conflict. When people in positions of authority, like members of Congress or representatives of major interest groups, are willing to speak out against the president, journalists may use such people as actors in a story of conflict between the president and an antagonist. By allowing the spokespeople for the two sides of conflict to speak, journalists may remain objective and professional or at least convey such an impression. As the supply of authoritative voices critical of the president increases, the amount of negative news should also rise. When this political environment is less hostile toward the president, the amount of negative news should drop.[11]

Two variables capture this aspect of the political context, whether government is divided (1 = divided, 0 = united) and the degree of party polarization in Congress (Hetherington 2001). The polarization measure utilizes the distance between the median Democrat and Republican on the first dimension of the DW-Nominate scores, from Poole and Rosenthal (1996). DW-nominate is the name of a scaling device that allows us to measure the position of a legislator relative to all the other legislators in that chamber at the same time and over time. The median value tells us the position of the middle legislator in each party. The difference between the two party medians thus indicates how far apart the middle members of each party are. This leads to two hypotheses, that divided government and higher levels of party polarization will be associated with a greater proportion of negative news.

## Presidential Agendas

Presidential agendas are in part a function of the political context and help to structure the political context. Presidents may pursue an ambitious agenda because they feel that they possess a mandate for change (Conley 2001); because of their own beliefs (Cohen 1997); or to repay interest groups, voters, and others for their support in the election. At the same time, when deep divisions exist between the parties and/or when the president's position with Congress is structurally weak, presidents may be inclined to scale back their agenda. This is more likely the case when presidents want to avoid being defeated in Congress. Thus while party polarization and divided government may increase the number of potential presidential critics, a less ambitious presidential agenda may limit the number of policies for critics to attack. The combination of these two factors may cancel out, leaving no discernible trace on the amount of negative news. In general, however, we expect that the more ambitious the president's agenda, the more likely this agenda will threaten the status quo, leading critics to mobilize against the president. To measure the ambitiousness of the president's agenda, I use Binder's (2002) measure of the number of major agenda items, under the hypothesis that as the president's agenda grows, the amount of negative news will rise.[12]

## Modeling Negative Presidential News as a Time Series

The dependent variable for this analysis is Ragsdale's negative news measure, the annual percentage of negative news about the president in the *New York Times* from 1949 through 1992. The discussion above identified the following independent variables: a Korea–Vietnam War dummy, Gulf War dummy, inflation, unemployment, a Watergate dummy, an Iran-Contra dummy, a New President dummy, a Divided Government dummy, party polarization, the size of the president's agenda, the percentage of households with television, and the percentage of households with cable television, a total of twelve independent variables. Appendix 5B, found on our supplementary webpage, presents a more technical and detailed discussion of the time series properties of the negative news variable. Because of that analysis, we are able to use the level of negative presidential news as the dependent variable in the analysis.

Table 5.1 presents the results of two estimations: a full model that includes all of the above independent variables save party polarization, and a reduced form model that excludes the insignificant variables.[13] After discussing these results, party polarization is added to the analysis for reasons that will become apparent. Results indicate that several of the hypothesized variables have no significant impact on negativity in presidential news. These insignificant variables are both of the economic factors (inflation and unemployment), the percentage of households with television, and the presence of divided government.[14]

Turning to the findings from the reduced-form OLS estimation, we see that during the Korean and Vietnam war periods presidents could expect to see 7 percent more negative news than in other years. The Gulf War also significantly affects presidential news, but contrary to initial expectations. During the year of the Gulf War, President George H. W. Bush received about 11 percent more negative news than presidents received in other years. This supports the alternative Gulf War hypothesis discussed above.

This alternative Gulf War hypothesis focuses on the great degree of public debate before the war, which lasted for months, in addition to the short period of actual hostilities, which did not generate much negative news according to this view. The division among the political parties, opinion leaders, and the mass public over the war option prior to the war likely produced many news

Table 5.1
Sources of negative presidential news, *New York Times*, 1949–92

| | Full (OLS) | | Reduced (OLS) | | Reduced (AR1) | |
|---|---|---|---|---|---|---|
| | b | p | b | p | b | p |
| War | 6.19 | .01 | 6.98 | .00 | 6.21 | .001 |
| Gulf War | 10.95 | .04* | 10.77 | .04* | 8.07 | .93* |
| Inflation | .19 | .24 | xxxx | | xxxx | |
| Unemployment | −.48 | .25 | xxxx | | xxxx | |
| Watergate | 29.84 | .00 | 32.73 | .00 | 30.78 | .00 |
| Iran-Contra | 24.76 | .00 | 24.95 | .00 | 24.39 | .24 |
| New president | −4.89 | .01 | −4.84 | .01 | −5.34 | .00 |
| Divided govt. | 2.86 | .06 | xxxx | | xxxx | |
| Pres. agenda | .15 | .00 | .16 | .00 | .16 | .00 |
| TV pct | .02 | .65* | xxxx | | xxxx | |
| CATV pct. | .11 | .04 | .14 | .01 | .14 | .04 |
| AR(1) | xxxx | | xxxx | | .29 | .08* |
| Constant | −1.27 | .78* | −2.18 | .55* | −1.22 | .79 |
| $R^2$/adjusted $R^2$ | .88 | .84 | .87 | .85 | xxxx | |
| Lag 1 Q/p | .79 | .37* | 2.43 | .12* | .00 | .99* |
| Lag 5 Q/p | 2.78 | .73* | 4.33 | .50* | 1.73 | .89* |
| Lag 10 Q/p | 11.28 | .34* | 15.97 | .10* | 9.65 | .47* |

*Sources:* See appendix 5A for details.

*Note:* N = 44.

* All coefficients are one-tailed *t* tests, except for the * coefficients, which are two-tailed tests because of incorrect signs or because no direction was predicted. The Q tests are two-tailed.

stories that either noted these policy divisions or that included the opinions of war opponents in news stories about Bush and his war policy. Moreover, in the aftermath of the war, critics also questioned the president for not completing the task of removing Saddam Hussein from power. Thus postwar stories also may have added to the amount of negative or critical news. The combination of these two sources of negative news may have easily outweighed the amount of positive news associated with the success and brevity of the war, but to test the veracity of this alternative Gulf hypothesis requires more finely grained time units than used here, although the results here are supportive of this interpretation.

The reduced-form results also reveal the impact of the devastating effects of scandal on presidential news coverage. During the years of the major scandals, Watergate and Iran-Contra, the amount of negative news ballooned, 33 percent in the case of Watergate and 25 percent in the case of Iran-Contra. An ambitious presidential agenda also increases the level of negative news coverage. Each additional proposal in the president's agenda will result in a 0.16 percent increase in negative news coverage. Such an effect appears trivial until we look at the actual size of the president's agenda. From 1949 through 1992, presidents averaged 118 agenda items, ranging from 70 to 160 per year. The least ambitious president, such as Eisenhower in 1959, who proposed only 70 items, saw his negative news level decline about 7.5 percent compared to an average president. In contrast, the most ambitious president, Reagan, who proposed 160 items in 1985, saw his negative news totals rise by nearly 7 percent compared to the average president. A one standard deviation shift in the size of the president's agenda, about 28 items, will shift the level of presidential news by about 4.5 percent. Being a new president, as hypothesized, reduces the level of negative presidential news. During their first year in office, presidents, no matter how they came to the office, see about 5 percent less negative news than in the other years.

Finally, we turn to the larger question that drives this study: Did the rise of the new media age have anything to do with the increased negativity in presidential news? The reduced-form results on table 5.1 indicate that as the percentage of households with cable television increased, the level of negative presidential news also rose. Each 1 percent increase in households with cable will increase negative news by about 0.14 percent. By the early 1990s, about 60 percent of households subscribed to cable. Thus a president in the early 1990s could expect a negative news level about 8 percent higher than presidents who served before cable television came online.

## A Question of Causality

Before accepting the conclusion that the new media age, here measured as cable television penetration, causally affects the tone of presidential news, recall that none of the equations yet presented includes the party polarization variable. Party polarization purposely was excluded from the above analysis because of its high correlation with the cable television variable. For the 1949–92 time span, the two correlate at 0.95. Further both correlate strongly with time.[15] The strong correlation between the level of negative news and time compounds our problem.[16] Figure 5.2 plots the cable television and party polarization variables. The plot reveals dramatically the resemblance of the time paths of the two variables. With such high intercorrelations, it may be impossible to separate out the effects of these two variables (cable TV and party polarization) on the level of negativity in presidential news.[17] Appendix 5C, on the webpage, presents a more detailed discussion of several attempts to deal with the problem of the high correlation between cable television and party polarization, none particularly satisfying.

Due to this problem, we are unable to say definitively whether the rise of cable television variable affects the level of negative news.[18] When both cable television and party polarization are entered together, neither appears significant. In equations with only one, both are statistically significant. Finally, adding the time counter also renders the cable and party polarization variables

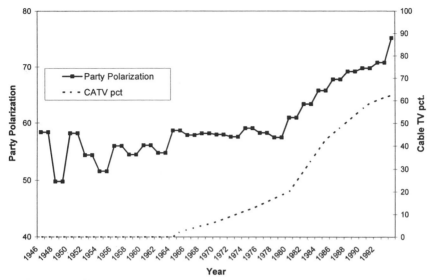

Figure 5.2 Trends in party polarization and cable television penetration, 1949–92. Source: Cable television, *Statistical Abstract of the United States*, various years. Party polarization, Poole and Rosenthal DW-Nominate scores, downloaded from Keith Poole's homepage, http://polisci.ucsd.edu/faculty/poole.

insignificant. With the data at hand we cannot pull apart the separate effects of cable television and party polarization on the level of negativity in presidential news.

## An Interactive Model

The high correlation between cable television penetration and party polarization may be coincidental in the sense that both have grown over time. But their high correlation may also suggest a close relationship between the two. Polarized parties may facilitate the reporting style of the new media age, the quest for conflict and controversy. Similarly, this appetite of the media may help the careers of certain types of politicians, those who are relatively extreme. In combination, the new media and polarized parties may increase the incidence of negative presidential news beyond what would be the case if only one existed. In other words, there may be an interaction effect between the new media and party polarization that affects the production of negative presidential news.

First, consider how polarized parties ease the production of negative presidential news in the age of new media. Facing stiff competition from other news organizations, as well as a decline in the audience for news, news organizations in the age of new media shift their news product to marginally more profitable news. The previous two chapters recorded how this has led to a decline in presidential and hard news. A similar logic may apply to the rise in negative news. For this discussion we will focus on one type of negative presidential news story—when an authoritative spokesperson named or quoted in the story criticizes the president. News professionals may think that such negative news holds some appeal to their news audience and might attract those who do not attend regularly to hard news.

Yet, national news organizations do not want to give up their professional norms, such as objectivity, in the pursuit of negative news stories. They do not want to be viewed as purveyors of tabloid journalism.[19] To preserve their reputation for objectivity, which helps maintain their credibility, as well as their social and political influence (Comstock and Scharrer 2005, 75–78, 81), journalists turn to authoritative spokespeople on both sides of an issue (Page 1996a). Authoritative spokespeople may be members of Congress, party officials, leaders of interest groups, or others who hold important positions in established institutions. In the case of presidential news, this may mean finding someone from among these authoritative leaders to criticize the president. To the president, a story that mentions or quotes an authoritative source criticizing the administration is a negative news story. To a journalist, it is a balanced story, presenting both sides of the issue, and thus is "objective" (Mindich 1998, Schiller 1981, Shoemaker and Reese 1996).

The supply of authoritative leaders willing to criticize the president publicly thus affects the ability of journalists to produce a negative news story. Even for a controversial decision, if authoritative elites uniformly line up in support of the president, a journalist seeking "balance" for his or her story will be unable to produce such a story unless the journalist decides to criticize the president him- or herself.[20] Yet professional norms tend to inhibit journalists from taking on such an active role in a news story. The heightening of party polarization over the past several decades, however, means that there exists a ready supply of administration critics. Even for presidential decisions and actions that are not highly controversial and that meet with the approval of a large segment of the populace, journalists may easily be able to locate a critic who is willing to go public given this context of polarized party politics.

Now consider the implications of the new media on the behavior of politicians, especially extreme politicians and those from the opposition who are willing to criticize the president. The new media age provides two venues for such politicians and other administration critics, the mainstream press and the more recent niche press. The mainstream press's appetite for administration critics in the new media age means that such critics, including relatively extreme ones, have easier access to the news media than they once did.[21] They will be quoted more often and appear in more news stories than in the past. Appearing more commonly in the pages and broadcasts of the major, mainstream news media may legitimate their relatively extreme or critical positions.

As their legitimacy grows and their appearance in the news increases, these politicians may be able to solidify and build their bases of political support, which in turn will increase their political influence. And as their influence increases, the news media may turn more frequently to them as a news source.

The rise of the niche news media in the new media age may also have career effects for these types of politicians, although through a different route. During the new media age, some news organizations decided to specialize, to distinguish their product from their competitors. Rather than seek to appeal to the broad mass public, these niche news media focus on a specific segment of the news audience, with the hopes of building "customer" loyalty within that audience segment. Fox Cable News, for example, has been quite successful with such a strategy, appealing especially to conservatives. The expansion in the ranks of these niche media has afforded administration critics and comparatively extreme political leaders venues to voice their positions and gain some measure of publicity. With access to these niche media, political careers can be built or enhanced in ways similar to the dynamic noted above. Some of these politicians will even be able to crossover from the niche media to the major, national media, thereby becoming national political figures in their own right.[22]

This suggests an interaction between the new media and party polarization. To create the interaction term, the party polarization and cable television penetration variables are multiplied together (Friedrich 1982). The mathematical logic of the interaction variable works this way. When both party polarization and cable television possess low values, the interaction variable will have a low value. When either party polarization or cable television has a low value and the other has a high value, the interaction term will have a medium value. Only when both cable television and party polarization have high values will the interaction term have a high value, and this is where the impact of the interaction will be felt most strongly. The interaction hypothesis suggests a joint effect of the new media (cable penetration) and party polarization above and beyond the independent impacts of each of these variables on the amount of negative news. That is, when controlling for the effects of cable penetration and party polarization, the interaction of the two will be statistically significant and positive.

Table 5.2 presents results of analyses to test this interaction hypothesis. The table presents the results of two estimations, one without the interaction term (the additive model) and one with the interaction term (interaction model). Also, the estimation includes a time counter (1949 = 1, 1992 = 44) to control for any trends, as well as all of the other variables from the reduced-form estimation. By all conventional standards, the interaction model outperforms the additive one. The interaction term is statistically significant, even though the estimation controls for the time counter.[23] Plus, the interaction term is properly signed—it adds to the level of negativity in presidential news. Third, the $R^2$ of the interaction model is higher than that of the additive model (0.89 to 0.87). An F test establishes that this incremental addition to the $R^2$ of 2

Table 5.2
Interactive effects of party polarization and cable television penetration on negative presidential news, 1949–92

| | Additive model | | Interactive model | |
|---|---|---|---|---|
| | b | p | b | p |
| War | 6.20 | .00 | 5.98 | .00 |
| Gulf War | 10.97 | .02 | 9.06 | .04 |
| Watergate | 32.16 | .00 | 31.99 | .00 |
| Iran-Contra | 24.93 | .00 | 25.50 | .00 |
| New president | −5.10 | .01 | −5.34 | .00 |
| Pres. agenda | .15 | .01 | .17 | .00 |
| CATV pct. | −.02 | .91* | −2.26 | .03* |
| Party polarization | .45 | .17 | .13 | .39 |
| Time | .08 | .35 | .35 | .07 |
| Interaction** | xxxx | | .03 | .02 |
| Constant | −26.58 | 31* | −13.14 | .60* |
| R² / adjusted R² | .87 | .84 | .89 | .86 |
| Lag 1 Q / p | 1.70 | .19 | .29 | .59 |
| Lag 5 Q / p | 2.93 | .71 | 5.20 | .39 |
| Lag 10 Q / p | 14.31 | .16 | 14.31 | .16 |

Source: See appendix 5A for details.
Note: n = 44.
* All coefficients are one-tailed t tests, except for the * coefficients, which are two-tailed tests because of incorrect signs or because no direction was predicted. The Q tests are two-tailed.
** CATV pct. x Party Polarization.

percent is significant.[24] Given that the base $R^2$ from the additive model is already so high, we would be hard pressed to improve on it. As such, the improvement appears slight, at about 2 percent. But this added increment to the $R^2$ represents about 15 percent of the remaining variance.[25]

Due to the multiplicative nature of the interaction term, it is hard to interpret substantively by merely inspecting the coefficient. Moreover, the interaction effect needs to be compared to the base effects of cable television and party polarization. To estimate the effects of the interaction thus requires specifying particular levels of cable television penetration and party polarization. The most relevant case for us is when both cable television penetration and party polarization are high compared to when they are both at lower levels. During the new media age, both cable penetration and party polarization are quite high by historical standards. Simulating the level of negative presidential news, presidents can expect to receive 10 percent more negative news when cable penetration and party polarization are high than when they are at average values.[26] This is a substantively important change in the president's news environment during an age of both the new media and high party polarization.

## Conclusion

From mid-century into the 1990s, presidents faced an increasing level of negative news. This chapter asked whether the rise of the new media had anything to do with this trend. Using an annual time series on the tone of presidential news in the *New York Times* from 1949 through 1992, we arrived at an equivocal answer. Controlling for other factors that affect the tone of presidential news, analysis found that the rise of the new media age, measured with the percentage of households subscribing to cable, is positively associated with the level of negativity in presidential news.

However, other trends also occurred at the same time as the diffusion of cable into households, in particular the increasing polarization of the parties. Party polarization and cable penetration are so highly correlated that it is impossible to separate the particular effects of these two trends. Thus we cannot say definitively that cable penetration or party polarization either affects or does not affect the degree of negativity in presidential news. Moreover, both of these trends are so highly correlated with a simple time counter that we cannot rule out the possibility that yet a third factor is the critical causal influence on negativity in presidential news.

Further analysis, however, found that an interaction between cable penetration and party polarization increased the level of negative presidential news above and beyond the effects of cable, polarization, and a time counter. During the age of new media, news organizations increased their appetite for stories in which someone would criticize the president, a type of negative news. Extreme politicians, who were in greater supply during this age, would willingly play the role of administration critic. Thus not only would the needs of the news media be satisfied, but the news media, by granting greater access to administration critics, would bolster the careers of politicians willing to criticize the president. Polarized parties and the new media, by facilitating each others' needs and ambitions, would further boost the amount of negative news.

Still, the interaction theory hinges on whether cable and polarization are the critical causal agents. The data at hand are not up to the task of fully sorting through all of the possible influences on negative presidential news. These tonality data are at too high a level of aggregation and do not span a long enough time period. And as long as time, cable penetration, and party polarization each follow the same time path, we will be unable to sort out their individual effects. Thus the analysis in this chapter must be taken with a grain of salt.

The next chapter turns to a different data set, the Patterson content analysis of more than five thousand news stories from 1981 through 1999. That data set will allow us to look at sources of negative presidential news at the individual story level, albeit only during the new media age. The next chapter assesses whether journalistic practices associated with the new media age are also associated with negative reporting on the president. If the Patterson data point in that direction, we can be somewhat more assured that the rise of the new media has something to do with the increase in negativity in presidential news.

## Appendix 5A: Variables Used in the Analysis

Note that further information about statistical methods employed in this book can be found online at http://press.princeton.edu/titles/8592.html.

### Dependent Variable

1. Negative Presidential News: Percentage of negative news stories about the president in the *New York Times*, 1949–92. Source: Provided to the author by Lyn Ragsdale, discussed in Ragsdale (1997).

### Independent Variables

1. War: Dummy variable for Korean and Vietnam War (1951–53, 1965–72 = 1, otherwise 0).
2. Gulf War: Dummy variable for Gulf War (1991 = 1, otherwise = 0).
3. Inflation Rate: Annual consumer price index, 1949–92. Source: Bureau of Labor Statistics CPI homepage, http://www.bls.gov/cpi/home.htm.
4. Unemployment Rate: Annual unemployment rate, 1949–92, Source: Bureau of Labor Statistics homepage, http://www.bls.gov/.
5. Watergate: Dummy variable for Watergate (1973–74 = 1, otherwise = 0).
6. Iran-Contra: Dummy variable for Iran-Contra (1987 = 1, 0 = otherwise).
7. New President: First year of a new president no matter how the president came to office (first year = 1, non-first years = 0).
8. Divided Government: Dummy variable for whether at least one house of Congress is controlled by the opposition party (coded = 1, united government = 0).
9. Party Polarization: Absolute difference in the party medians on the first dimension of the Poole-Rosenthal DW-Nominate scale. Downloaded from Keith Poole's homepage, http://voteview.com/dwnl.htm.
10. Agenda Size: Number of major items on the president's agenda. Source: Binder (2002).
11. Television Percent: Percentage of households with free broadcast television. Sources: *Historical Statistics of the United States* and various volumes of the *Statistical Abstract of the United States*.
12. Cable Television Percent: Percentage of households that subscribe to cable television. Sources: *Historical Statistics of the United States* and various volumes of the *Statistical Abstract of the United States*.

# CHAPTER 6

# Sources of Negativity in Presidential News during the Age of New Media

Presidents receive a higher proportion of negative news during the age of new media than during the golden age of broadcasting. Using the Ragsdale data analyzed in chapter 5, on average 20 percent of presidential news was negative during the years 1949 through 1979 compared to 28 percent from 1980 through 1992. The analysis in chapter 5 opened up the possibility that the rise of the new media spurred some of this increase in negativity. However, that analysis was limited in a number of senses. First, the negative news data were highly aggregated and ended with 1992. Plus, the primary indicator of the new media age, cable penetration, correlated strongly with another variable that trended similarly over time, party polarization, and both cable and party polarization correlated highly with a simple time counter. Thus the rise of the new media may have had something to do with the increase in negativity in presidential news, but the analysis in chapter 5 is far from definitive.

This chapter turns to Thomas Patterson's content analysis of more than five thousand randomly generated news stories from 1980 through 1998. The great strength of Patterson's data for our purposes is that we can gauge the factors that influence negativity at the individual story level. But Patterson's data exist only for the new media age, which will constrain any ability to make comparisons between the broadcasting and new media ages. Yet Patterson's data allow us to address whether factors that characterize reporting in the age of new media are associated with negativity in presidential news at the individual story level. The existence of such an association helps establish a link between journalistic practices in the new media age and negativity in presidential news. In this chapter, the new media age characteristics perspective will also be tested against two rival explanations that might affect negativity in presidential news, characteristics of presidential (hard) news reporting and the outer environment. The guiding question for this chapter is: Is there something about journalistic practices in the new media age that increases the likelihood of negativity in presidential news and how well does this explanation fare against rival explanations?

## Patterson's Lexis-Nexis Data: Basic Trends and Properties

Although Patterson's study focused on the rise of soft news, he collected a considerable amount of information pertinent to this research. His data consist of 5,331 randomly sampled news stories from Lexis-Nexis from 1980 through 1998 from 33 news outlets.[1] Fortunately, presidential news is quite common—950, or 17.8 percent, of the stories in Patterson's data set concern the president or the administration.

Unlike Ragsdale, who only distinguished between negative, positive, and neutral stories, Patterson codes for degree of negativity or positivity, and further distinguishes between neutral and balanced stories, that is, stories that are neither positive nor negative from those that are equally positive and negative. For this analysis, I collapse the neutral and balanced categories, leaving five categories: (5) clearly negative, (4) more negative than positive, (3) neutral or balanced, (2) more positive than negative, (1) clearly positive.[2]

Presidential news tilts in a decidedly negative direction, as one would expect, in the new media age. Overall, 26.8 percent of presidential news stories are clearly negative, 25.5 percent more negative than positive, 14.2 percent equally negative and positive (balanced), 15.2 percent more positive than negative, 8.9 percent clearly positive, and 9.4 percent neutral. Combining the two negative categories produces a total of 52.3 percent.[3]

Although one must be cautious in doing so, one can aggregate the news stories by year to create an annual percentage of clearly negative and more negative than positive news stories. Figure 1.1 previously displayed those data. Figure 6.1 redisplays these data and adds a linear trend line. Despite the fact that this series begins in 1980, there is still an unmistakable trend of increasingly negative news in the aggregate, which echoes the results derived from Ragsdale's *New York Times* series. The linear regression indicates that for each additional year from 1980 to 1998, the amount of negative news increases by 0.87 percent. For instance, in 1980, 41.8 percent of news stories have some level of negativity. At this pace of change, by 1998 presidents could expect 58.3 percent of their news to be negative.

That the series ends in 1998, the year of the Lewinsky scandal and Clinton impeachment process, may account for the upward trend in negativity in these data. To control for this, a dummy variable for scandal is added, coded 1987 and 1998 equal to "1," to pick up the effects of the Iran-Contra and Lewinsky scandals on presidential news. Even with controls for these scandals, the time trend remains significant, although somewhat weakened. The regression coefficient drops to 0.64 from 0.87, which tells us that for each year in the series, presidential news will get more negative by 0.64 percent.[4] Across the nineteen-year series, this cumulates to 12.2 percent increase in the amount of negative news. Assuming again the 41.8 percent of stories were somewhat negative in 1980, presidents can expect 54 percent of stories to be so in 1998. The scandal variable also is highly potent, as expected.[5] However, the value of the Patterson data is not its use at the aggregate level, but at the individual story level. The next sections turn to such an analysis.

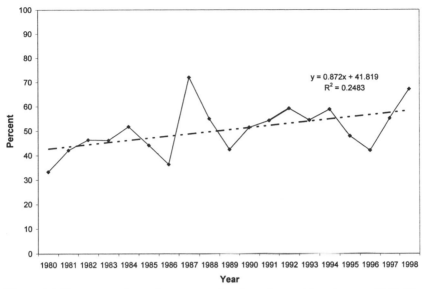

Figure 6.1 Percentage of negative news stories about the president, by year, 1980–98. Source: Patterson (2000).

## New Media Age Reporting Practices and Negativity in Presidential News

Throughout, the argument here has been that there is something different about news production in the new media age compared to the golden age of broadcasting. The last several chapters, using the market model of news production, suggested that the rise of the new media in part accounted for the decline in the amount of presidential news and the rise of negativity in news, with the caveats on the latter point as noted throughout. Likewise, Patterson (2000) argues that the types of news stories reported and the way that news is reported changed across the 1980s and 1990s, that is, during the age of new media. He also attributes these changes in part to the increased economic competition that news organizations face in the new media age.

The changes from the golden age of broadcasting to the new media age have altered the characteristics of news. For instance, Patterson charts the rise in soft news. He defines soft news as news that is not hard news, that is, news that does not refer to "breaking events involving top leaders, major issues, or significant disruption in daily life, such as an earthquake or airline disaster. Information about these events is presumably important to citizens' ability to understand and respond to the world of public affairs" (3).

Other aspects of news in the new media age have also changed. For instance, according to Patterson, fewer stories contain a public policy emphasis, while stories are also more likely to be written in a sensationalistic and/or human interest fashion. Use of collective terms, a sign according to Patterson of hard news reporting, has also ebbed, while reporter self-references have increased.[6] Crime and disaster stories also have become more common. Although Patterson does not single out scandal stories, others suggest that this kind of reporting has become more common in recent decades (Sabato 1991; Kerbel 1999; Farnsworth and Lichter 2006, chap. 6). Thus we can define reporting in the new media age as soft, sensational, human-interest oriented, and with a nonpolicy emphasis. If new media age reporting practices lead to negative presidential news stories, then we can establish a link between new media age reporting styles and the rise of negativity in presidential news.

## Nonpolicy Content and Negativity

According to Patterson, articles with policy content declined in frequency across the 1980s and 1990s. It is not clear whether a story with policy content will lead to negative or positive presidential news. Moreover, it is not clear that policy content declined in presidential news, as Patterson suggests that it has for news in general. Taking the second point first, presidential news is more policy oriented than nonpresidential news. Patterson finds that the bulk of presidential news stories are either substantially (58.6 percent) or somewhat (15.5 percent) relevant to public policy; only 25.9 percent of presidential news stories lack policy relevance. In contrast, 46.8 percent of nonpresidential news lacks policy relevance. From this comparison it appears that presidential news may have resisted the trend away from policy content. Although we can not compare the policy content of presidential news in the broadcasting age with the new media age, we can look more closely at time trends within the new media age, arguing that as time has progressed, the new media age may have set in more firmly to affect news. Bisecting the 1980–98 years into two sets reveals that there was an increasing amount of nonpolicy presidential news in 1980–89 and 1990–98—16.8 percent for 1980–89 and 29.8 percent for 1990–98, nearly a doubling in the incidence of nonpolicy presidential news.

But does the policy/nonpolicy distinction affect the negativity of presidential news? One can argue, for instance, that a policy story might include passages in which antagonists to the president's policy voice their opposition. Such a story may possess a negative attribute, the voice of presidential critics. But policy stories may also present the president as a leader offering a policy solution to a problem, which may cast the president in a positive light. Whether or not a story contains policy content may not be related to tonality. The correlation between policy content and negativity is faint—stories lacking policy content are slightly more negative than stories containing policy content ($r = -0.05$, $p = 0.095$), but not by much.

## "News You Can Use" and Negativity

Patterson codes stories for whether they employ a "news you can use" frame, that is, whether their major purpose is to offer personal advice. Despite the seeming appetite that the public has for personal advice news, Patterson's data do not pick up much of this type of news in either presidential or nonpresidential news. This may be a function of his sample selection process, which was limited to the front page and local news sections of newspapers. Personal advice news may be more common in other sections of the newspaper. Patterson finds that less than 4 percent of presidential news stories are either primarily or secondarily "news you can use" stories, while only about 5 percent of nonpresidental news is either primarily or secondarily of this sort. "News you can use," thus, may not be highly relevant here and is not significantly related to negativity in presidential news (r = −0.03, p = 0.29).

## Human Interest Stories and Negativity

Human interest stories, another common type of new media age story, are more common in presidential news reporting than "news you can use" stories. Patterson defines human interest stories as those that use one or more of the following: "use a human example or put a 'human' face on an issue or problem; go into the private or personal life on an actor (in the story); employ adjectives or personal vignettes that generate feelings of sympathy/empathy/outrage" (25). Almost one-quarter of presidential news stories display a high or moderate degree of human interest, in contrast to slightly more than 40 percent of nonpresidential news stories.[7] Presidential news displays no strong trend of increasing human interest content, with slightly more than 20 percent displaying such an element for the 1980–89 period and 25 percent for the 1990–98 period. Perhaps most significant is that human interest frames are absent in about 56 percent of presidential news stories.

Human interest stories provide the administration with an opportunity to portray the president and his family in a positive light, perhaps as human beings for the nation to relate to. Ronald Reagan initiated the practice of "personalizing" or "humanizing" his State of the Union Addresses by directing the audience to a specific individual, whom the president could use as an example of a more general point that he was trying to get across to the nation. Presidents since Reagan have followed suit in their major addresses. Some indication exists that presidents understand the power of human interest themes to manage their image, as the Reagan example illustrates (Waterman et al. 1999).

Farnsworth and Lichter (2006) argue that George W. Bush used a media strategy throughout his term in which cabinet secretaries and other administration spokespeople would announce policy and other substantive actions, especially if these actions were controversial. The president's media appearances would be reserved generally for occasions that would allow him to be portrayed in a more positive light, either through a ceremony, commander-in-chief, or some type of personal activity. As a result, Bush's news was consistently more positive that that of his administration or the executive branch in general. At the zero-order level, however, human interest content does not appear strongly related to negativity (r = −0.04, p = 0.24) in these data.

## Sensationalism and Negativity

Many commentators suggest that sensationalism strongly characterizes news in the new media age (Farnsworth and Lichter 2006, Kerbel 1999, Patterson 2000, Sabato 1991, West 2001). Sensationalism has roots in the yellow journalism of the late nineteenth century. Some argue that the new media age reinvigorated sensationalism as a style of news reporting, through, for instance, "feeding frenzies" (Sabato 1991) and tabloid style journalism (Esser 1999, Glynn 2000). Patterson describes sensationalism in his codebook instructions as news stories "presented as something so earthshaking / unsettling / remarkable that everyone should take notice" (26).

Although sensationalism does not dominate the news stories in Patterson's sample, about 30 percent of presidential news stories contain a moderate or high degree of sensationalism, compared to 33 percent for nonpresidential news. Thus the bulk of presidential news contains no sensational element or frame. Moreover there is no trend toward increasing sensationalism in presidential news, although nonpresidential news sees a modest increase in sensationalism from about 28 percent to 35 percent from the 1980s to the 1990s. Sensationalism, however, appears somewhat related to negativity in presidential news in these data (r = 0.17, p = .000).

## Scandal and Negativity

Although scandal is related to sensationalism, it is useful to treat scandal reporting as a separate category. Farmsworth and Lichter (2006), among others, suggest that scandal reporting has become a more common feature of political news in the new media age. The Gary Hart bid for the Democratic presidential nomination in 1984, which was derailed because of his sexual improprieties, was perhaps the first such incident with career implications to touch the presidency, although several members of Congress saw sex scandals undo their careers somewhat earlier. In contrast, neither John F. Kennedy's nor Franklin Roosevelt's affairs were made public during their time in office. Nor did Eisenhower's prepresidential affair become a public issue when he ran for office in 1952. Such behavior among these presidents and presidential candidates only came to public attention when biographers and historians began to publish information on the affairs, usually after these presidents left office or died.[8]

Further, because of their complexity, which made reporting about them diffi-cult, some scandals did not become major news items. Corporate corruption scandals such as Enron, which emerged in the early 2000s, are good examples of this. But scandal stories that maintain their presence in the news may pro-duce negative news and harm the president.

While scandal news did not dominate presidential news, in Patterson's data, scandal news comprises about 8.5 percent of all presidential news, compared to 3 percent for nonpresidential news. These data also indicate a very modest uptick in scandal news across the two periods here, 6 percent for 1980–89 but 9.5 percent for 1990–98, much of that rise due to the Lewinsky scandal of 1998. In 1998, fully 21 percent of the news reported on Clinton dealt with scandal. Despite the strategies that presidents use to deflect the negativity of scandal, such as going on the offensive and attacking critics (Farnsworth and Lichter 2006, chap. 6), in these data news scandal is strongly related to negativ-ity (r = 0.27, p = .000).

## Soft News and Negativity

Finally, we turn to soft news, the focus of Patterson's study. To a degree, soft news is a summary indicator of the other characteristics reviewed above. Soft news correlates strongly with sensationalism (r = 0.25, p = .00), human interest (r = 0.44, p = .00), and nonpolicy news (r = 0.21, p = .00); weakly correlates with scandal (r = 0.05, p = 0.10); and does not correlate with "news you can use" (r = 0.01, p = 0.69), perhaps because of the lack of variance on the last variable.[9] Soft news is not common in presidential news writing—only about 10 percent of presidential stories are coded as definitely or mostly soft news. Another 12 per-cent are mixed, while fully 77 percent are mostly or definitively hard news. In comparison, 19 percent of nonpresidential news is definitely or mostly soft. Moreover, there is no trend toward increasing softness in presidential news, un-like other news, as Patterson discusses. But contrary to our overarching hypothe-sis, soft news is less likely to be negative than hard news (r = 0.10, p = 0.001), perhaps because of the strong human interest dimension in soft news, which tends to be associated with positive, rather than negative, presidential news.

## Summing Up: New Media Age Reporting Practices and Negativity

This discussion suggests that some aspects of reporting in the age of new media may be associated with negativity in presidential news. For instance, scandal and sensationalism, two common story characteristics in the new media age, correlate with negativity, but soft news, another important characteristic of news in the new media age, is associated with positive coverage of the president. This section pulls together the above discussion into a multivariate analysis of all the new media age characteristics on the tone of presidential news coverage.

Before proceeding, a technical note is in order. The possibility exists that selection bias may affect analysis of the subset of presidential news stories taken from Patterson's study because Patterson did not design his study to look at presidential news in particular, but news in general. Appendix 6B (on the web-page) presents details of a statistical technique, Heckman's two-step selection model, which can correct for this problem. The results of the Heckman analysis suggest that there is no selection effect, that the subset of presidential news stories is not a biased sample. The analysis presented below and throughout this chapter uses multiple regression techniques on the 950 presidential news cases from the larger Patterson sample of news stories. Model 1, table 6.1 presents OLS results of regressing negative news on the six new media age variables: nonpolicy news, "new you can use," human interest, sensationalism, soft news, and presidential scandal.[10]

Several of the new media age reporting style characteristics are statistically significant predictors of the tone of presidential news. Both sensationalism and scandal are associated with negativity in presidential news. Each one unit change in the three-point sensationalism scale increases the degree of negativity by 0.43 units on the five-point negativity scale (5 = clearly negative, 1 = clearly positive). Moving from the least to most sensational reporting will increase the degree of negativity a full 1.3 units. A scandal story itself will increase the degree of negativity by nearly the same amount, 1.15 steps. From another perspective, both of these factors can alter the degree of negativity by nearly one standard deviation unit of the negativity scale (standard deviation = 1.27).

Contrary to expectations, however, several of the new reporting style characteristics lessen the degree of negativity in presidential news. When presidential news is soft, which it rarely is, presidential news gets less negative. The effect is modest, however. Each one unit change in the five-point soft news scale moves negativity by only 0.17 steps. Going from the hardest presidential news story to the softest will alter the degree of negativity 0.85 units, less than one full unit. Similarly, when presidential news is framed as a human interest story, negativity eases, but the effect is modest. Each one unit change in the four-point human interest scale moves negativity a mere 0.09 units: from the least to most human interest frame, presidential news will move 0.36 units in negativity.

In these results we can see the incentives for presidential image management (Waterman et al. 1999). News about the president as a person, his family, and presidential appearances at ceremonial events, all tend to produce positive news reports, which they are designed to do. The impact of these types of stories, however, pale in comparison to sensationalism and scandal reporting. Image management may not be a potent enough strategy to overcome these aspects of reporting in the new media age. And we must not lose sight that hard news reporting, the bulk of presidential news, may be a major source of negative news because of the potential for controversy and conflict inherent in hard news reporting. Even if soft and human interest news has a more positive cast

Table 6.1
Impact of soft news reporting style, hard news reporting characteristics, and environmental conditions on negativity in presidential news

| | Model 1 | | Model 2 | | Model 3 | | Model 4 | | Model 5 | |
|---|---|---|---|---|---|---|---|---|---|---|
| | $b$ | $p$ | $b$ | $p$ | $b$ | $p$ | $b$ | $p$ | $b$ | $p$ |
| Straight news | — | | .37 | .09 | — | | −.07 | .76 | — | |
| Mixed news | — | | .36 | .11 | — | | −.03 | .91 | — | |
| Analysis | — | | .38 | .09 | — | | .10 | .65 | — | |
| Urgent call | — | | .57 | .00 | — | | .58 | .00 | .58 | .00 |
| Call | — | | .27 | .05 | — | | .28 | .05 | .28 | .00 |
| Action taken | — | | −.24 | .03 | — | | −.27 | .02 | −.27 | .02 |
| Conflict | — | | .64 | .00 | — | | .59 | .00 | .59 | .00 |
| Context | — | | −.08 | .43 | — | | −.08 | .45 | — | |
| Ambition | — | | .07 | .45 | — | | .06 | .51 | — | |
| Cooperation | — | | −1.01 | .00 | — | | −.96 | .00 | −.96 | .00 |
| Soft news | −.17 | .00 | — | | — | | −.21 | .00 | −.19 | .00 |
| Sensationalism | .43 | .00 | — | | — | | .20 | .00 | .21 | .00 |
| Human interest | −.09 | .05 | — | | — | | −.02 | .65 | — | |
| News you can use | −.04 | .81 | — | | — | | .19 | .24 | — | |
| Nonpolicy | .03 | .54 | — | | — | | .15 | .00 | .15 | .00 |
| Scandal | 1.15 | .00 | — | | — | | .68 | .00 | .71 | .00 |
| Inflation | — | | — | | −.25 | .33 | −.33 | .12 | — | |
| Unemployment | — | | — | | −.00 | .99 | −.04 | .46 | — | |
| Consumer confidence | — | | — | | −.00 | .97 | .00 | .74 | — | |
| Consumer expectations | — | | — | | .00 | .97 | .00 | .60 | — | |
| Gulf War | — | | — | | .03 | .95 | .16 | .66 | — | |
| Lewinsky period | — | | — | | .35 | .07 | .07 | .65 | — | |
| Iran-Contra period | — | | — | | .43 | .12 | .36 | .13 | — | |
| Positive event period | — | | — | | .01 | .94 | −.10 | .39 | — | |
| Negative event period | — | | — | | −.08 | .54 | .13 | .26 | — | |
| Party polarization | — | | — | | −1.92 | .26 | −2.50 | .08 | — | |
| Divided government | — | | — | | −.06 | .67 | .08 | .44 | — | |
| New president | — | | — | | .00 | .97 | .13 | .24 | — | |
| Cable TV % | — | | — | | .006 | .13 | .01 | .08 | — | |
| Approval-lag | — | | — | | .00 | .79 | −.01 | .22 | — | |
| Constant | 3.30 | .00 | 1.81 | .00 | 4.03 | .00 | 3.38 | .01 | 1.97 | |
| N | 950 | | 950 | | 949 | | 929 | | 950 | |
| F | 21 | | 37.8 | | 1.14 | | 17.7 | | 55.2 | |
| Prob. > F | .00 | | .00 | | .32 | | .00 | | .00 | |
| R-squared | .12 | | .29 | | .02 | | .36 | | .35 | |
| Adjusted R-squared | .11 | | .28 | | .00 | | .34 | | .34 | |

Source: Patterson (2000) and data collected by author. See appendix 6A for details.

than other presidential news stories, one must wonder if soft and human interest news about the president has much impact on public opinion.

As to the remaining two variables, neither "news you can use" nor policy news affects the tone of presidential news story. Nonpolicy news tends to be soft news, which may account for this finding, while a "news you can use" frame is exceedingly rare in presidential news.

Finally, the overall model fit is modest ($R^2 = 0.12$), although the equation F test is strongly significant ($F = 21.31$, $p = .0000$). One possible reason for the modest explained variance is that human coding of story tone is difficult and likely prone to some error. Moreover, many of the predictor variables also require judgment from coders, which also may induce some coding error. Deciding whether a story should be classified as high or moderate in sensationalism or human interest may be quite difficult. We need to take measurement error like this into consideration, and as a result the magnitude of the $R^2$ of 0.12 may not be as modest as it first appears.[11]

These results do establish a causal link between new media age reporting practices and negative presidential news and suggest that the rise of the new media may be part of the explanation for the increase in negativity in presidential news. However, the modest $R^2$ may suggest that more than the reporting practices of the new media age affect the tonality of presidential news. Plus, how well do these results about new media age reporting practices hold up in the face of rival explanations? The next section turns to the impact of characteristics of hard presidential news, the bulk of the news on the president, while the following section looks at the impact of the larger environment.

## Hard News Reporting and Negativity in Presidential News

The analysis thus far suggests that the reporting styles of the new media age affect presidential news, but not always as predicted. Further, the new media age variables together account for only a modest proportion of the variance in the tonality of presidential news at the story level. Two other important findings also emerged from the above analysis. First, most presidential news is hard rather than soft. Second, hard news is more likely to be negative than soft news. These points suggest that we should look more closely at characteristics of hard news reporting to understand the tone of presidential news.

Hard news stories can be written in several ways, emphasizing some characteristics or elements over others. These varying emphases may produce a negative tone in presidential news stories. Fortunately, Patterson coded news stories on a number of dimensions relevant to these matters. For instance, it may matter whether a story is presented as straight news versus news analysis, whether the story calls for the president to take action on an issue, whether the story possesses a conflict theme involving the president, whether the story portrays the president as ambitious and as a power seeker, and/or whether the story is written thematically or episodically.

## Straight News versus Analytic Stories

Newspapers developed editorial and columnist (op-ed) pages to present a place for opinion and analysis, even a political slant. By restricting such "bias" to these pages, news organizations could protect their reputation for journalistic professionalism and objectivity, maintain an image of political independence, and still engage in public debate through their opinion pages. As interpretive journalism became more common (West 2001) and interpretive and analytical stories began to be located outside of the editorial and op-ed pages, they were often labeled as news analysis, again to protect the professionalism, objectivity, and independence of "straight" news reporting.

Analytic stories present journalists with an opportunity to criticize the president in the guise of news analysis. Although analytic stories may focus on presidential successes, more commonly analytic stories will delve into reasons for failure. Obviously, presidents will view stories that focus on their failures as negative or bad news. Straight news reporting offers journalists less opportunity to offer judgments about presidential success or failure, and thus on average should be less negative (or positive) in tone.

Patterson codes straight versus analytical stories into four categories— straight news, news analyses, stories that mix the two, and features. Features are uncommon among presidential news, accounting for only 3 percent of the total. Straight news accounts for 34.7 percent of presidential news stories, mixed stories 37.8 percent, and news analyses 24.5 percent.[12] News analyses do not become more common from the 1980s to the 1990s, but as expected, a slight tendency exists for analysis to be more negative than straight news. Forty-seven percent of straight news stories are somewhat or mostly negative, compared to 56 percent and 59 percent for mixed and analytic stories.[13]

## Calls for Action

Presidents prefer the news to present them as taking charge, as leading, as active. Such attributes are commonly associated with a positive presidential image (Cronin and Genovese 1998, Waterman et al. 1999). Although Patterson does not code whether presidents are so portrayed, he codes for whether the story calls for action utilizing four coding categories: (1) no action is required, (2) action is already taken, (3) action is needed urgently, or (4) if it is not urgent, action is still required.[14] Calls for action imply that the president needs to be doing something about a problem, either because he has overlooked a problem or because his policy is not working. Either may undermine a president's leadership image.

A substantial number of the presidential news stories fall into the two "call for action" categories: 8 percent cite urgent calls, 16 percent cite nonurgent calls. But the bulk of stories (62 percent) note an action already being taken, while 13 percent make no reference to action or its need. Calls for action categories are more likely to be negative than the other categories: 82 percent of urgent calls are negative as are 66 percent of nonurgent calls, while only 47 percent of action being taken and 43 percent of no calls for action have a negative tone.

## Conflict

Presidents prefer news stories that show other actors supporting rather than challenging them. When other leaders support the president, the president can point to this support as evidence of the quality of his leadership and the wisdom of his policy course. When other leaders criticize the president, when they withhold their support, the president's ability to proclaim the quality of his leadership is undermined.

Journalists, however, like stories with conflict among the major actors. Journalists find conflict between major actors interesting and think that conflict generates reader interest. Conflict is also a useful way of organizing the information presented in a news story; conflict provides a structure for readers to make sense of what is going on and why it is going on. Patterson codes stories as containing either substantial levels of conflict (56 percent of presidential news stories), some conflict (22 percent), or no conflict (22 percent). Conflict is highly related to negative news at the zero order level, as expected, with a Pearson's r of 0.47 (p = .0000).

## Thematic versus Episodic Context

Seminal research by Iyengar and Kinder (1987) found that stories written thematically were more likely to negatively affect viewers' presidential approval levels than those written episodically. Thematic contexts link a story to broader social, political, and/or economic environment, and these contexts provide frames of reference that help readers make sense of or interpret the story, albeit from that frame of reference. Negativity, then, may be more likely to be found in thematic than episodic stories. However, if those contexts paint a positive picture, then a thematically rendered story may not produce negative news. As others have found (Graber 2001), here most presidential news is episodic (85 percent), but episodic news appears unrelated to story tone (r = 0.05, p = 0.12).

*Major Frame or Story Theme*

A story's major frame can be thought of as its key theme or plotline. Although journalists possess a variety of frames that they can employ, they tend to employ only a handful, to which they continually return (Gans 1979). Patterson coded stories for five major themes that may be relevant to understanding the tone of presidential news: (1) whether the story revolves around *power and ambition*, (2) *conflict* among major actors, (3) *cooperation*, (4) *solving a problem or policy*, or (5) *human interest*.

The American political culture holds ambivalent attitudes about power and ambition. Ambition is often lauded in stories of personal success, like in the Horatio Alger myths, but our political culture prefers that politicians serve in the public interest, not in their personal self-interest. Rarely does our political culture recognize that self-interest and the public interest may coincide rather than collide. Thus stories written with such a frame are likely to be associated with negative news. In contrast, cooperative stories may present actors who are willing to overcome their personal differences and/or may show actors supportive of presidential efforts. Thus cooperative frames may be associated with positive presidential news.

In Patterson's data, policy frames are most common (43.2 percent), followed by conflict (30.9 percent) and ambition/power (15.8 percent) frames in presidential news. Cooperation and human interest frames are less common (4.2 percent and 5.4 percent, respectively). There appears to be a correlation between major frame and negativity. Over three-quarters (77.2 percent) of conflict stories are negative, while cooperation and human interest stories rarely are (2.5 percent and 27.5 percent negative). Sadly, from the president's perspective, cooperative stories are rare compared to conflict stories. In an age of divided government and polarized parties, one might be hard pressed to find cooperative politicians, who possess few incentives for cooperation across party lines. The other frames, ambition and policy/problem solving, are more evenly balanced with 53.3 percent and 42.7 percent, respectively, possessing a negative tone.

*Summing Up Hard News Reporting: A Multivariate Analysis*

The above discussion detected several strong relationships between hard news characteristics and story tone. Table 6.1, model 2, presents the results of a multivariate OLS analysis that regresses news tone on the following variables: straight news dummy, mixed news dummy, news analysis dummy, urgent call for action dummy, call for action dummy, action taken dummy, conflict frame scale, ambition/power frame dummy, and a thematic/episodic context dummy. The variables are described more fully in Appendix 6A, located at the end of this chapter.

Compared to the new media factors employed in model 1, this estimation fits the data more strongly, with an $R^2$ of 0.29. Conflict frames appear the most important factor in affecting story tone. The variable is highly significant, with a massive t value of nearly 14.0. The higher the level of conflict presented in the story, the more likely that the news story will have a negative tone. Moving one unit on the three-step conflict scale increases the degree of negativity 0.64 units. Moving the entire range, from the lowest to the highest level of story conflict will increase the degree of negativity 1.3 units on the five-point negative news tone scale. Cooperation frames also strongly affect news tone and are highly significant with a t value of 5.55. When a story presents a cooperative frame, negativity eases by one full unit. One reason that presidential news on balance is more negative that positive is that conflict framing is more common than cooperative framing.

Calls for action also demonstrate hypothesized effects. With no call for action as the omitted or reference category, we find that an urgent call for action increases negativity by 0.57 units, which is about twice the impact of a nonurgent call for action. In contrast, stories about action already underway move story tone in the opposite direction by about 0.24 units, slightly less than half the impact that urgent calls for action have in increasing the negative tone of a story. Story type (e.g., straight news versus analysis) seems to have no effect on tone. Results indicate that compared to features, all three story types (e.g., straight news, mixed news, and analysis) promote a negative story tone at about the same magnitude. Last, neither episodic-thematic context nor ambition significantly affects story tone.

## The Environment of News Production

Chapter 5 found that certain environmental factors, such as the economy, major scandals, the honeymoon period, and possibly the era of new media, helped to explain the aggregate trend in negative presidential news. These factors may likewise affect the degree of negativity in news stories at the individual level. We must bear in mind, however, that the individual-level data used here do not span as long of a time frame as the aggregate data in chapter 5. Critically, these individual-level data used here exist primarily within the new media age. Thus many variables, including the dependent variable, will possess less variance than for the aggregate analysis of the last chapter. For example, divided government is nearly a constant and party polarization is always high in the 1980–98 period compared to the 1949–92 time span of the aggregate data. Owing to this restricted variance issue, factors found significant in the aggregate analysis may not prove to be so in this analysis.

Based on the theory and analysis of the last chapter, the environmental variables used here are roughly categorized into several sets—economic context, political context, and event context, along with the cable penetration variable. For comparability, as much as possible, this analysis includes variables from the aggregate analysis, modified when necessary and appropriate. For instance, instead of annual data, when available monthly data are used. In several instances, variables that could not be used for one reason or another in the aggregate analysis are added into this analysis, when possible. Appendix 6A details the variables used in this analysis.

## Economic Context

In chapter 5, unemployment and inflation were used as independent variables, but neither was found to be significant predictors. They are used again here, now measured in monthly time units. In addition, the indices of Current Consumer Confidence and Consumer Expectations, from the Survey of Consumers of the University of Michigan, are also used as independent variables. Here the guiding hypothesis is that the worse the objective or perceptual economy, the more likely that presidential news will be negative.

## Political Context

The previous chapter found that new presidents tend to receive a higher proportion of positive news, and that polarization between the parties may also contribute to negativity.[15] Variables for each of these are included here, as well as a dummy variable for divided government, which was used in the aggregate analysis but was not found to be statistically significant in that analysis. The aggregate analysis also found that war was associated with negativity. During the 1980–98 period, the United States was engaged in only one major war, the Gulf War of January–February 1991, which is also used here.

Public support for the president may also affect whether news about him takes a negative turn. When the president is popular, other politicians may restrain themselves in criticizing and/or opposing the president, wanting either to be associated with a popular president or at least not be seen as highly antagonistic. In contrast, when a president's popularity wanes, opposition party leaders will likely heighten their attacks on the administration. Political weakness may also embolden leaders from the president's party to challenge the incumbent. From this greater supply of critics when popularity is low, we can expect to see greater negativity in presidential news.

Declining polls may also affect journalistic news production decisions independent of the behavior of political elites. The market model of news production suggests that news organizations attempt to feed the public with news that the public wants. Hence, as the public becomes less sanguine about the president, its appetite for critical news may rise, creating an incentive for news organizations to produce negative news about the president. In contrast, when the president is popular, the public may be less tolerant of critical news. News organizations will tone down the negativity in news reports about the president so as not to alienate readers or viewers.[16] To measure this effect, I use the monthly Gallup approval rating, lagged one month, to insure that causality runs from the poll rating to the news.

## Event Context

Events are the raw material of news. Much of what journalists do is report on transpiring events. Events may reflect poorly or well on the president, inasmuch as journalists tie events to the president and/or the public holds presidents responsible for the event. Considerable research on presidential approval finds that events affect presidential approval, with events classified as positive often boosting approval in the short run, and events classified as negative deflating approval (Ostrom and Simon 1985, 1989; Brace and Hinckley 1992; Gronke and Brehm 2002; Newman 2002). Brody (1991) argues that news mediates the impact of events on approval. Thus we might expect that some events will produce negative news and others positive news. Several major studies have classified events as either positive or negative and used them to account for presidential approval (Brace and Hinckley 1992, Gronke and Brehm 2002, Newman 2002). Not surprisingly, in general those studies found that the presumed direction of an event, whether it was coded as positive or negative, statistically affected presidential popularity. For this research, I used these studies' classification of events to build two variables, which count the number of positive and negative events for the month of the news story.[17]

Scandal proved among the most important predictors of negative news in the aggregate analysis. Scandals, which are negative almost by definition, may occupy a significant fraction of news space and crowd other stories off of the news agenda. Alternatively, scandal may affect a president's image and reputation, thus spilling over onto other presidential news stories. By entering dummy variables for the two scandals, Iran-Contra and Lewinsky, while also controlling for the scandal time period variable used above, we can test which of these mechanisms is at work. Such an analysis will also inform us as to the success of presidential strategies to deal with scandals. Bill Clinton's strategy, for instance, involved having the president actively engaged in the duties of his office and speaking on important policy issues, in other words, looking presidential (Farnsworth and Lichter 2006, chap. 6).

## Results of the Impact of Environmental Factors on Negativity

Model 3 on table 6.1 presents the results of regressing these environmental variables on story tone. The Heckman selection effects for this analysis find a significant selection effect. However, the substantive results are nearly identical to the OLS results. (The Heckman results are reported in appendix 6B on the webpage.) The following discussion refers to the OLS results. Compared to the new media and hard news characteristics, this model does a poor job of explaining variance, with a meager $R^2$ of 0.02 and an insignificant equation F ($p = 0.26$). A reduced-form model detected that three variables—Iran-Contra, Lewinsky dummy, and cable television—may be significant predictors of the tone of presidential news stories.

Those results suggest that during the Lewinsky and Iran-Contra periods, presidential news is 0.30 ($p = 0.02$) and 0.52 ($p = 0.05$) units more negative. However, when controlling for the presidential scandal variable used above (that is, whether the story referred to scandal), both of the scandal period variables fall below conventional significance levels, while the presidential scandal variable maintains its significance.[18] From this result it appears that scandals do not spill over to affect other presidential news during the same time period, perhaps because presidential strategies, such as Clinton's, to contain the news damage of scandal, may be effective.

These reduced form results also suggest that cable penetration is associated with negative news. The regression coefficient indicates that each 1 percent increase in cable penetration leads to a 0.006 unit increase in negativity. Over the 1980–98 period, cable penetration increased from about 20 percent of households to about two-thirds of households. This approximately 45 percent increase in cable penetration leads to about a 0.25–0.30 unit change in negativity on the five-point scale.

Chapter 5 found that cable penetration, party polarization, and a simple time counter were all highly correlated and that it was impossible to disentangle their separate effects on aggregate trends in negativity. Again, the three are highly related, with correlations at the story level ranging from 0.91 to 0.97. Estimations (not shown) that replace the cable variable with either party polarization or the time counter find that neither of these substitutions attains statistical significance. When either polarization or the time counter are added into estimations that also includes the cable variable, the cable variable no longer appears significant either, but this is what one would expect given such high multicollinearity. This evidence suggests that cable television, rather than the other variables, affects negativity in presidential news at least during this period.

## The Comparative Impacts of New Media Reporting Practices, Hard News Reporting, and Environmental Factors on Negativity in Presidential News

Thus far, this chapter has produced some evidence that each of the three perspectives—new media reporting practices, hard news reporting practices, and the environment of news production—may contribute to our understanding of the tone of presidential news. This section pulls together these three perspectives into a multivariate framework and asks how well they fare when pitted against each other. Models 4 and 5 of table 6.1 present OLS results of using all variables from each of the three perspectives. (Appendix 6B on the web presents results of the Heckman selection model, which are substantively identical to the OLS results.) Model 4 is a full or saturation model that uses all variables; model 5 is a reduced-form estimation that only includes variables found to be significant or variables that raised the $R^2$ by a significant increment.[19] The discussion below focuses on the reduced-form OLS results.

Overall model fit is reasonably good, with an $R^2$ of 0.35 (adjusted $R^2$ of 0.34). Given the difficulty in coding the story tone, this is impressive. As indicated in the above analysis, environmental factors fail to contribute to our understanding of story tone. Not one environmental variable proved statistically significant with controls for the new media and hard news reporting variables. If the environment affects the tone of individual stories, it does so through its effects on new media and/or hard news reporting styles. We will return to this point below.

Three new media factors affect story tone—soft news, sensationalism, and a nonpolicy story emphasis. Contrary to the overarching hypothesis, soft news is associated with positive, not negative, presidential news. Each one unit step toward the soft news end of the scale reduces the negativity of a presidential news story by 0.19 units. This amounts to a full step in the five-category news tone variable if a story moves from the hardest to the softest category.

In contrast, stories lacking policy content are more likely have a negative tone than stories with a policy focus. Each one unit increase in the nonpolicy content scale leads to a 0.15 increase in the negativity of a presidential news story, or a 0.45 change in negativity from a story with policy content to one without policy content at the maximum level (recall, the policy content variable has three categories, from no policy content to substantial policy content). Given that the bulk of presidential news stories contain some policy content, this may too work in the president's favor. But as noted above, presidential news stories without policy content have become more common in the 1990s (29.8 percent) than the 1980s (16.8 percent).

Sensationalism also affects story tone. As hypothesized, sensationalism is associated with a negative news tone. Each one unit increase in sensationalism affects negativity by 0.21 units. Moving from the least to the most sensational story will render it 0.63 units more negative. But as sensationalism is rare in presidential news (6 percent), this may have little practical implication for presidential news tone overall.

Finally, scandal coverage greatly affects the tone of presidential news coverage. A scandal story will be some 0.7 units more negative than a nonscandal story. Importantly, with this variable as a control, the Lewinsky and Iran-Contra period effects dummies are no longer significant. This suggests that scandals do not spill onto nonscandal stories, as noted above. But also recall that the aggregate analysis found strong effects of the Watergate and Iran-Contra scandals on trends in presidential news tone. In combination, these two findings suggest that scandals affect news tone by altering the composition of the news. That is, scandals become major news stories and thus may push other potential news stories off of the news hole. At the same time, the negative coverage in scandal stories does not seem to affect the tone of other news stories about the president occurring during the period of the scandal.

Turning to the hard news reporting practices, we also find several variables that significantly affect news tone. First, the amount of conflict reported in the story strongly affects news tone. Each one unit increase in conflict increases negativity by 0.58 units, with a 1.16 difference in negativity between the least and most conflict ridden stories. Since conflict is found in many presidential news stories, the conflict frame plays a large role in accounting for negativity in presidential news. Counterbalancing conflict, cooperation themes lead toward a positive tone. And like conflict, the effect of cooperation in stories is large—cooperative stories are 0.96 units less negative than stories lacking a cooperation frame. But unlike conflict, cooperation frames are found rarely in presidential news—less than 5 percent of presidential news stories. The environment of the new media age—divided government, party polarization—may lend toward the greater production of conflict frames, while limiting the production of cooperation frames in presidential news, a point we will turn to below.

Finally, the action component of presidential news stories also affects tone. When a story cites a call for action, negativity increases by 0.28 units over a story that makes no call for action. When action is urgently needed, the story becomes even more negative, another 0.30 units (or 0.58 more than stories that do not refer to any call for action). But when the story discusses action already being taken, news tone moves in a positive direction. Such a story will be 0.27 units less negative than a story making no reference to a call for action, or 0.55 units less negative than one that calls for action. Working in the president's favor is that many more stories cite an action already taken (62.3 percent) than call or urgently call the president to take action (24.3 percent).

This finding has broader and perhaps deeper implications. An assumption of much writing on presidential images and the public reaction to such images suggests that the public prefers presidents who appear to be active (Cronin and Genovese 1998). Here we find that taking action leads to news that is less negative. It would be of interest for future research to link this characteristic of presidential news to public support for the president. If the president is portrayed as taking an action, does his approval rise? Do specific characteristics of the president's action, such as its scope, speed, timeliness, or likelihood of success, affect the public's opinion of the president? And how reliably does the news media report that presidents are taking action?

## An Assessment: The Impact of the New Media Age on the Tone of Presidential News

Presidential news in the age of new media is more negative and critical than it was during the golden age. The analysis in chapter 5, using aggregate times series data, indicated that something about the new media age added to the level of negativity of presidential news, but that analysis could not isolate the mechanism(s) at work, due to high multicollinearity among the cable penetration, party polarization, and time counter variables. This chapter turned to an analysis of stories themselves, but the stories exist only for the age of new media. The environmental context did not seem to affect the level of negativity directly, although aspects of reporting in the age of new media appear to have strong impacts. However, contrary to our stereotypes of new media age reporting, the rise of soft news, sensationalism, and other features of this era, while often significant in explaining the degree of negativity, at times displayed results contrary to expectations (e.g., soft news leading to positive news). Attributes normally associated with hard news reporting seem to better account for negativity in presidential news.

Scholars of the age of new media often focus on soft news, sensationalism, the lack of policy content, and other characteristics to distinguish news reporting in the new media age from the previous era (Davis and Owen 1998; Patterson 2000; Baum 2003a, 2003b). But standards of hard news reporting may have also changed. Some note, for instance, that news analysis is more common now than it used to be (West 2001). Perhaps the attributes of hard news reporting that lead to negativity are more common in the new media age than before. For instance, hard news reporting may be more likely to emphasize conflict or refer to a call for action than used to be the case. If the attributes of hard news reporting that affect negativity in presidential news have become more or less common, then we have unearthed one mechanism to understand the rise in negativity in presidential news reporting. Plus, if this is the case, then we have found another aspect that distinguishes reporting in the new media age from previous eras. Reporting in the age of new media is not only softer: hard news reporting in the new media age may emphasize conflict and call for action themes more than reporting in the earlier era.

We can provide an initial test of this idea by correlating the factors from model 5, table 6.1, with time. Several of these variables were found to be more common in the 1990s than the 1980s. While this correlation with time will not tell us whether reporting in the new media age differs from golden age reporting, it will tell us if the likelihood of conflict themes, for instance, have become more common as the new media age has matured. Table 6.2 presents the correlations with a monthly time counter.

Table 6.2
Correlations between select variables
and a monthly time counter, 1980–98

| Variable | r | Significance |
| --- | --- | --- |
| Urgent call | .004 | .91 |
| Call | .03 | .35 |
| Action taken | −.05 | .05 |
| Conflict | −.03 | .42 |
| Cooperation | .01 | .81 |
| Soft news | .003 | .93 |
| Sensationalism | .05 | .11 |
| Nonpolicy | .16 | .00 |
| Scandal | .12 | .00 |

Neither of two new media age characteristics, soft news and sensationalism, show any trend over time. However, scandal reporting is more likely as time progresses, but this might be a function of the Lewinsky scandal in 1998. When I restrict the correlation to 1997, the size of the relationship weakens slightly to 0.10 from 0.13, but it is still highly significant (p = 0.002). The rise of scandal reporting may be one source of the increase in negative presidential news in the new media age. Similarly, policy content in presidential stories has declined as time progresses (r = 0.16, p = .000). As the lack of policy content is associated with negativity in presidential news, this too may account for the increasing negativity in presidential news.

Most of the "hard news" reporting characteristics are not related to time. Neither calls for action, nor conflict, nor cooperation frames shows any relationship to time, yet stories that mention an action being undertaken are slightly less likely to be noted in news stories as time progresses (r = −0.05, p = 0.05). Again, as action taken is associated with a positive tone, the modest decline in the likelihood of an action taken-story will reduce the amount of positive news coverage that the president receives in the new media age. Figure 6.2 plots the trends in the "policy" and "action taken" series.[20] For the action taken series, each data point is based on the annual percentage of presidential news stories that either refer to an action already taken or being taken. The policy series plots the annual percentage of presidential news stories that contain a substantial amount of policy content. Regression trend lines are superimposed and results of regressing each series on an annual time counter (1980 = 1 . . . 1998 = 19) are also presented.

Both trends display a downward slope, although the decline in policy content is the steeper of the two. Based on the regression analysis, each year sees an additional decline of 0.75 percent in stories containing a substantial amount of policy content. Across the nineteen-year time span, this accumulates into a 13.5 percent decline. Alternatively, in 1980 approximately 67.4 percent of

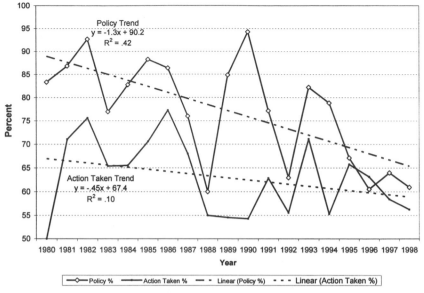

Figure 6.2 Percentage of presidential news that includes a policy element and reports that an action has been taken, 1980–98. Source: Patterson (2000).

presidential news stories contained a substantial amount of policy content; in 1998, only 53.9 percent would. The regression results indicate that for each year there is a decline of 0.27 in the percentage of stories that refer to action being taken, or a cumulative decline of 4.9 percent across the series. In 1980, about 61.4 percent of presidential news stories made an action reference; in 1998, only 56.5 percent would, based on the linear trend.

As stories citing action reduce negativity, their lower frequency over time will generate more negativity in presidential news. The declining frequency of policy content will also lead to greater negativity. Thus the rise of new media age reporting style, in particular the shift from policy to nonpolicy stories, has had major implications for the tone of presidential news. But changes in hard news reporting, specifically the decline in the percentage of stories that refer to action being taken, has also steered presidential news in a more negative direction.

The forces that lead to the new media age help account for the rise of non-policy reporting, but it is not clear why journalists are less inclined to refer to action being taken in the late 1990s than the early 1980s. One hypothesis is that presidents have actually taken fewer actions than they once did. Perhaps Bill Clinton's announcement in his 1996 State of the Union Address of the end of the era of big government indicates less activity on the part of presidents and government, which may get reflected in the news.

But the rise of divided government and the gridlock that it produces may also have an effect here, either deterring presidents from proposing as much legislation as they once did or stymieing their efforts to see their legislation enacted into law. Thus there were fewer stories to write in which presidents were taking or proposing governmental action. In other words, there may be something in the environment of the new media age that affects whether journalists write stories with an action component, conflict themes, and the like.[21] The next section turns to the question of whether the environment during the new media age affects the characteristics of stories that in turn affect the tonality of presidential news stories.

## Environmental Effects on New Media and Hard News Reporting Practices in the Age of New Media

Chapter 5 found that some environmental factors help explain the rise of negativity in presidential news in the new media age and that aspects of the new media age may have contributed to this increase in negative news. In this chapter, however, environmental factors do not affect the tonality of presidential news directly, although some characteristics of reporting in the new media age do. In particular, sensationalism and nonpolicy reporting, two aspects that distinguish new media age reporting from reporting in the broadcast age, increase the likelihood of negativity in presidential news. But soft news reporting, another distinguishing attribute of new media age reporting, promotes a positive tone in presidential news.

Can we reconcile the finding of environmental effects on tonality from chapter 5 with the lack of such impact in this chapter? Differences in the time frame and of level of analysis likely account for much of the divergence in results. The shorter time frame of the data in this chapter truncates the variance in many variables. Plus the fact that the data used in this chapter all come from the new media age means that we cannot make comparisons across the new media age and the earlier broadcast age. Thus the questions posed in these two chapters are slightly different. While the previous chapter asked whether the *change to* the new media age contributed to the rise in negativity in presidential news, this chapter asked if something intrinsic to the new media age affects the tone of presidential news.

Certain new media age reporting practices, as well as hard news reporting practices, affect the tone of presidential news. Does the environment, however, affect whether reporters employ these reporting practices in producing presidential news? In other words, is the environment an indirect influence on the tone of presidential news? To address this question, I took each of the variables from table 6.1 that were found to be significant predictors of negativity in presidential news and regressed them on the environmental factors, also from

Table 6.3
Impact of environmental factors on new media and hard news reporting
characteristics in presidential news

| Dependent | Independent | b | p | $R^2$ | Eq. F or $\chi^2$ | p of F or $\chi^2$ |
|---|---|---|---|---|---|---|
| Action taken | Unemployment | .07 | .03 | .01 | 4.79 | .03 |
| Call for action | Lewinsky period | .31 | .08 | .01 | 6.48 | .04 |
| | Negative event | .29 | .04 | | | |
| Urgent call | Divided govt. | −.44 | .01 | .02 | 9.58 | .02 |
| | New president | −.38 | .04 | | | |
| | Approval-lagged | .01 | .05 | | | |
| Conflict* | none | | | | | |
| Cooperation | none | | | | | |
| Soft news* | Unemployment | −.15 | .00 | .02 | 5.85 | .02 |
| | Consumer confidence | −.03 | .00 | | | |
| | Expectations | .02 | .00 | | | |
| | Approval-lagged | −.01 | .07 | | | |
| Sensationalism* | none | | | | | |
| Nonpolicy* | Polarization | 2.07 | .00 | .04 | 14.72 | .00 |
| | Divided govt. | .25 | .00 | | | |
| | Approval-lagged | −.01 | .00 | | | |
| Pres. scandal | Expectations | .03 | .00 | .07 | 40.92 | .00 |
| | Iran Contra | .85 | .00 | | | |

* Multiple regressions, all other equations use multivariate probit. For the probit models, the $R^2$ is the pseudo-$R^2$ and instead of the equation F, the $\chi^2$ is reported.

table 6.1.[22] Table 6.3 presents the results of this analysis. To make it easier to digest the mass of results, given the large number of dependent (9) and independent variables (14), the table only presents environmental variables found to be significant predictors.

The first thing to notice from table 6.3 is the paucity of significant environmental predictors of new media age and hard news reporting characteristics. Of a possible 126 relationships (9 × 14), only 15 attained statistical significance. Second, no environmental variable consistently predicts to these reporting characteristics. Third, the $R^2$ (or pseudo-$R^2$ in the case of the probit models) are weak, never rising above 0.07. But the stronger equations in terms of explained variance tend to be for the new media age reporting characteristics (e.g., scandal, nonpolicy news, soft news) than the hard news reporting ones. Overall, however, environmental factors during the new media age do little to explain the employment of these types of reporting practices in presidential news. This is not to say that environmental factors have no impact on the tonality of presidential news. It may be that the role of environmental factors on presidential news changed from the broadcast to the new media age. To identify such changes, we need data like these here, but spanning the new media and broadcast ages.

## Conclusion

Chapters 3 through 6 have reviewed a mountain of evidence documenting that there is less presidential news, but it is more negative in tone, in the new media age than the broadcast age. These analyses also indicate that the new media, which began to appear in force in the late 1970s to mid 1980s, may have something to do with both of these trends. Using a market model of news production as a theoretical foundation, results in chapter 4 detect a linkage between the diffusion of cable television, one indicator of the new media age, and the decline in presidential news among the traditional, major national news media. Although presidential news is definitely more negative in the new media age than the broadcast age, the results of the analyses in chapters 5 and 6 are less definitive in establishing a causal link between the new media age and this increased negativity

Chapter 5's results cannot rule out that other factors, such as increased party polarization, rather than the rise of the new media, may be the primary explanation for the rise in negativity in presidential news. However, the new media and increased polarization may reinforce each other, producing a higher level of negativity than would be the case if only one affected presidential news tone.

This chapter explored in detail the impact of attributes of reporting in the new media age on the tone of presidential news. From this analysis, certain reporting practices associated with the new media age, such as the rise of sensationalism and the displacement of policy-based news stories with nonpolicy ones, seem to lead to negativity in presidential news. But countering these trends, another new media practice, the rise of soft news, seems to lend toward a positive news tone. The increased emphasis and skill of the White House with regard to presidential image management may explain why soft news about the president is positive. Presidential news management strategies may also account for the rise of soft news in presidential news, presenting the president in ceremonial and other occasions, where other administration figures do the dirty job of making more controversial announcements, as Farnsworth and Lichter (2006) argue was the practice of the George W. Bush administration.

However, even in the new media age, and despite rising amounts of soft news, most presidential news still has a policy focus. Presidential news stories that contain conflict themes and/or suggest that action needs to be taken tend to be negative in tone, whereas stories that portray the president as already having taken an action are more positive in tone. From the 1980s to the 1990s, the latter type of story has become somewhat less common, another reason for the rise in negativity in presidential news. It is not clear, though, why such stories are less common. It may be due to decreasing presidential (and national government) activity levels, the barriers that divided government and party polarization erect that inhibit presidential policy aims, or something else about journalism in the new media age that diverts journalist attention from such stories.

Thus even though this and previous chapters provide some answers to account for these two trends in presidential news, these analyses also open up new questions, while not fully resolving all of the questions set out in this research either. The next two chapters turn to two other trends in the mass public—the decline in news attentiveness and the erosion of public confidence in the news media—and ask: Has the rise of the new media had anything to do with these two trends?

## Appendix 6A: Variables Used in the Analysis

Note that further information about statistical methods employed in this book can be found online at http://press.princeton.edu/titles/8592.html.

### Dependent Variable

*Negative News*: 5 = clearly negative, 4 = more negative than positive, 3 = neutral or balanced, 2 = more positive than negative, 1 = clearly positive. Source: Patterson (2000).

### Independent Variables

NEW MEDIA AGE REPORTING PRACTICES

*Soft News*: 5 = definitely soft news, 4 = mostly soft news, 3 = mixed evenly, 2 = mostly hard news, 1 = definitely hard news. Source: Patterson (2000).

*Sensationalism*: A three point scale coded 1 = low sensationalism, 2 = moderate sensationalism, 3 = high sensationalism. Source: Patterson (2000).

*Human Interest*: 1 = no human interest content, 2 = slight human interest content, 3 = moderate human interest content, 4 = high human interest content. Source: Patterson (2000).

*News You Can Use*: 1 = not the primary purpose of the story, 2 = a secondary purpose of the story, 3 = the primary purpose of the story. Source: Patterson (2000).

*Nonpolicy*: 1 = substantially policy relevant story, 2 = somewhat policy relevant story, 3 = non-policy-related story. Source: Patterson (2000).

*Scandal*: 1 = scandal story, 0 = no scandal, from Patterson's major topic code variable, code 3 (political scandal). Source: Patterson (2000).

CHARACTERISTICS OF PRESIDENTIAL NEWS

*Straight News*: 1 = straight news, 0 otherwise, from Type of Story variable. Source: Patterson (2000).

*Mixed News*: 1 = mixed news, 0 otherwise, from Type of Story variable. Source: Patterson (2000).

*Analysis*: 1 = analysis, 0 otherwise, from Type of Story variable. Source: Patterson (2000).

*Urgent Call for Action*: 1 = Story says/implies that urgent action is needed, 0 otherwise, from Action/No Action Frame variable. Source: Patterson (2000).

*Call for Action*: 1 = Story says/implies that nonurgent action is needed, 0 otherwise, from Action/No Action Frame variable. Source: Patterson (2000).

*Action Taken*: 1 = Story says action has been taken, 0 otherwise, from Action/No Action Frame variable. Source: Patterson (2000).

*Conflict*: 3 = substantial level of conflict, 2 = some conflict, 1 = no conflict or so slight as to be inconsequential, from Conflict/No Conflict Frame variable. Source: Patterson (2000).

*Context*: 1 = Episodic, 2 = Thematic, from Context Frame Variable. Source: Patterson (2000).

*Ambition*: 1 = if ambition and power serve as the story's major frame, 0 = otherwise, based upon Major Context Frame variable. Source: Patterson (2000).

*Cooperation*: 1 = if cooperation serves as the story's major frame, 0 = otherwise, based upon Major Context Frame variable. Source: Patterson (2000).

ENVIRONMENTAL FACTORS

All environmental factor variables are measured for the month of the story unless otherwise noted:

*Inflation*: Monthly change in the Consumer Price Index, 1949–92. Source: Bureau of Labor Statistics CPI homepage, http://www.bls.gov/cpi/home.htm.

*Unemployment*: Monthly unemployment rate, 1949–92, Source: Bureau of Labor Statistics homepage, http://www.bls.gov/.

*Consumer Confidence*: Monthly Index of Consumer Confidence, Survey of Consumers, University of Michigan.

*Consumer Expectations*: Monthly Index of Consumer Expectations, Survey of Consumers, University of Michigan.

*Gulf War*: "1" for the period of major fighting, January and February 1991, and 0 otherwise.

*Lewinsky Period*: 1 = January–December 1998, 0 otherwise.

*Iran-Contra Period*: 1 = December 1986–December 1987, 0 otherwise.

*Positive Event*: A count of the number of positive events that occurred in the month of the news story. Source: Gronke and Brehm (2002). The variable ranges from 0 to 2.

*Negative Event*: A count of the number of negative events that occurred in the month of the news story. Source: Gronke and Brehm (2002). The variable ranges from 0 to 2.

*Party Polarization*: Absolute difference in the party medians on the first dimension of the Poole-Rosenthal DW-Nominate scale for the year of the news story. Downloaded from Keith Poole's homepage, http://voteview .com/dwnl.htm.

*Divided Government*: A dummy variable whether at least one house of Congress is controlled by the opposition party, coded divided = 1, united government = 0.

*New President*: A dummy variable for the first year of a new president no matter how the president came to office, coded first year = 1, non-first years = 0.

*Approval-lagged*: The Gallup approval score of the president in the month before the news story.

*Cable Television Percent*: percentage of households that subscribe to cable television. Sources: *Historical Statistics of the United States* and various volumes of the *Statistical Abstract of the United States*.

HECKMAN FIRST STAGE VARIABLES

*Time*: monthly counter, 1–224. January 1980 = 1, February, 1980 = 2, etc.

*Local News Outlet*: 1 = local or regional news source (26 in all), 0 = national news source (*New York Times, Washington Post, Wall Street Journal*, ABC, NBC, *Time, Newsweek, USA Today*). Source: Patterson (2000).

*Unemployment*: Monthly unemployment level of the month that the story appeared. See above.

# CHAPTER 7

# The Declining Audience for News and the New Media Age

The news media, the public, and the president comprise the three legs of the presidential news system. That system underwent a transformation from the golden age of television (Baum and Kernell 1999) of the 1960s through the mid 1970s to the current age of new media. The preceding chapters documented the transformation of one leg of the system, the news media. News reporting in the new media age offers less news on the president and that news is more negative than was the case in the broadcasting age.[1] This and the next chapter turn to a second leg of the presidential news system, the mass public, to address changes in the behavior and opinion of the mass public with regard to news and the news media.

Compared to the broadcast era, the new media age features a mass public that consumes less news and harbors less trusting attitudes toward the news media. Many kinds of data, from television ratings, to newspaper circulation totals, to survey responses indicate a general decline in the news attentiveness of the average person across almost every medium of news delivery, which I document below for some forms of news attention, save for a select few, like talk radio (Davis and Owen 1998).[2] Similarly, the public trusts the news media less now than it did in the broadcasting age (Cook and Gronke 2001, 2002; Cook, Gronke, and Rattliff 2000; Hibbing and Theiss-Morse 1995, 2001, 2002; Moy and Pfau 2000). In this chapter I ask whether the rise of the new media has anything to do with the decline in news consumption, while in chapter 8 I ask whether the rise of the new media accounts for some of the decline in public trust and confidence toward the news media.

The decline in news use and media trust parallel other changes in the mass public, such as the drop-off in turnout, the increase in cynicism, the rise of independents, and the more general decline in social capital (Bennett 1998; Chanley, Rudolph, and Rahn 2000; Hansen and Rosenstone 1993; Hetherington 2001; Hibbing and Theiss-Morse 2001, 2002; Putnam 2000). Thus much of the explanation for the decline in news consumption and media trust is likely be found in the factors that have lead to these other changes in mass behavior and attitudes. But this research departs from that literature by focusing on the particular effects of the new media.

News attention can be conceptualized as a form of political and/or social participation (Hansen and Rosenstone 1993, Putnam 2000). As past research on participation shows, different forms of participation are not always or easily substitutable (Verba and Nie 1972). This chapter focuses on four major forms of news attentiveness—reading newspapers, reading weekly newsmagazines, watching television news, and listening to news on the radio. Although there is considerable overlap across these types of news attention, these four forms of news attention also differ in some important respects as detailed below.

Extant literature suggests two mechanisms through which the rise of the new media may have affected the decline in news attention. One mechanism looks at the impact of the variety of programming offered on cable television. This argument suggests that some people who once consumed network news abandoned those programs for lighter entertainment fair on cable television (Baum and Kernell 1999, Welch 2000, Prior 2005).[3] A second mechanism looks at the characteristics of news reporting in the age of new media and the public response to that style of news reporting (Patterson 2000). As detailed in chapter 6, news reporting in the new media age is softer, more cynical toward authorities, and more fixated on scandal than was the case during the broadcasting age (Cappella and Jamieson 1997, Kerbel 1999, Patterson 2002). Has this new reporting style alienated some news consumers, leading them away from the news media that most heavily rely on this style of news reporting?

## Reporting Styles in the New Media Age and the Public Response

Thomas Patterson's (2002) new media age reporting style thesis links changes in the way news is reported to declining trust in the news media and news consumption. He argues that in response to the competitive environment of the new media age the style of news reporting changed: "News outlets have softened their coverage. Their news has also become increasingly critical in tone" (2).

Increased competition sensitized news organizations to the news tastes of consumers. News organizations used several types of information about consumer tastes that led them to substitute soft news for hard news. First, news producers noticed the decline of audiences, especially the major network evening broadcasts. Viewer decline not only affected revenues, because advertising rates are pegged to audience size, but also forced news producers to question why their audiences were shirking. In many cases, market research, to which many news organizations turned, found that consumers possessed only a limited interest in traditional hard news, while desiring perhaps a greater quantity of soft news in their news diet (McManus 1994, Underwood 1998). Furthermore, the success of new news formats, which mixed entertainment and news values (e.g., talk radio, *Crossfire* on CNN, etc.), provided news producers with another model of news programming to offer consumers. Some of these new style "news" programs proved highly successful, and in several cases ratings of dedicated hard news programs showed some improvement once their content was softened.[4] Thus in the new media age, several forces converged to soften the news product offered to consumers.

Patterson argues that this change to softer news affected people's evaluations and consumption of news. Some people disliked this turn to softer news, especially those who preferred a hard news diet. These types of people ceased watching news programs that added a higher quotient of soft news than they preferred. At the same time, those with a taste for the softer over hard news were less often likely to consume news of any type and turned, instead, to entertainment shows, their preferred choice.

Patterson finds some support for his thesis in a survey that he conducted in October 2000. His survey found that by large margins people say that the news is depressing rather than uplifting (84 percent to 16 percent) and that it is negative rather than positive (77 percent to 23 percent). About one half of his respondents described news as superficial, biased, and not enjoyable (6). But most important, and counter to the market research that points to the public's preference for soft over hard news,[5] respondents by a wide margin said that they prefer hard to soft news (63 percent hard news to 24 percent soft, with 13 percent wanting an equal mix of the two).[6] Noting the possibility of response bias in this last item, Patterson presented respondents with twenty-one headlines and asked if they would be interested in reading such a story. Respondents again showed a preference for hard news stories over the softer variety (7).

Patterson's survey findings raise the thorny issue of whether the public prefers soft or hard news. First, just because people say that they prefer hard news does not mean that when given the choice between hard news and something else (e.g., soft news, entertainment) that they will select hard news. King et al.'s (1999) analysis of the Pew News Interest Index, which asks people if they have been following certain major news stories, does not find high levels of interest in traditional hard news stories. More crucially, Nielsen ratings indicate a steady erosion of the audience for the network evening news broadcasts (West 2001, 132); little indication exists that those fleeing the network news have flocked to the cable or other news outlets, such as the news sites on the internet. The cable news networks, like CNN and Fox News, possess small audiences, and while an increasing percentage of people are using the internet for news, most internet news users also follow news from more traditional news sources. People who commonly do not use other news sources have not turned to the internet for news but use the internet for other purposes (Rainie et al., 2005).

In sorting through this issue of whether the public prefers hard or soft news or some mix of the two, it may be useful to distinguish those in the mass public who prefer hard news to soft news (or entertainment) from those who prefer soft news (or entertainment) to hard news (Prior 2005). Most contend that those who prefer hard news constitute the smaller of the two groups (e.g., Zaller

2003). Prior (2005) presents some data from surveys in 2002 and 2003 that allow an estimate of the relative sizes of the two groups during that time frame.

Rather than ask people if they like or appreciate hard news, as Patterson did, Prior gives respondents a list of ten program category choices and asks them to rank these choices. News was one of the ten genres, along with science fiction, comedy and sitcoms, drama, soap operas, reality TV, sports, game shows, documentaries, and music videos. Prior allowed respondents to select up to four preferred genre selections in rank order from first most liked on to fourth most liked. After the four liked genres were selected, respondents were allowed to designate one that they "really disliked" (581).

Prior found that while few disliked news (3 percent), it rarely ranked among the top viewing choice for many: 5 percent ranked it first, 11 percent second, 14 percent third, and 17 percent fourth. Notably 50 percent were indifferent, neither ranking it nor disliking it (581). Thus while news was rarely the leading viewing choice, a large number of people rated it among their top four viewing choices. Prior's estimates suggest a potentially large number of individuals like news and might be upset by the increasing softness found in so many newscasts, as Patterson's hypothesis suggests. Still, Prior's study does not distinguish whether those who rank news prefer the hard or soft variety.

Patterson's argument appears most appropriate for understanding the behavior of those with a preference for hard news over soft news. He argues that the market strategy of news organizations, which targets soft news consumers, is counterproductive. First, soft news consumers tend not to tune into the news in large numbers. Second, even if soft news attracts those who prefer soft news, the high soft news diet has alienated viewers who prefer hard news.[7] Thus Patterson links changing news reporting styles to changing news consumption habits and attitudes about the news media. Patterson's argument has a causal chain—changes in news reporting styles have alienated those who prefer hard news to soft news. As a result of the diminishing supply of hard news on network broadcasts (and other traditional news media), the audience for these traditional media has shrunk.


## Cable Television and Public Consumption of News

Baum and Kernell (1999; also Prior 2005) offer another, not incompatible, model of the impact of the new media environment, what I will call the "viewing opportunity" model, to explain the decline in the size of the audience for news. The Baum and Kernell model employs standard utility assumptions, which they apply to viewing presidential addresses and debates, and which may be applicable, with modifications, to news consumption (see Prior 2005).

This model assumes that people engage in an activity when its benefits outweigh the costs. The introduction of cable television altered the cost calculation of television viewing for many people. According to Baum and Kernell, prior to cable, viewing choices were limited. For instance, all three networks aired the major, prime-time presidential addresses and few localities had anything other than the three networks during this time period. With few viewing alternatives, people watched the presidential addresses in numbers comparable to entertainment programming (101). The introduction of cable altered the opportunity costs of watching a presidential speech over a more preferred entertainment program increased. Watching a presidential speech would mean that viewers would have to forego watching an entertainment program that they might like better. This cost could be far from negligible if a person preferred the entertainment program to the presidential speech, but not if the person preferred the speech to the entertainment program.

Baum and Kernell use several types of evidence to support their model. Using 1996 ANES data, they find that cable subscribers were less likely to watch either the first or second presidential debates than noncable respondents. They also find that highly politically informed cable subscribers viewed the debates at higher levels than less informed cable subscribers. Yet levels of information had little impact on the debate watching behavior of highly and poorly informed *noncable* respondents. Last, at low levels of information, cable subscribers were less likely to watch the debates than noncable respondents. Baum and Kernell also show that as the network audience share has declined, a function largely of cable television, presidential speech ratings also declined (107–8). Importantly, neither political trust nor government confidence appears to affect debate watching or presidential speech ratings in their analysis.

The Baum-Kernell viewing opportunity model may be applicable to television news and other news media consumption generally, and not merely to major political events, like presidential addresses and debates. While Prior (2005) does not look at the impact of preferences and new media access on news consumption, he finds that those with cable and internet access, and who also like entertainment over news, possess much less political information than those who also prefer entertainment to news but lack access to cable and the internet.[8]

However, where Baum and Kernell find that political trust and government confidence have no impact on speech and debate viewing, trust in the media may affect news consumption habits. First, we should not necessarily expect political trust or confidence in the government to affect watching a presidential speech or the presidential election debates. Prime-time presidential speeches are relatively rare events. When presidents address the nation during prime time, it is usually to signal something of importance. Many addresses concern foreign policy crises; others, such as State of the Union addresses, are moments of high ceremony and/or are instances of state tradition. Cynical and noncynical alike may tune into these events because of their importance. Presidential debates, too, may attract viewers with cynical political attitudes. People who are cynical of government may tune into the debates in search of a candidate to support, perhaps a candidate who reflects their cynical attitudes. In 1992 and 1996, Ross Perot's presidential candidacy targeted such individuals. While they may or may not have voted for Perot in the general election, or voted at all, they may have tuned into the debate(s) to satisfy their curiosity about him as it related to their political discontent. Thus these types of major events may attract people irrespective of their degree of political distrust or cynicism about the government.

Plus, political trust and cynicism toward the government, while related to presidential approval, are system-level properties. Many people may approve of the president, while simultaneously distrusting government. Some politicians, like Ronald Reagan, in part built their personal popularity from the roots of such discontent. Even though evidence suggests that Reagan's popularity ameliorated political cynicism somewhat during his term in office (Citrin and Green 1986), his popularity did not stem the tide of increasing cynicism, nor was his personal support so strong that the public became more trusting of government than distrusting during his tenure.

But media distrust and cynicism, as opposed to political distrust, may affect news media use, as Patterson suggests. People may use the news for information on important events and conditions that may affect them. When people begin to distrust the news, because they think that news reports are inaccurate or politically biased, they may reduce their consumption of news. In other words, if the utility of news declines, we may see people using the news less. Similarly, if people use news for information about the world, but find that the news has gotten softer, they may find that the news contains less information than they want or need, and thus consume less of it.

The Patterson and Baum-Kernell (and Prior) ideas offer two mechanisms through which the new media may affect news consumption habits. Patterson's model suggests that the new reporting style affects both media trust and news consumption levels and that declines in media trust will depress news consumption across all forms of news. This is because the new reporting style is a general attribute of journalism and not particular to any one news medium. However, those who have a stronger preference for hard over soft news will be the people most likely to be alienated by the shift to softer news. Baum and Kernell's viewing opportunity model predicts that cable television access will lower levels of news consumption, but mainly for those less interested in news. Furthermore, the costs will most greatly affect television news consumption, and not other news forms, like newspapers, because the different forms of news are not fully substitutable. Finally, their model suggests no relationship between access to cable and news media attitudes but does not rule out that such a linkage may exist. These two mechanisms focus on different pieces of the puzzle of declining news attention.

Providing definitive or strong tests of these two ideas is not possible. A definitive test requires individual-level data on the content of the news to which people are exposed, their attitudes to the news, their news viewing habits, and their cable access and cable use habits over a long period of time, preferably in a panel design and preferably stretching into the days prior to cable television. Such data do not exist. Hence I employ several different types of data and analyses to test the various predictions of these two models.

## Trends in News Consumption since Mid-century

Whether measured with audience ratings, circulation figures, or survey self-reports, Americans consume less news now than they did a generation ago. Some evidence on this point is presented below. This decline in news consumption is ironic given the greater availability of news due to 24/7 cable news networks and the internet.[9] Of the older news technologies, only radio has witnessed any audience growth. The growth in the radio audience is a function of the creation of a new radio format, talk radio, which attracts a highly selective audience.

### Trends in Broadcast Network News Ratings, 1970–2004

Audience ratings for the early evening broadcast networks news programs provide a direct measure of how many people are watching the news. Although these ratings give us a look at a relatively long trend in news viewing, comparable indicators of others types of news attention do not exist, which limits the utility of audience ratings data. Still, these ratings data are important in that more people use the evening network broadcasts for their news than any other source.

Figure 7.1 traces the trend in the combined ratings and share of the three broadcast networks (ABC, NBC, CBS) from the 1970–71 through the 2004–5 seasons.[10] The audience ratings data suggest quite high and stable viewer levels across the 1970s. Ratings, the percentage of total U.S. households tuned into the programs, ranged between 35 and 40 percent across the 1970s, while audience share, the percentage of television viewers at that time slot who tuned into one of the three broadcast, hovered in the 72–77 percent bracket across the decade. Both lines indicate a decline that begins about 1979–80, approximately when subscriptions to cable television began to grow strongly. By 2004–5, audience share was 36 percent, one-half of its level in the 1970s, while ratings declined to 18.8 percent, again one-half its peak in the late 1970s. Neither decline appears to be flattening; how long these audiences will continue to erode is an open question. It may not be entirely coincidental that the erosion in these news audiences began just as growth in cable began to accelerate, a finding consistent with the Baum-Kernell model discussed above.

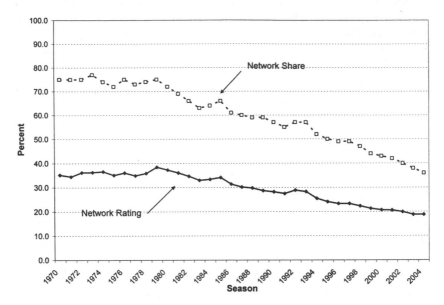

Figure 7.1 Trends in early evening network news broadcasts ratings and share, 1970–2004 seasons. Source: Nielsen media research.

## Survey Trends: ANES, 1952–2000

Since the early 1950s, the American National Election Study (ANES) has been asking respondents about their use of newspapers, television, newsmagazines, and radio for news about the election campaign.[11] The ANES questions possess some notable limitations (Price and Zaller 1993). For one, they only ask about campaign news, not news in general. Second, the ANES questions do not discriminate between heavy and light news media use. Respondents are merely asked if they watch "any programs about the campaign on television" or "did you read about the campaign in any newspaper?" Third, the ANES questions lack specificity about the program or news outlet that respondents use. Respondents may also overstate their degree of news media use. Given the low threshold that allows a person to respond affirmatively merely by seeing a news story on television or reading a newspaper article (perhaps only the headline), one should expect inflated news use totals. Still, these data, despite their measurement problems, provide information that can be compared over time.

Figure 7.2 plots the mean number of news sources out of four (television, radio, newspapers, newsmagazines) that a person uses for presidential years from 1952 to 2000.[12] The mean scores readily display the inflation in news media use that one would expect with such questions. From 1952 until the

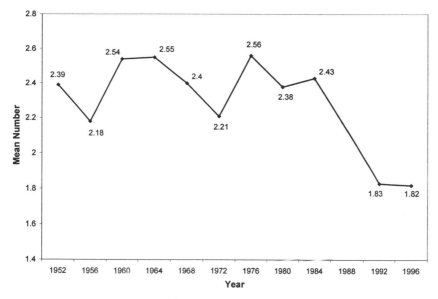

Figure 7.2 Mean number of media used for news about the campaign, 1952–96. Source: ANES, 1952–2000.

mid 1980s, respondents claim on average to use from 2.18 to 2.56 news sources. These figures indicate a modest increase in the number of news sources used from the 1950s to the 1960s. In 1952 and 1956, people claim to use 2.39 and 2.18 sources, respectively. The mean increases to 2.54 in 1960 and hovers in that range through 1976. In 1980 and 1984, the average number of news media sources used dips to 2.38 and 2.43, which then slides precipitously to 1.8 in 1992–96. In the 1990s, people on average used less than two media sources for news about the presidential election campaign.

A major problem with such a summary index as this is that it equates each medium, assuming that one can substitute one for another. But different media may attract different users, and therefore, may not be highly substitutable.[13] For instance, the correlations for use across media sources range only from 0.09 to 0.29.[14] Moreover, some of these media have changed remarkably over the years. In the 1950s, radio was a mainstream news source, tied to the national radio networks. In the 1980s, talk radio emerged, becoming an important political information source, attracting an audience that differed considerably from the radio news audience of the 1950s. For instance, the talk radio audience tended to be more politically conservative than the population in general (Davis and Owen 1998). The media exposure index masks such differences and also masks the differing use trends across the second half of the twentieth century.

Figure 7.3 plots separately the percentage of people who claim to use each news source. The four news sources display somewhat different use patterns

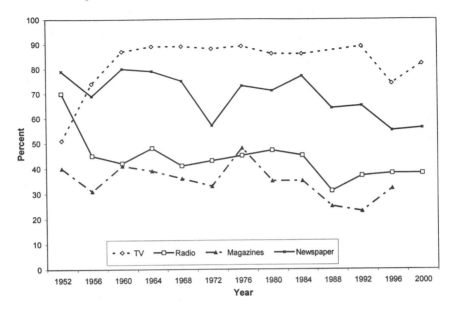

Figure 7.3 Percentage of respondents using each medium for presidential campaign news, 1952–2000. Source: ANES, 1952–2000.

over time. For instance, radio use plummets from nearly 70 percent in 1952 to 45 percent in 1956, remaining at that level until 1988, when it sharply drops to 31 percent. But in 1996 and 2000, it rises to nearly 40 percent.

Newsmagazines also display a unique time trajectory. About one-third to two-fifths of respondents report reading a newsmagazine article about the campaign from the early 1950s through 1984, although there is considerable variability from campaign to campaign. Television's appearance in the 1950s, from these data, did not seem to affect newsmagazine reading habits. But in the late 1980s, magazine readership fell to one-quarter, although it did return to the one-third level in 1996, the last year for which we have data.

Newspapers, the dominant news source for such a long time, show slow erosion in use across the 1950s and 1960s. By 1972, newspaper readership had plummeted to 57 percent from the nearly 80 percent in 1952. A large drop in newspaper use occurred between 1952 and 1956, a time of massive television diffusion. During that time period, the number of households with television doubled from about one-third to two-thirds.[15] Newspaper readership seemed to rebound from the mid 1970s to 1984, when it reached 77 percent, but from the late 1980s to 2000, readership again eroded, settling at 59 percent in 2000, nearly the lowest figure in these data.

Television also shows a time path that differs from the other media. As a new medium in the 1950s, television diffused quickly into nearly every household by the early 1970s. With televisions so ubiquitous in American households, it not only became the primary entertainment medium, but a major news source. In 1952, barely half of respondents reported watching a campaign story on television; more people used radio or newspapers for campaign news than television in 1952. This changed in 1956, when nearly three-fourths of respondents reported seeing a campaign story on television, a 50 percent increase from 1952. Television had outpaced all other news sources in popularity, a position that it has held thereafter.

Television popularity as a news source continued to grow, topping 80 percent by 1960, where it stayed until 1992. Then in 1996 we see a dip in television use to 75 percent, its 1960 level. While this might have been a function of the lack of drama of the 1996 election, with Bill Clinton assured of an easy reelection, in 2000, a very close election year, there was only a small rebound in television use, to 83 percent.

That television use for news about the presidential campaign should decline in the 1990s is somewhat odd, given the greater availability of news through cable and the increasing amount of time that Americans seem to be spending watching television. For instance, one time use study found that Americans aged eighteen to sixty-four increased their television watching from 10.5 hours per week in 1965 to 15.1 in 1985 (Mayer 1993, 606). General Social Survey (GSS) data spanning from 1975 to 2000 find virtually no change in the number of hours spent watching television daily, with Americans on average watching television about three hours daily.[16] The arrival of the internet in the mid 1990s might account for the decline of television viewing in the mid 1990s.

Although each of the four major news media sources displays a different time path, all show declines in use in the late 1980s and 1990s, except for radio, which rebounded in use during the 1990s. This radio rebound is probably a function of talk radio and its mobilization of conservative, alienated, and antiestablishment listeners.[17]

## Frequency of Media Use: ANES and GSS

The ANES questions fail to distinguish between heavy and light users of the different media. Beginning in 1972, the GSS began asking respondents about the frequency of their use of newspapers with the question: "How often do you read the newspaper—every day, a few times a week, once a week, less than once a week, or never?" The major limitation of this question for our purposes is that it does not ask about news. People may turn to the sports pages, comics, and other features, and ignore the news sections. In 1984, ANES began asking people political news use questions modeled on the GSS frequency question: (1) "How many days in the past week did you watch national news on TV?" and (2) "How many days in the past week did you read a daily newspaper?" Notably, neither question refers to the election campaign and the television

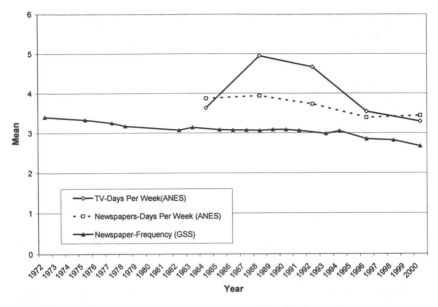

Figure 7.4 Mean number of days per week that respondents watch television news or read a newspaper. Source: GSS, 1972–2000, ANES, 1984–2000. *GSS Question*: "How often do you read the newspaper—every day, a few times a week, once a week, less than once a week, or never?" where every day = 4, a few times a week = 3, once a week = 2, less than once a week = 1, or never = 0." *ANES questions*: "How many days in the past week did you read a daily newspaper (watch national news on TV)?" The ANES values range from 0 to 7.

question points to national news. Figure 7.4 presents plots of the ANES and GSS series.

The GSS series indicates a slow decline in the frequency of newspaper use. To plot the GSS values, I scored "every day" readers a "4," "few times a week" readers a "3," "once a week" readers a "2," "less than once a week" readers a "1," and nonreaders a "0." In 1972, the first year of this series, the 3.4 value suggests that on average people read a newspaper from a few times a week to everyday. By 2000 that value had dropped to 2.7, suggesting that on average people were reading a newspaper once or twice a week. The ANES data, which begins much later, in 1984, shows a gentler decline. Newspaper reading fell from 3.9 days per week in 1984 to 3.4 in 2000, a loss of a half day per week. The frequency of watching national television news also declined in the 1990s. In 1984, people claimed to watch television news 3.6 days per week, which rises strongly to nearly five days per week in 1988. The figure slides to 3.3 days per week in 2000.

No matter which series we look at, with the possible exception of radio, we see erosion in the frequency of news attention.[18] Our primary question, however, is whether the rise of the new media had anything to do with these trends in news attention. The next section turns to an analysis of the ANES questions at the individual level to address this question.

## The Decline in News Consumption: A Pooled Survey Analysis

This section uses the 1952–2000 ANES pooled data at the individual level to address whether the rise of the new media affect the public's attention to news. Before turning to the analysis, some analytic issues need to be addressed. As done in previous chapters, access to cable television will be the primary indicator of the sweep of the new media.[19] Obviously factors besides access to cable television will affect news consumption. Demographics, attitudes, and participation affect news consumption, and many of these attributes that affect news consumption have also changed over the past several decades. Plus, levels of political interest, strength of party identification, political efficacy, and political participation, all of which may affect news consumption, have declined in recent decades.[20] Fortunately, we can control for the effects of these types of factors on news consumption because the ANES studies include such items.[21] Furthermore, we can control for other contextual factors that might affect news consumption, such as whether there was a presidential election. The analytic strategy here asks: Does the spread of cable television, a sign of the new media age, affect individual-level news consumption above and beyond a baseline model composed of individual attributes and contextual factors?

Each of the four news media sources (newspapers, radio, television, newsmagazines) is analyzed separately. As above, the primary independent variable of interest will be the percentage of households that have access to cable television. This variable is less than ideal for present purposes. This variable will only tell us if people use different news media more or less as cable availability increased over time, not whether those with cable television watch less news, as the viewing opportunity model suggests. Later in this chapter I turn to an analysis of the 2000 ANES survey, which includes a cable access item for each respondent. That analysis, however, loses the dynamic component of this pooled analysis.

### Building a Baseline Model of News Media Use

The appendix to this chapter presents the complete list of variables and their question wordings from the 1952–2000 pooled ANES surveys that are used as controls. Demographic controls include age, gender, black, Hispanic, education, income, South, union member, Protestant, Catholic, Jew, urban resident, and suburban resident. In general, we expect women, blacks, and Hispanics to be negatively associated with all news media save television, where we do not expect any effect of these demographics. A positive association between media use and both income and education is hypothesized, except that education should be negatively associated with television use (Patterson 2000, Putnam 2000). The three religious categories, Protestant, Catholic, and Jewish, are hypothesized to be positively associated with all types of news media use. Research has found a positive association between religiosity and some forms of political and social activity (Putnam 2000) and with watching presidential debates (Baum and Kernell 1999). Lacking a religiosity measure, religion is used as a substitute, even though as researchers we are aware that many who claim a religious affiliation are not necessarily active in religious organizations. Union membership is also hypothesized to be positively associated with news use. Union members tend to be higher in most forms of political and social participation than nonunion workers. No hypothesis exists for the other demographics (e.g., urban, suburban, and southern residence), which are included in order to build as fully specified of a baseline model as possible.[22]

The analysis also controls for political attitudes often found to be strongly related to political engagement: political interest, strength of party identification, political efficacy, and an index of political participation. Conceptualizing news consumption as a form of social and political participation makes it reasonable to expect these attitudes about the political world to affect news attention. However, as these attitudes are often highly correlated, we find that not all are related to news media use.

Last, the baseline model includes variables for whether the survey was conducted during a presidential or midterm election and the percentage of households with television. The expectation here is that there will be greater news attention in presidential than midterm election seasons. The drama of the presidential race, covered copiously in the news media, may lead people to watch more news than they otherwise would. Second, the importance of the presidency may motivate some people to watch more news than they traditionally do. Finally, an aggregate television household variable parallels the cable television indicator and is used to capture the effects of broadcast television diffusion on news consumption. We expect television diffusion to be positively associated with watching television news, but negatively associated with the other news media, although if different news forms are not substitutable, then we would expect no television impact on them.

*Results of the Analysis*

Results of the analysis are presented on table 7.1. Probit is used because the dependent variables are dichotomous. Many of the control variables affect use of the four news media. Those that are significantly related to news use at the 0.05 level are high-lighted in bold. Notably, while the set of variables that is associated with news media use varies somewhat from one medium to the next, as we would expect if the news sources are not fully substitutable, some factors are consistently associated with news media use irrespective of medium. For instance, age, political interest, political efficacy, and political participation are always positively associated with using each news medium. Being female, black, and a southerner, is generally negatively associated with news use. Education and income are usually positively associated with news use too. The other factors are occasionally associated with use of one or two news media, and no factor fails to be associated with at least one of the four news media. Numbers in bold in table 7.1 indicate statistically significant results.

On the table, associations that run counter to expectations are underlined. Multicollinearity with other variables is the source of the incorrect sign for strength of partisanship and newsmagazines, income and radio use, and union membership and newsmagazine use. The midterm variable is properly signed for television and newsmagazines, but for radio and newspapers it is unexpectedly positively signed and statistically significant. It is unclear what is driving these incorrect signs. Last, as expected, as the percentage of households with television grew, so did use of television. At the same time, growth in television undercut use of radio and newspapers, while having no apparent effects on newsmagazine use.

## The Impact of Cable Diffusion on News Media Use

Our major question asks whether cable television diffusion affects use of the four news media. Results on table 7.1 suggest that the aggregate spread of cable is associated with declining use of each of the four news media. Since probit coefficients are not intuitively interpretable, I convert them into probabilities setting all variables at their means.

The probabilities indicate that each 10 percent increase in cable penetration at the aggregate level is associated with a 0.03 decline in the probability of reading a newsmagazine, a 0.0027 decline in reading a newspaper, a 0.01 decline in watching television news, and a 0.001 decline in the probability of listening to campaign news on the radio. Considering that cable penetration moved from "0" in the 1950s and 1960s to about 70 percent by 2000, this means that the probability of reading a newsmagazine declined by 0.21 from before cable's onset to the end of the series. The comparable probability declines for the other three media are 0.19 for newspapers, 0.70 for television, and 0.07 for radio. These are all substantial effects, although the effect on television seems especially large and likely overstated. Still, the Baum-Kernell viewing hypothesis implies that we might find that cable television has larger effects on television news viewing than for the other three media. In part this derives from the large number of television watchers who prefer entertainment programming to news. At the same time, that the effects of cable appear general across the four media lends support to Patterson's news reporting hypothe-

Table 7.1
Impact of cable television on use of four news media, 1952–2000

| | TV Model 1 | | | Radio Model 2 | | | Newsmagazines Model 3 | | | Newspapers Model 4 | | |
|---|---|---|---|---|---|---|---|---|---|---|---|---|
| | b | SE | p | b | SE | p | b | SE | p | b | SE | p |
| Age | .005 | .0007 | .000 | .005 | .0006 | .000 | .003 | .0007 | .000 | .012 | .0006 | .000 |
| Female | .018 | .022 | .397 | −.190 | .018 | .000 | −.043 | .021 | .036 | −.159 | .020 | .000 |
| Income | .103 | .011 | .000 | −.021 | .009 | .023 | .114 | .010 | .000 | .127 | .010 | .000 |
| Education | −.015 | .014 | .289 | .083 | .012 | .000 | .368 | .013 | .000 | .288 | .014 | .000 |
| Black | −.082 | .038 | .032 | .178 | .033 | .000 | −.126 | .039 | .001 | −.160 | .034 | .000 |
| Hispanic | −.169 | .060 | .005 | .061 | .055 | .270 | .091 | .067 | .173 | −.125 | .057 | .027 |
| Urban | .064 | .030 | .030 | −.036 | .025 | .149 | −.027 | .027 | .321 | .157 | .027 | .000 |
| Suburban | .021 | .026 | .412 | −.011 | .022 | .610 | −.0001 | .025 | .998 | .070 | .024 | .004 |
| South | .075 | .026 | .004 | −.072 | .022 | .001 | −.088 | .025 | .000 | −.097 | .024 | .000 |
| Union | .044 | .027 | .099 | −.038 | .022 | .088 | −.083 | .025 | .001 | .010 | .025 | .683 |
| Protestant | .183 | .036 | .000 | .022 | .033 | .507 | −.066 | .038 | .059 | .068 | .070 | .067 |
| Catholic | .237 | .040 | .000 | .010 | .036 | .773 | −.078 | .041 | .059 | .050 | .040 | .210 |
| Jew | .330 | .088 | .000 | .988 | .068 | .198 | −.029 | .073 | .690 | .103 | .083 | .214 |
| Polit. interest | .468 | .016 | .000 | .243 | .013 | .000 | .363 | .015 | .000 | .447 | .015 | .000 |
| Strength PID | .042 | .011 | .000 | .009 | .010 | .348 | −.035 | .011 | .001 | .018 | .011 | .095 |
| Pol. efficacy | .001 | .0003 | .000 | .0005 | .0002 | .047 | .002 | .0002 | .000 | .002 | .0003 | .000 |
| Particip. index | .169 | .021 | .000 | .175 | .015 | .000 | .230 | .016 | .000 | .221 | .019 | .000 |
| Midterm | −.509 | .024 | .000 | .201 | .023 | .000 | −.201 | .030 | .000 | .232 | .023 | .000 |
| TV pct. | .021 | .0007 | .000 | −.010 | .0006 | .000 | −.001 | .0006 | .060 | −.004 | .0007 | .000 |
| CATV pct. | −.005 | .0006 | .000 | −.002 | .0005 | .000 | −.090 | .0006 | .000 | −.090 | .0005 | .000 |
| Constant | −2.80 | .088 | .000 | −.315 | .074 | .000 | −2.37 | .085 | .000 | −1.81 | .086 | .000 |
| N | 22318 | | | 22080 | | | 20449 | | | 22585 | | |
| Pseudo-$R^2$ | .16 | | | .05 | | | .17 | | | .18 | | |
| Wald chi-sq. | 2758.55 | | | 1549.65 | | | 3457.86 | | | 3518.57 | | |
| Prob. chi-sq. | .0000 | | | .0000 | | | .0000 | | | .0000 | | |

Source: ANES cumulative file, 1948–2000.
Note: Robust standard errors, sample weighted probit estimation. Underlines indicate that sign is opposite of expectations.

sis. Since each media form will include some people who enjoy hard news, according to Patterson's thesis, each of the four media will see a decline in consumers as cable came online and affected the style of news reporting across all four news media forms.

A major limitation of the above analysis is the lack of individual-level data on cable access. These aggregate cable impacts on individual-level behavior may not be due to the diffusion of cable but from other social trends that covary with the diffusion of cable television. We can indirectly test this hypothesis by controlling for a time counter (e.g., 1952 = 1, 2000 = 48), asking whether these cable effects persist in the face of this control. Such a control, however, is

Table 7.2
Comparative impact of cable TV and a time counter
on use of four news media, 1952–2000

| Medium | Variable | b | p | Effect |
|---|---|---|---|---|
| TV | Cable TV% | .0005 | .81 | .0001 |
| | Time | −.01 | .01 | −.003 |
| Magazines | Cable TV% | −.02 | .000 | −.008 |
| | Time | .03 | .000 | .012 |
| Newspapers | Cable TV% | −.005 | .01 | −.0016 |
| | Time | −.009 | .05 | .003 |
| Radio | Cable TV% | −.02 | .000 | −.008 |
| | Time | .04 | .000 | .016 |

*Source:* ANES cumulative file, 1948–2000 and data collected by the author. See text and appendix 7 for details.

*Note:* Robust standard errors, sample weighted probit estimation. Also includes all other variables from table 7.1 as controls.

Marginal effects calculated with all variables at their mean values.

limited in that it does not directly measure other trends over time and also assumes linearity to these trends. But since cable diffusion at the aggregate level correlates highly with time, such a control is useful. Our confidence in the effects of cable diffusion on individual-level behavior will be strengthened if those effects persist in the face of a control for time.

Table 7.2 reports the effects of cable and the time counter, controlling for the other variables used in table 7.1 (The results of those variables are not reported. They are nearly identical to the results in table 7.1.) These results indicate that the effects of cable television remain with controls for time in three of four cases. Only for television do we now find insignificant cable effects. In two cases, newsmagazines and radio, the effects of cable actually seem to grow. The probabilities, also reported on table 7.2, indicate that for each 10 percent increase in cable television penetration the probability of reading a newsmagazine drops by 0.08. The comparable declines for newspaper reading and radio listening are 0.016 and 0.08, respectively, while we observe essentially no effect on television.

Figure 7.5 graphically presents the impact of cable television on the probability of using each of the four news media at different levels of cable penetration with all other variables set at their means. Here we clearly see the strong effects of cable penetration on newsmagazine reading and radio listening; each has a strong downward slope. At high levels of cable penetration, the average person essentially will not read a newsmagazine or listen to news on the radio. The effects on newspaper reading are less severe, but still noticeable. Presumably the weaker effects of cable on newspaper reading might have much to do with the habit that people developed in reading newspapers. Moreover,

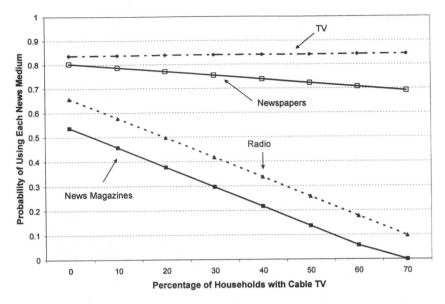

Figure 7.5 Probability of using each of four news media at different levels of cable television diffusion.

newspaper readers might not as readily substitute cable television for reading the newspaper. Even with the advent of 24/7 cable news networks, newspapers still provide deeper coverage of some news stories than cable news networks are able to provide. Such depth may be attractive to newspaper readers and may be one reason that newspaper reading does not suffer as much from the diffusion of cable as newsmagazine reading and radio listening.

Finally, it is not entirely clear why cable does not seem to affect television news viewing when controlling for time. First, the ANES question does not differentiate between broadcast and cable television. Perhaps some television news viewers switched from broadcast to cable network news. In answering the ANES question, they might still say that they watched television news. Moreover, the linear time counter might have picked up the effects of other trends that also affect television viewing, such as the advent of the remote control, the VCR, and the internet. In combination, these other changes may have been more consequential for television news viewing than cable television, although it is more likely that these several tends, including the diffusion of cable television, interact to divert audiences away from television news. Without better data, we will not be able to sort through these issues. Still it is notable that the effects of cable television persist in the face of the time control for three of the four news media.[23] And recall that from the vantage point of the larger argument being made here, which concerns the effects of the new media age, we need not distinguish among these different aspects of the new media. The cable diffusion variable is but one indicator of the advancement of the new media age.

## The Effects of Media Trust and Cable Access on News Media Use: A Cross Sectional Analysis, 2000

The above analysis is limited in several regards. First, the aggregate measure of cable television cannot tell us which individuals have been affected by the growth of cable television, only that as cable grew, people's news consumption for most types of news media declined. Both the viewing opportunity and new reporting style hypotheses, however, are individual-level hypotheses and the aggregate measure of cable television does little to tell us whether each of these two mechanisms affect the trend of declining news use.

This section turns to the 2000 ANES study, which asks respondents about both their level of media trust as well as whether they subscribe to cable television. Thus we can assess the relative effect of these two mechanisms on news attention. However, as the analysis relies on cross-sectional data, we cannot estimate the impact of these two mechanisms on the trends discussed throughout this chapter. Still, we are able to test the implications of the viewing opportunity and reporting style hypotheses, that is, that access to cable for some voters and distrust in the media will be associated with lower media consumption levels.

The dependent variables here are two items that ask respondents how many days in the previous week they watch television news or read the newspaper. The two independent variables of interest ask whether or not the respondent has access to cable television and the respondent's attitudes toward the news media. The cable question is worded: "Do you have either cable or satellite television?" coded "1" if the respondent has cable or satellite television, "0" otherwise. The media trust item asks, "How much of the time do you think you can trust the media to report the news fairly?" (my recodes are in parentheses): Just about always (4), most of the time (3), only some of the time (2), or almost never (1).

The viewing opportunity hypothesis suggests that cable access will depress news consumption, but only for individuals less interested in and/or informed about politics (Baum and Kernell 1999). To test this conditional effects hypothesis, I created a series of interaction terms between cable access and respondent information level, following Baum and Kernell's (1999) procedure. Respondents' information level is measured with the interviewer's assessment (VAR 001033). From this variable, the "very high" and "fairly high" categories are combined, now labeled *high information*, "average" becomes *medium information*, and "fairly" and "very low" become *low information*. Then the cable subscribers and noncable respondents are classified into one of the three information categories, producing a total of six dummy variables. The viewing opportunity hypothesis suggests that there will be no association between level of information and news consumption among respondents who *do not have* access to cable. In contrast, as information levels decline for cable subscribers, so should news consumption.

The media trust variable does not measure reporting styles directly, nor does it even measure respondent's perception of reporting styles. Still, the reporting style hypothesis argues that changes in reporting style have led to greater cynicism and lower levels of regard for the news media. As attitudes to the news media turn more negative, people's news consumption levels will decline, according to this hypothesis. The media trust item allows us to test this implication of the reporting style hypothesis, that individuals with less positive assessments of the news media will consume less news than those with more positive assessments.

As more than cable access and media trust will affect news consumption habits, controls for a battery of demographic and attitudinal characteristics that past research has found to be associated with either political participation (Hansen and Rosenstone 1993, Putnam 2000) and/or debate watching (Baum and Kernell 1999) are applied. In creating variables from the 2000 ANES, I followed Baum and Kernell's procedures as closely as possible.[24] The appendix to this chapter presents details on these control variables.

Another complication is that media exposure may lead to less trusting attitudes toward the media. Patterson's reporting style hypothesis suggests just such a dynamic over time—as people watch the news and encounter more news stories presented in the new reporting style, they will reduce their news consumption. With cross-sectional data, we can only test the cumulative effects of exposure to the new reporting style, which suggests that those with more negative attitudes to the news media will consume less news.

But it is also possible for people to rationalize their lack of news consumption by saying that they distrust the news media. To guard against this possible reversed causality, I estimated a two-stage least squares equation, with Bennett et al. (1998, 1999) as a guide in building the equation used to estimate the media trust instrument. Two-stage least squares requires that at least one variable predict media trust but not be associated with television or newspaper use. Several variables used to create the media trust instrument fit this restriction, including thermometer ratings for Bill Clinton and Al Gore, traditionalism, and misanthropy. Appendix table 7.1, which is located on the webpage for this book, presents details of the first-stage estimation.

Results of the 2SLS estimations are presented on table 7.3, which indicate that media trust affects newspaper reading and television news watching.[25] The regression coefficient suggests that each category improvement in media trust will lead to an additional 0.88 days of newspaper reading per week, a massive effect given that the newspaper reading variable can only range from zero to seven. The most trusting person will read a newspaper about 3.5 more days

Table 7.3
Impact of media trust and cable access on news consumption:
second-stage 2SLS regression results

| | Newspaper | | | TV | | |
|---|---|---|---|---|---|---|
| | B | SE | p | b | SE | p |
| Age | .049 | .006 | .000 | .040 | .005 | .000 |
| Female | −.297 | .176 | .092 | .113 | .161 | .483 |
| Hispanic | −.737 | .391 | .060 | −.337 | .357 | .345 |
| Black | −.604 | .271 | .025 | .094 | .247 | .703 |
| South | .066 | .180 | .714 | .185 | .165 | .260 |
| Education | .100 | .064 | .118 | −.087 | .058 | .138 |
| Income | .060 | .031 | .057 | .010 | .029 | .714 |
| Strength PID | −.093 | .087 | .287 | .040 | .080 | .611 |
| Employed | .168 | .189 | .374 | −.179 | .173 | .300 |
| Pol. interest | .081 | .159 | .611 | .309 | .145 | .033 |
| Discuss politics | .530 | .235 | .024 | −.172 | .215 | .425 |
| Public affairs int. | .436 | .118 | .000 | .265 | .108 | .014 |
| Gen. camp. int. | .275 | .155 | .077 | .683 | .142 | .000 |
| Pres. camp. int. | −.146 | .119 | .221 | .278 | .109 | .011 |
| Care who wins | −.619 | .241 | .010 | −.431 | .220 | .050 |
| Close election | −.551 | .249 | .027 | −.053 | .228 | .815 |
| Expect to vote | .442 | .292 | .130 | .153 | .267 | .566 |
| Party contact | .156 | .175 | .374 | .009 | .160 | .956 |
| Org. memberships | .178 | .057 | .002 | .017 | .051 | .745 |
| Internal efficacy | .145 | .189 | .441 | .069 | .173 | .691 |
| External efficacy | −.075 | .113 | .510 | −.037 | .104 | .719 |
| CATV-lo | −.242 | .367 | .510 | .184 | .335 | .582 |
| CATV-med | .102 | .299 | .734 | .865 | .274 | .002 |
| CATV-hi | .360 | .281 | .200 | 1.109 | .257 | .000 |
| No CATV-lo | −.767 | .463 | .098 | .358 | .434 | .398 |
| No CATV-med | −.542 | .439 | .218 | −.158 | .401 | .695 |
| Govt. trust | .011 | .101 | .915 | −.227 | .093 | .015 |
| Media trust | .883 | .453 | .051 | .896 | .415 | .031 |
| Constant | −2.67 | 1.11 | .016 | −4.45 | 1.02 | .000 |
| RMSE | 2.63 | | | 2.41 | | |
| $R^2$ | .20 | | | .25 | | |
| F | 12.02 | | | 15.21 | | |
| P of F | .0000 | | | .0000 | | |
| N | 1132 | | | 1130 | | |

*Source:* 2000 ANES. First stage results to create the Media Trust instrument is on appendix table
7.1

per week than the least media trusting person (4 * 0.88 = 3.52). The effect of media trust on television news watching is of similar magnitude, with a regression coefficient of 0.9. As with newspaper reading, the most media-trusting individual will watch on average 3.6 more days of news than the least media-trusting person (4 * 0.9 = 3.6). That media trust affects both forms of news consumption is consistent with Patterson's argument that the new style of reporting is a general property of news and not specific to any news format.

The results also indicate that cable access affects television news consumption, but not newspaper reading. Figure 7.6 graphically illustrates the impact of cable access on news consumption. The figure is based on regressions with five dummies for various combinations of cable access and information levels and a constant on television news watching and newspaper reading. These six variables combined account for all combinations of cable access and information levels. I use these results merely for illustrative purposes and because it is so difficult to produce estimates based on the multivariate results from table 7.3. The major difficulty arises because there are other dummy variables in the equation. This means that the constant represents not merely the omitted category from the six cable-information variables but also from each of the other dummies.

Still, the estimates from figure 7.6 present the theoretical relationships faithfully, even if we cannot take the numerical impacts literally. The results show that as information level increases, so does newspaper reading for cable subscribers and noncable respondents alike. The only difference between cable subscribers and noncable respondents in newspaper reading levels is that cable subscribers have a higher level of newspaper reading at all levels of information, because cable subscribers are more affluent and better educated than noncable respondents (recall that the estimates on figure 7.6 do not control for these demographics or other factors than distinguish cable and noncable respondents).

However, cable access affects television news watching. We see no difference in television news watching for noncable respondents, but television news watching increases as information levels rise. This repeats Baum and Kernell's finding with regard to debate watching. Also, poorly informed cable subscribers (shown as "low" on figure 7.6) watch much less television news than poorly informed noncable respondents, an effect that Baum and Kernell's viewing opportunity hypothesis also suggests. Medium and highly informed cable subscribers, in contrast, display higher television news watching levels than noncable respondents. Cable access affects television watching but not newspaper reading, which is consistent with the viewing opportunity perspective.

## Conclusion: The New Media Age and Attention to the News

Public consumption of news from traditional news sources has declined relative to the golden age of broadcasting, and there is little indication that people have

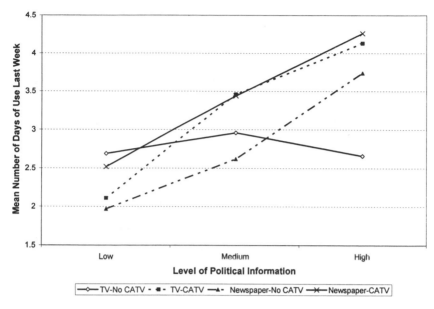

Figure 7.6 Impact of cable television access on television and newspaper use by information level. 2000 ANES.

been substituting new media age news sources, such as the 24/7 cable news networks and internet news sites for traditional media such as newspapers and broadcast television. Ironically, attributes of the new media age may have played a part in the public's declining attention to news.

This chapter has surveyed considerable evidence on the role of the new media age in the public's decreasing attention to news. Results of analyses using the pooled 1952–2000 ANES study suggest that the aggregate spread of cable television, a key technology of the new media age, is strongly associated with declines in public use of newsmagazines and radio for news. The aggregate spread of cable also, albeit somewhat less strongly, has depressed newspaper reading, although it is unclear from these data whether cable affects the viewing of broadcast television news.

Analyses that used the 2000 election study allowed us to investigate two mechanisms through which the new media age might affect news attention: the cable viewing opportunity model (Baum and Kernell 1999, Prior 2005) and the reporting style model (Patterson 2000). Support for both mechanisms was found. These results confirm the idea that we should conceptually distinguish the different forms of news attention and that in at least one important respect newspaper reading differs from other forms of news attention—the arrival of cable television seems to have modest impacts on newspaper reading compared to the other media (although one must keep in mind the ambiguous effects of cable television on the trend in television watching).

One implication of Patterson's reporting style theory is that the reporting style of the new media age should lower regard for the news media, which in turn will lower news attention levels. This new reporting style is characterized, among other attributes, as presenting increasing amounts of soft, cynical, and scandal news. Analysis of the 2000 ANES provided indirect support for the second leg of the casual chain, that as trust in the media falls, so does news attention for both newspapers and television. That distrust of the media reduces use of both newspapers and television supports another implied aspect of Patterson's theory, that the new reporting style can be found across all types of news media and that the effect of this new reporting style on news use is general across types of news media (also see Cappella and Jamieson 1997).

## Appendix 7: Variables from the 1948–2000 ANES Cumulative File for Tables 7.1 and 7.2

Note that further information about statistical methods employed in this book can be found online at http://press.princeton.edu/title/8592.html.

*Age*: VARCF0101
*Female*: VARCF0104
*Income*: VARCF0114
*Education*: VARCF0110
*Black*: VARCF0106a
*Hispanic*: VARCF0106a
*Urban*: VARCF0111
*Suburban*: VARCF0111
*South*: VARCF0112
*Union*: VARCF0127
*Protestant*: VARCF0128
*Catholic*: VARCF0128
*Jew*: VARCF0128
*Political Interest*: VARCF0310
*Strength PID*: VARCF0301
*Political Efficacy*: VARCF0648
*Participation Index*: VARCF0723a
*Public Affairs*: VARCF0313
*TV*: VARCF0724
*Radio*: VARCF072
*Magazines*: VARCF0726
*Newspapers*: VARCF0727
*Newspaper Days*: VARCF9033
*TV Days*: VARCF9035
*Midterm*: 1 = Midterm Election Year, 0 = Not a Midterm Election Year.

*TV pct.*: Percent of households with Television, *Statistical Abstract of the United States*.

*CATV pct.*: Percent of households with Cable Television, *Statistical Abstract of the United States*.

## Variables from the 2000 ANES Survey for Tables 7.3 and Appendix Table 7.1

*Age*: VAR000908
*Female*: VAR001029
*Hispanic*: VAR001006a
*Black*: VAR001006a
*South*: VAR000092
*Education*: VAR000913
*Income*: VAR000995
*Strength of PID*: VAR000523 folded
*Employed*: VAR000918
*Political Interest*: VAR001201
*Discuss Politics*: VAR001204
*Public Affairs Interest*: VAR00136
*General Campaign Interest*: VAR000301
*Presidential Campaign Interest*: VAR001648
*Care Who Wins*: VAR000302
*Close Election*: VAR000486
*Expect to Vote*: VAR000792
*Party Contact*: VAR001219
*Organization Memberships*: VAR001495
*Internal Efficacy (politics is too complicated)*: VAR001529
*External Efficacy*: additive index of VAR001528 + VAR001527
*Government Trust Index*: additive index of VAR001534 + VAR001535 + VAR001536 + VAR001537
*Media Trust*: VAR001429
*Cable TV*: VAR000334
*Party ID*: VAR000523
*Presidential Thermometer*: VAR000359
*Information*: VAR001033
*Gore Thermometer*: VAR000360
*TV Days*: VAR000329
*Newspaper Days*: VAR000335
*Traditionalism*: additive index of VAR001530 +VAR001531 + VAR001532 + VAR001533
*Misanthropy*: additive index of VAR001475 + Var001477

# CHAPTER 8

# Declining Trust in the News Media
# and the New Media Age

Paralleling the decline in news consumption is the decline in trust and confidence in the media. As observed in the last chapter, the decline in news consumption in part reflects a secular decline across many forms of social and political activity. Similarly, there has been a secular decline in confidence and trust toward many major social and political institutions besides the news media (Cook and Gronke 2001, 2002; Cook, Gronke, and Rattliff 2000; Dautrich and Hartley 1999; Gillespie 2004).[1] The erosion in public confidence in the news media, however, appears steeper than for most other major institutions.

For instance, using General Social Survey (GSS) data, which has tracked confidence in institutions since the early 1970s, the average level of confidence for eleven institutions other than the press and television stood at 2.17 on a three-point scale in 1976.[2] Mean confidence in the press and television stood at 2.11 and 1.91 that year, somewhat below the average for all major institutions. By 2000, the average for the eleven institutions other than the press and television dropped slightly, 0.04, to 2.14.[3] Confidence in the press and television fell more sharply by 2000, 0.24 for television (to 1.67) and a whopping 0.42 for the press (to 1.69).

The fact that confidence has fallen for most institutions, but has fallen more sharply for the press and television, suggests two components to the slide in confidence toward the media. First, the secular forces pushing confidence down across all institutions had some effect on the slide in confidence toward the media. Second, factors intrinsic to the media also seem to be depressing public confidence in the media. This chapter asks whether the rise of the new media is one of those media-specific forces that has been deflating public trust and confidence in the news media.

Patterson's (2000) news reporting style thesis suggests a linkage between the style of reporting during the new media era and lower levels of public confidence. For instance, his October 2000 survey found that a majority of respondents think that the quality of the news has deteriorated. Moreover those who follow the news closely and those who think that the news has softened are even more likely to say that news quality has deteriorated (Patterson 2000, 6; also see Bennett et al. 1998, 1999).[4] David Jones (2004) finds that media exposure affects media trust, but the effect is only significant for those who listen to talk radio. Both Patterson and Jones suggest that exposure to the news lowers media trust.

In this chapter, rather than look at the individual and cross-sectional correlates of media trust, as Patterson and Jones do, I follow the tack of the previous chapter and look at the association between the spread of cable television, an indicator of the new media age, and change in public confidence toward the news media.

## Trends in Public Confidence and Trust toward the News Media

Since the early 1970s, the GSS and Harris poll have asked people about their confidence in major institutions, including the press and television news. The length of these series is especially important for present purposes, which is to track the decline in public regard for the news media. The GSS and Harris question reads: "I am going to name some institutions in this country. As far as the people running these institutions are concerned, would you say you have a great deal confidence, only some confidence, or hardly any confidence at all in them?"

These confidence questions have their limitations. They are vague in identifying the institution that people are asked to assess. The television confidence question does not point to television news in particular but television in general. When responding to this question, people may be thinking of television entertainment as well as or instead of television news. Plus, the television question does not distinguish between broadcast and cable television. Like the television question, the press question does not discriminate among the various forms of the press (e.g., print, television, radio, and other forms). Again, different people may imagine different types of the press in answering this survey question. Finally, respondents are asked about the leaders of these institutions, not the performance of these institutions. Although respondents may equate performance with leadership, they may still distinguish between institutional leadership and institutional performance (Cook and Gronke 2001, 2002; Cook, Gronke, and Rattliff 2000; Hibbing and Theiss-Morse 1995).

Figures 8.1 and 8.2 present the series from these two survey organizations. Following Cook, Gronke, and Rattliff (2000), I create a mean value for the GSS series by scoring "a great deal confidence" a "3," "only some confidence" a "2," and "hardly any confidence at all" a "1." The Harris data come from the Roper online poll archive. The Roper archive generally only reported the percent responding that they had a great deal of confidence; thus figure 8.2 plots this percentage instead of the mean score.[5]

Taking into account the limitations noted above, both series display a remarkable drop in public confidence toward these media. The GSS series shows the press sliding at a somewhat steeper rate than television. The Harris data

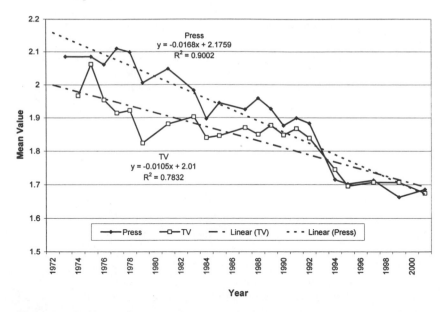

Figure 8.1 Public confidence in the press and television, 1973–2000. Source: General Social Survey. *Question Wording*: "I am going to name some institutions in this country. As far as the people running these institutions are concerned, would you say you have a great deal of confidence, only some confidence, or hardly any confidence at all in them? TV, Press."

also show decreases in public confidence. The Harris data, shown in figure 8.2, indicates that confidence in television peaked in 1979, with 37 percent expressing a great deal of confidence in the medium. At the end of 2002, only 21 percent of respondents felt that way. Press confidence, which also peaked in 1979 at 28 percent, plummeted to 15 percent in 2002.

Other, more specific, poll questions also detect a decline in public regard for the media. For instance, in 1985 the Times Mirror poll queried respondents about whether they could believe what they read or heard in the news from particular news organizations, not merely the media in general. In the late 1990s and 2000, the Pew Center for People and the Press asked these same questions in several of its surveys. Believability in news is critical if the news media are to help the public hold political leaders accountable. The specific question posed to respondents reads: "Now, I'm going to read a list. Please rate how much you think you can believe each organization I name on a scale of 4 to 1. On this four scale, '4' means you can believe all or most of what the organization says. '1' means you believe almost nothing of what they say. How would you rate the believability of (Name of organization) on this scale of 4 to 1?"

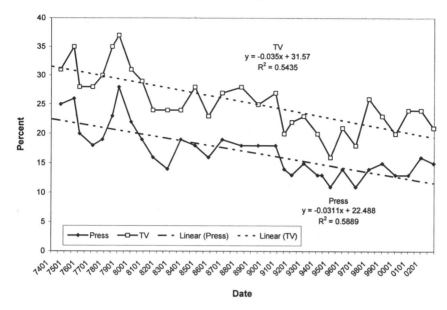

Figure 8.2 Public confidence in the press and television, Harris polls, 1974–2002. Source: Harris surveys, 1972–2002. The figure plots the percentage with a great deal of confidence. *Question Wording:* "I am going to name some institutions in this country. As far as the people running these institutions are concerned, would you say you have a great deal of confidence, only some confidence, or hardly any confidence at all in them? TV, Press."

Robinson and Kohut (1988), in analyzing the 1985 data, created a "believability index" by subtracting the percentage of respondents who give scores of 1 and 2 (those who lean toward "believing almost nothing") from the percentage giving scores of 3 and 4 (those who lean toward "believe all or most"). By wide margins in 1985, the public seemed to believe almost all types of news organizations. Results are displayed on table 8.1. The networks scores range from 66 to 72, making them the most believed news organizations at that time. Daily newspapers and the newsmagazines follow closely behind with net scores of 65 and 50+, respectively. Only the tabloids, *People* magazine and the *National Enquirer*, and the youth-oriented magazine, *Rolling Stone*, had net negative index scores. The public found the traditional, mainstream press highly believable and credible in the mid 1980s.

By the late 1990s, public willingness to believe in the mainstream press had declined substantially, although on average more people still believed than disbelieved these news organizations. Network believability declined by 25 to 33 percent, depending on the network. Local television news displayed comparable declines, while the weekly newsmagazines exhibited losses of more than

Table 8.1
Believability of the press, 1985–2002

|  | Net believability | | | | Trend |
|  | 2002 | 2000 | 1998 | 1985 | 2002–1985 |
|---|---|---|---|---|---|
| Network TV |  |  |  |  |  |
| ABC News | 40 | 36 | 49 | 71 | −31 |
| NBC News | 41 | 35 | 46 | 66 | −25 |
| CBS News | 39 | 36 | 44 | 72 | −33 |
| Cable TV |  |  |  |  |  |
| CNN | 45 | 46 | 57 | 36 | 9 |
| MSNBC | 33 | 27 |  |  |  |
| Fox News cable | 27 | 19 |  |  |  |
| TV magazines |  |  |  |  |  |
| *Dateline NBC* | 33 | 32 | 38 |  |  |
| *60 Minutes* | 49 | 44 | 45 |  |  |
| *20/20* | 37 |  |  |  |  |
| Other TV |  |  |  |  |  |
| C-SPAN | 27 | 28 | 30 |  |  |
| *NewsHour* | 15 | 10 | 19 | 27 | −12 |
| Local TV news | 36 | 44 | 45 | 67 | −31 |
| *Inside Edition* |  |  | −30 |  |  |
| Newsmagazines |  |  |  |  |  |
| *Time* | 30 | 30 | 38 | 53 | −23 |
| *Newsweek* | 30 | 25 | 38 | 52 | −22 |
| *US News* | 32 |  |  |  |  |
| Newspapers |  |  |  |  |  |
| *USA Today* | 26 | 21 | 27 | 24 | 2 |
| *Wall Street Journal* | 36 | 36 | 47 | 40 | −4 |
| Daily newspaper | 25 | 29 | 32 | 65 | −40 |
| Influential paper |  |  |  | 36 |  |
| Radio |  |  |  |  |  |
| NPR | 17 | 11 | 23 |  |  |
| *All Things Considered* | 10 |  | 17 | 21 | −11 |
| Radio news |  |  |  | 61 |  |
| Print tabloids |  |  |  |  |  |
| *People* | −19 | −24 | −21 | −10 | −9 |
| *National Enquirer* | −63 | −70 | −73 | −54 | −9 |

Table 8.1 (*cont.*)
Believability of the press, 1985–2002

|  | Net believability | | | | Trend |
| --- | --- | --- | --- | --- | --- |
|  | 2002 | 2000 | 1998 | 1985 | 2002–1985 |
| Miscellaneous |  |  |  |  |  |
| AP | 20 | 19 | 21 | 47 | −27 |
| *Parade* |  |  |  | 4 |  |
| *Reader's Digest* |  |  |  | 51 |  |
| *Rolling Stone* |  |  |  | −19 |  |

*Question*: "Now, I'm going to read a list. Please rate how much you think you can believe each organization I name on a scale of 4 to 1. On this four scale, '4' means you can believe all or most of what the organization says. '1' means you believe almost nothing of what they say. How would you rate the believability (name of organization) . . . on this scale of 4 to 1?"

*Source:* 1998–2002, Princeton Survey Research Associates, 1985: Times Mirror poll.

*Note:* Net believability is calculated by subtracting the percentage answering 1 and 2 from those answering 3 or 4.

20 percent. Daily newspapers show the most severe losses here, at 40 percent. The tabloids, *People* magazine and the *National Enquirer*, also show declines in believability, which is remarkable in the latter case given the already low score in 1985. Only two news organizations bucked these trends. *USA Today* shows almost no change in believability (24 in 1985, 26 in 2002). CNN truly counters the trend with its believability score rising by nine points, from 36 in 1985 to 45 in 2002, although CNN's believability score peaked in 1998 at 57.

One limitation of the believability question is that it does not ask people why they might not believe the news. People may, for instance, believe that the facts are accurately reported but disagree with the interpretation of the facts. Or people may disbelieve the press because they feel that the important facts are left out of news reports. People may also disbelieve the press because they think that factual inaccuracies exist and/or that the news media may at times make up or manufacture the news, perhaps for political, partisan, ideological, or some other reason. Several recent incidents, such as those involving Jayson Blair at the *New York Times* and Dan Rather at CBS News, may provide disbelievers with examples that buttress their disbelief.

From the early 1990s, the Pew Center for People and the Press has been asking people whether they think news reports are accurate or not. Results are presented in table 8.2. Somewhat disheartening, people often perceive inaccuracy in news reports. Of the eight administrations of the question since 1992, only twice did more people think that the press got the facts straight than possessed inaccuracies (January 1992 and November 2001), although only by very shallow margins.

More commonly, people tend to think that inaccuracies better typify press reports, sometimes by wide margins. In February 1998, the margin shifted to

Table 8.2
Trends in press accuracy

| Date | Get facts straight | Often inaccuracies | Don't know |
|---|---|---|---|
| January 1992 | 47 | 44 | 7 |
| February 1997 | 37 | 56 | 7 |
| February 1998 | 34 | 63 | 3 |
| August 1998 | 33 | 58 | 9 |
| February 1999 | 37 | 58 | 5 |
| September 2001 | 35 | 57 | 8 |
| November 2001 | 46 | 45 | 9 |
| July 2002 | 35 | 56 | 9 |

*Question:* "In general, do you think news organizations get the facts straight or do you think that their stories and reports are often inaccurate?"

*Source:* Pew Center for People and the Press.

its widest mark when 29 percent more people felt that news reports were inaccurate than accurate (63 to 34). The high percentage of people who view press reports as inaccurate, from nearly half to almost two-thirds of the public in the 1990s and early 2000s, is indeed sobering and has major implications for democratic accountability. Based on this question, at a most basic level, the public appears suspicious of what it reads or hears from the news. This question, however, does not tell us whether people think that the news is systematically inaccurate or only occasionally so, or whether they think that inaccuracy is purposeful or accidental.

Media bias questions may indirectly address the notion of whether people think that press inaccuracy is systematic and/or purposeful. Since 1987, the Pew Research Center has been asking people whether they notice partisan bias in news reporting of the presidential campaigns with this question: "In the way they have been covering the Presidential race in (year) so far, do you think that news organizations are biased in favor of the Democrats, biased in favor of the Republicans, or don't you think news organizations have shown any bias one way or the other?" Results of the five administrations of this question from 1987 to 2000 are presented in table 8.3.

These data indicate a slight increase in the percentage of people noticing some type of partisan bias since 1987. In 1987, 27 percent of respondents said that they detected a partisan bias. That figure rose to 32 percent in 2000, a modest gain of about five points. Moreover, respondents also saw slightly more favoritism toward Democrats than Republicans, although the Democratic edge is usually marginal at 5–6 percent. But the percentage seeing no bias fell from 62 percent in 1987 to 48 percent in 2000, a 14-percentage-point drop. A sizable and increasing proportion of the electorate sees partisan bias in news re-

Table 8.3
Perceptions of bias in coverage of the presidential campaigns, 1987–2000

|  | Year | | | | |
| --- | --- | --- | --- | --- | --- |
|  | 2000 | 1999 | 1996 | 1988 | 1987 |
| Democratic bias | 19 | 19 | 20 | 22 | 16 |
| Republican bias | 13 | 14 | 14 | 7 | 11 |
| No bias | 48 | 52 | 53 | 58 | 62 |
| DK | 20 | 15 | 13 | 13 | 11 |
| Total bias | 32 | 33 | 34 | 29 | 27 |
| Bias/opinions | 40 | 39 | 39 | 33 | 30 |

*Question:* "In the way they have been covering the Presidential race (year) so far, do you think that news organizations are biased in favor of the Democrats, biased in favor of the Republicans, or don't you think news organizations have shown any bias one way or the other?"

*Source:* Pew Research Center.

*Note:* Cells are calculated as the percent seeing a bias divided by the total percent with an opinion.

porting about presidential election campaigns. Consistent with the trend of declining confidence, the public has increasingly come to see the press as not believable, inaccurate, and biased.

Finally, a set of questions ask respondents about the social benefit of the news media, another type of summary orientation toward the news media. A growing body of research now views the news media as a governing institution, and not merely a watchdog over government, public officials, and other power centers (Cook 1998; Sparrow 1999). As a governing institution, the news media do not make authoritative decisions about policies. But in this role the news media may steer the agenda in certain directions, create hurdles and barriers to leaders bent on certain policies, while at other times facilitating policy choice.

Starting in the 1990s the Pew Center began asking people questions that tap into this governing role. One question refers to the news media's social role: "Which of the following two statements about the news media do you agree with more? The news media helps society to solve its problems. Or, the news media gets in the way of society solving its problems." A second question refers to the impact of news organizations on the actions of government leaders: "Some people think that by criticizing leaders, news organizations keep political leaders from doing their job. Others think that such criticism is worth it because it keeps political leaders from doing things that should not be done. Which position is closer to your opinion?" From these questions we can gain a sense of whether people feel that the press plays a positive or corrosive role in society and governance.

Table 8.4
Perceived impact of the news media on society and government

| | Society* | | | Government** | | |
|---|---|---|---|---|---|---|
| Date | Helps society | Gets in the way | DK | Keep from doing job | Keep from doing wrong | DK |
| July 1994 | 25 | 71 | 4 | 24 | 55 | 8 |
| March 1995 | 33 | 57 | 10 | 32 | 56 | 12 |
| February 1997 | 36 | 54 | 10 | 39 | 66 | 10 |
| January 1998 | 31 | 63 | 6 | | | |
| February 1998 | 29 | 65 | 6 | 31 | 58 | 11 |
| September 2001 | 31 | 58 | 11 | 25 | 60 | 15 |
| November 2001 | 35 | 51 | 14 | 32 | 54 | 14 |
| July 2002 | 31 | 58 | 11 | 26 | 59 | 15 |

Source: Pew Center for People and the Press.

* Question: "Which of the following two statements about the news media do you agree with more: The news media helps society to solve its problems, or the news media gets in the way of society solving its problems."

** Question: "Some people think that by criticizing leaders, news organizations keep political leaders from doing their job. Others think that such criticism is worth it because it keeps political leaders from doing things that should not be done. Which position is closer to your opinion?"

Before proceeding, we should note some limitations of these questions. First, the social role question does not ask respondents in what ways the media may interfere or aid society in solving its problems. Second, the phrase in the government question, "keeps political leaders from doing things that should not be done," is ambiguous. Does the phrase refer to personal malfeasance in office or does it refer to policies that government might take? Noting these ambiguities, results are presented in table 8.4.

In both cases, large fractions of the public feel that the media have harmful rather than beneficial effects. By margins that sometimes exceed two-to-one, people feel that the news media get in the way of society solving its problems rather than helping. From 1995 through 2002, only 30 percent give the news media positive marks, compared to about 60 percent who grade the media negatively. The public is less antagonistic to the news media, however, when assessing its governmental role. Here only about one-quarter to one-third feel that news organizations stand in the way of leaders from doing their job, in comparison to about 60 percent who think that the media keep leaders from doing things that should not be done.

Thus the public on average sees the media as socially harmful, but the public is less inclined to view the media that way when asked about its relationship to government. What accounts for this difference? Part of the answer may be because the public thinks of political leaders in a more negative light than the news media. Moreover, the social effects question, unlike the governmental one, does not ask people to compare the news media with other organizations. Had the governmental question been rephrased in such a manner, we might see the highly negative assessment of the news media reemerge.

All evidence points to declining public regard toward the news media over the past thirty years (Cook and Gronke 2001, 2002; Cook, Gronke, and Ratliff 2000). One reason for the decline in regard toward the media lies in the general decline in trust and confidence across social and political institutions (Cook and Gronke 2001; Bennett et al. 1998, 1999), but factors intrinsic toward the news media may also be a part of the story. The next section turns to the question of whether the rise of the new media helps explain this decline in public regard toward the news media.

## The New Media Age, Cable Diffusion, and Changing News Media Attitudes

This section uses the GSS confidence questions to investigate the impact of the spread of cable television on the decreasing level of trust toward the news media. Again, the cable television variable serves as an indicator of the new media age. One advantage of the GSS data for present purposes is that they span a fairly long time period and are available at the individual level. Further, the GSS surveys contain a reasonable number of variables that can be used as controls, although the GSS lacks the range of political attitudes and behaviors for use as controls as found in the ANES polls used in the previous chapter. Yet, since the GSS series begins long after broadcast television diffused into virtually every American household, we will not be able to control for the effects of broadcast television on media attitudes.

Perhaps the greatest strength of the GSS surveys, other than the relatively long time frame, is the GSS battery of confidence measures regarding other social and political institutions. This provides us with an unusually strong control variable, given that past research finds that confidence in one institution is strongly (although not perfectly) correlated with confidence in other institutions (Cook and Gronke 2001, 2002; Cook, Gronke, and Ratliff 2000). By controlling for confidence in these other institutions, we can assess whether cable diffusion affects media confidence above and beyond the effects of confidence in other institutions, in this way parceling out the effects of general secular decline in confidence without having to identify its sources.

This analysis resembles that in chapter 7, on the decline in public consumption of news. The aggregate indicator of cable diffusion (the annual percentage of households with cable subscriptions) serves as the primary independent variable of interest, again recognizing the limitation of this variable as discussed in chapter 7. Three dependent variables are used here: confidence in television, confidence in the press, and a media confidence index that sums the responses between the television and press items. Following Cook, Gronke, and Rattliff (2000), "hardly any confidence" is scored −1, "some confidence" 0, and "a great deal of confidence" 1. The additive media confidence index thus ranges from −2 to 2.

As in chapter 7, the analysis begins by building a baseline model. Past research, especially Cook, Gronke, and Rattliff (2000), and the availability of questions from GSS, identifies the components of the baseline model. The baseline model controls for demographics (age, gender, race, education, and income), political attitudes (ideological and partisan identification, and strength of partisanship), economic attitudes (job satisfaction, satisfaction with family finances, retrospective personal economic assessments), church attendance, and confidence in other institutions. Following Cook, Gronke, and Rattliff (2000), confidence in other institutions is an additive index for eleven other institutions: banks and financial institutions, business, Congress, courts/legal system, executive branch, government, medicine, military, labor, organized religion, scientific community, schools/education system, and the Supreme Court.[6] This index ranges from −11 to 11. The appendix provides details on variables used in the analysis.

## Results

Table 8.5 presents regression results of the impact of demographics, political and economic attitudes, confidence in other institutions, and cable diffusion on the three media confidence variables. The results from multiple regression analysis closely resemble those from ordered probit estimation. But as regression results are easier to interpret than probit, here I present the results of the regression analysis. Readers may contact me for the ordered probit results. Numbers in bold in the table indicate statistically significant results.

Many of the controls perform as expected, replicating Cook, Gronke, and Rattliff (2000). Importantly, results indicate that the index of confidence in the other institutions strongly affects confidence in the media, television, and the press. Overall, model fit is comparable to other analyses of these survey data, with adjusted $R^2$s of 0.22, 0.15, and 0.16 for the media index, television, and press estimations.

Turning to our main variable of interest, cable television, results indicate that as the percentage of households with cable television grows, confidence in the media, television, and the press falls. It is remarkable that in the face of controls for the institutional confidence index, that the cable effects are as strong as they are. For the cable diffusion variable, each 10 percent increase in households with cable is associated with a drop of 0.08 in media confidence. Approximately 55 percent of households added cable from 1976 to 2000. This growth rates converts into a decline of 0.44 in the media confidence index, which is about 20 percent of the range of the index. The index shows an actual

Table 8.5
Impact of cable television diffusion on confidence in the press and television, 1972–2000: OLS results

| | Media index | | | Television | | | Press | | |
|---|---|---|---|---|---|---|---|---|---|
| | *b* | *SE* | *p* | *b* | *SE* | *p* | *b* | *SE* | *p* |
| Age | −.002 | .001 | .003 | −.001 | .0004 | .007 | −.001 | .0004 | .046 |
| Female | −.03 | .015 | .091 | −.018 | .010 | .057 | −.008 | .010 | .427 |
| Black | −.064 | .050 | .200 | .026 | .031 | .403 | −.087 | .032 | .007 |
| White | −.153 | .046 | .001 | −.060 | .029 | .037 | −.090 | .030 | .002 |
| Education | −.029 | .003 | .000 | −.026 | .002 | .000 | −.003 | .002 | .092 |
| Income | −.022 | .003 | .000 | −.015 | .002 | .000 | −.007 | .002 | .001 |
| Ideology | −.052 | .006 | .000 | −.018 | .004 | .000 | −.035 | .004 | .000 |
| Party ID | −.038 | .004 | .000 | −.010 | .003 | .000 | −.029 | .003 | .000 |
| Strength PID | −.003 | .008 | .759 | .013 | .005 | .016 | −.015 | .005 | .005 |
| Satis. job | .001 | .010 | .929 | −.016 | .006 | .009 | .017 | .006 | .006 |
| Fin. alter | −.008 | .011 | .467 | .002 | .007 | .775 | −.010 | .007 | .159 |
| Sat. fin. | −.002 | .012 | .849 | .001 | .007 | .908 | −.004 | .008 | .619 |
| Attend church | -.044 | .003 | .000 | −.026 | .002 | .000 | −.017 | .002 | .000 |
| Confid. index | .110 | .002 | .000 | .056 | .001 | .000 | .055 | .001 | .000 |
| CATV pct. | −.008 | .0004 | .000 | −.002 | .0003 | .000 | −.006 | .0003 | .000 |
| Constant | 1.289 | .090 | .000 | .629 | .056 | .000 | .662 | .058 | .000 |
| n | 15574 | | | 15613 | | | 15617 | | |
| F | 301.96 | | | 190.77 | | | 204.48 | | |
| prob. F | .0000 | | | .0000 | | | .0000 | | |
| R²/adj. R² | .23 | .22 | | .16 | .15 | | .16 | .16 | |
| Root MSE | .93 | | | .58 | | | .60 | | |

*Source:* GSS, 1972–2000. See text and appendix for details on the variables used.

drop of 0.69 during this period. Cable television, by these estimates, accounts for about two-thirds (0.44/0.69) of the drop in media confidence.

A similar story is told when turning to the separate television and press items. For television confidence, we find a drop of 0.02 for each 10-percentage-point increase in households with cable subscriptions, or a drop of 0.11 due to the full growth of cable (55 percent * 0.02). During this time frame, television confidence overall dropped from −0.033 to −0.325, or 0.292. Cable may account for about 40 percent of the decline in television confidence. The impact of cable diffusion on press confidence is even stronger, at 0.06 for each 10-percentage-point increase in households with cable subscriptions. From 1973 to 2000, confidence in the press fell from 0.085 to −0.314, or 0.399. Cable's cumulative impact is 0.33 (55 *0.06) or possibly 80 percent of the fall in press confidence.

Why is the drop in press confidence so much more than for television? Part of the answer may reside in the questions themselves. The television item does not reference television news, nor does it single out free broadcasting from cable from local television from public television, etc. The press item focuses on the news media, although it does not distinguish print from broadcast, or national from local news. Despite the bluntness of these items, the press confidence item may tap into attitudes about the news media more directly than the television item.

The major limitation of this analysis is the aggregate nature of the cable variable. It cannot tell us whether those individuals most exposed to the new media are the ones with the lowest levels of news media confidence, as Patterson's theory implies. Moreover, the aggregate trend in cable correlates very strongly with a simple linear time counter, 0.98 (p = .00) at the individual level. Such a high correlation precludes entering both into the same equation. In fact, when both time and the cable variables are simultaneously entered, the time counter proves strongly significant and negative, while the cable variable reverses sign, becoming positive. We should not make much of this sign reversal other than referring to the perverse effects of multicollinearity. Hence we cannot definitively say that the spread of cable television depresses confidence in the press and television or whether some other process, which is similarly trending over time, is the true casual agent. Still, the results lend some plausibility to the notion that the spread of cable may be one reason for the decline in confidence in the news media.

## Conclusion: The New Media Age and the Public

The presidential news system has transformed over the past two to three decades. Previous chapters looked at the decline of news coverage and the increase in negative news reporting of the president in major, traditional news outlets. This and the previous chapter looked at changes in the public's use of and attitudes toward the news media, in particular the decline in news attention and the erosion of confidence in the news media.

One value of the presidential news system concept is that it directs attention not only to the impact of external forces on the system, but how changes in one element of the system may reverberate onto other segments of the system. Thus while large secular forces, such as changing population demography, declining political participation, eroding social capital, and waning trust in political and social institutions, have affected news consumption and attitudes toward the news media, changes within the system may have also affected the mass public. This and the last chapter looked at how the spread of cable television, an indicator of the rise of the new media, affected public use of and attitudes toward the news media.

Although the analysis is far from definitive, due to the aggregate level of the key independent variable, cable diffusion, the results suggest that the spread of cable may have depressed levels of news attention across many types of news media and also contributed to the decline in public confidence toward the news media. In looking at the decline in news attention, both Baum and Kernell's viewing opportunity model and Patterson's reporting style model received support. We were able to identify some of the mechanisms through which the new media age affects the news attention behaviors of individuals. However, the lack of direct, individual-level measures of cable access, exposure to new media reporting styles, and media trust limits how definitive we can be about asserting these claims.

Even if the rise of the new media system did not lead to diminished news consumption or confidence in the news media, presidents in the new media era face a public that consumes less news than it once did, as well as a public that has grown increasingly negative toward the news media. These changes, along with the declining levels of presidential news coverage and the mounting negative tone of that coverage, have implications for presidential leadership in the new media age, the subject of the next chapter.

## Appendix 8: Variables Used in the Analysis

Find below variables used from the 1972–2000 GSS Cumulative File for table 8.5. I downloaded the GSS data from their website: http://www.icpsr .umich.edu:8080/GSS/homepage.htm. The mnemonic that GSS uses for each variable is indicated in capital letters.

*Age*: AGE
*Female*: SEX
*Black*: RACE
*White*: RACE
*Education*: EDUC
*Income*: INCOME
*Ideology*: POLVIEWS
*Party ID*: PARTYID
*Strength PID*: This variable folds PARTYID, such that Independents = 1, Independent Leaners = 2, Weak Partisans = 3, Strong Partisans = 4
*Satisfaction with Job*: SATJOB
*Financial Alteration*: FINALTER (change in financial situation)
*Attend Church*: ATTEND,
*Confidence Index*: The confidence index is a summation in the confidence for 11 institutions:
Banks and financial institutions, *CONFINAN*
Business, *CONBUS*
Congress, *CONLEGIS*

Courts/legal system, *CONCOURT*
Executive branch, *CONFED*
Government, *CONGOVT*
Medicine, *CONMEDIC*
Military, *CONARMY*
Organized labor, *CONLABOR*
Organized religion, *CONCLERG*
Scientific community, *CONSCI*
Schools/education system *CONEDUC*
Supreme Court, *CONJUDGE*
*Confidence in TV*: *CONTV*
*Confidence in the Press*: *CONPRESS*
*Media Index*: Additive index of *CONTV* and *CONPRESS*
*CATV pct.*: Percent of households with Cable Television, *Statistical Abstract of the United States*, various years.

# CHAPTER 9

# The Implications of the New Media on the Presidential News System and Presidential Leadership

This book opened with a puzzle—the news does not seem to affect public evaluations of the president as strongly in the age of new media as it did in the age of broadcasting. Previous chapters have examined changes in the structure of the news media, the style of news reporting, the amount of news that people consume, and how they feel about the news media. The major, traditional news outlets, such as the *New York Times*, offer less news on the president in the new media age than they did in the broadcasting age. News on the president in the age of new media is more negative and critical in tone than it was during the broadcasting age. Plus, the public consumes less news in the new media age than it did in the broadcast age, while public confidence and trust in the news media have also waned.

This chapter brings these elements together in an attempt to build a general theory of news media effects on presidential evaluations. By using this theory, we will have something to say about the nature and limitations of presidential leadership in the new media age. As I will argue below, presidential leadership has changed as a result of the transformation from the broadcasting to the new media age. Presidents find it more difficult to lead the broad mass public. As a result they focus their leadership on mobilizing segments of the public already predisposed to support them.

## The Implications of the New Media Age I: The News Media and the Public

The presidential news system transformed in the 1980s and 1990s, as the relationships among the news media, the public, and the president changed. For instance, the style of news reporting changed, with soft news replacing hard news (Patterson 2000) and the amount of news on the president, the prototypical hard news story, declining.[1] News about the president in the new media age took a decidedly negative, critical, and cynical turn. At the same time, the audience for news shrank and the public became increasingly distrustful of the news media. These changes hold important implications for the democratic linkage role of the mass media as well as for presidential leadership and governance.

## A Signaling Theory of News and Public Opinion

A puzzle motivated this study: Why does news seems to have less effect on public evaluations of the president in the new media age than it did in the broadcasting age? For instance, despite a heavy barrage of bad press in 1999 due to the Monica Lewinsky scandal and congressional impeachment, Bill Clinton's polls barely seemed to budge. And, in general, the tone of presidential news seems uncorrelated to public approval of the president (Gaines and Roberts 2005), in contrast to studies of the broadcast age, which found a sizeable connection between news tone and presidential evaluations (Brody 1991). How can we account for the apparent lack of impact of news tone on presidential evaluations in the new media age?

A theory to account for the lack of news tone impact in the new media age should also account for the impact of news tone on public evaluations during the broadcast age. In building such a theory, I begin with the common assumption that most people are not highly interested and informed about politics and that it is not rational for them to expend much time, energy, or other resources learning about government and public affairs. Instead, people delegate to the news media, and perhaps other organizations such as interest groups and political parties, the task of monitoring government. People will only spend time or energy attending to news when certain circumstances motivate them to do so. Second, the presidential news system mediates the impact of news on people's political opinions. The transformation of that system in the 1980s and 1990s helps account for the decreased impact of news on public evaluations of the president.

The major changes in the presidential news system with relevance to this problem are (1) the increase in competition across news organizations, (2) the decline in hard news, (3) the rise of negativity in presidential news, (4) the decline in the size of the news audience, and (5) the erosion of trust in the news media. A theory of news impacts requires an understanding of the recipient, the communicator or message source, the relationship between the communicator and the recipient, as well as the message itself. These five factors correspond to recipient, source, source-recipient relationship, and message characteristics (Page, Shapiro, and Dempsey 1987).[2]

UNIFORMITY IN THE NEWS

During the golden age of broadcasting, we could expect the news to affect public opinion, especially with regard to the presidency. First, the news production sector was fairly concentrated and centralized, with relatively little economic competition across news organizations compared to the level of competition during the new media age. During the broadcasting age, the networks and a handful of elite news outlets defined the news; other news organizations followed their lead (Grossman and Kumar 1981). This resulted in a relative uniformity in the news across news providers. No matter which news outlet a person used, that person was likely to receive essentially the same news in terms of content, emphasis, and tonality.

West (2001, esp. chap. 4) argues that the news during this period was essentially homogenous (51, 53, 65). According to West, several factors promoted homogeneity in news, including broad journalistic adherence to professional norms that promoted a common understanding of what constituted news (51–53). First, communications technologies, like the telegraph in the 1800s and radio and television in the 1900s, allowed some news organizations to target a large, mass audience, with important implications for news. The telegraph, for instance, led to the creation of wire services and newspaper syndicates. Local newspapers subscribed to the wire services for news content that they could not collect on their own. To sell their content to as many newspapers as possible, the wire services and syndicates squeezed out "personal bias and local idiosyncrasies" (West 2001, 52), which resulted in many newspapers around the country offering their readers similar news content. Similarly, radio "encouraged journalists to wring partisan and commercial excesses out of their programming in order to attract more listeners" (West 2001, 53). The same could be said of television. The high barriers to broadcast entry for radio and television, a function of government policy and technology, also limited competitive pressures (Hamilton 2003).

Second, reliance on advertising, which began with the rise of the commercial newspaper in the late 1800s, created other incentives to reach as many readers as possible, which again meant a news product consisting of "relatively impartial stories" that would also attract advertising "from disparate business organizations . . . each of which had their own political viewpoints" (West 2001, 52).

Another source of similarity in news content across news outlets was that many news organizations tended to look to the *New York Times* and other major news outlets for guidance in selecting news stories and their tone. In developing their agenda-setting model of the news media, Comstock and Scharrer (2005, 181) argue that "there is considerable consonance among the media in what is covered as a consequence of competition and similarities in news gathering." Comstock and Scharrer (2005, 180) argue that such "intermedia agenda setting" is especially true for news about the president.

Despite these forces promoting consonance in news across news organizations, we must be careful in suggesting complete uniformity in news and a lack of competition among news organizations during the broadcast age. Surely the three broadcast networks competed with each other; each provided nightly news broadcasts and sought high ratings for their individual news programs. But the big three networks competed for the same viewers, which would lead to some degree of convergence in their news product.

Anthony Downs's (1957) model of party competition can help us understand the dynamics of competition among the three networks during the broadcasting age. Imagine the distribution of public opinion with regard to news as being unimodal, that is, single peaked. The three networks will offer a news product that converges toward the preferences of the median viewer. Economists suggest this as a fair description of the competitive system during the age of broadcasting (Hamilton 2003). Thus, rather than characterize the news as homogeneous or uniform, as West does, it is perhaps more accurate to suggest that the news during the broadcast was *more* homogeneous than it would be during the new media age.

Ample empirical evidence demonstrates convergence of news across the major news media during the era of broadcasting. Lemert's (1974) seminal study found considerable duplication of news stories across the three evening news network broadcasts in the early 1970s, a finding repeated numerous times (Stempel 1985; Foote and Steele 1986; and Riffe et al. 1986). Altheide (1982) found similarity in coverage of the Iran Hostage crisis across the three broadcast networks, while Grossman and Kumar (1981, 255–56) report relatively similar news coverage of the president in their content analysis across several major news media. In his study of the news coverage of ten issues in the *New York Times*, thirty periodicals in the *Readers' Guide to Periodical Literature*, and CBS News, Neuman (1990) finds a high degree of similarity across these news providers.[3]

Doris Graber (1974), in an important early study, compared the coverage of the 1968 presidential election campaign of sixteen daily newspapers, selected to generate diversity across the campaign. Importantly for our purposes, her study was conducted during the height of the broadcasting age. She comes to the conclusion that

> our sample revealed substantial, nationwide uniformity in the type of campaign information available in the daily newspapers and the proportions of coverage allotted to various issues and presidential qualities. Region, community size, party politics, endorsements, or any other criteria potentially responsible for differences in coverage did not seem to matter. Uniformity also characterized the proportional amounts of coverage given to presidential and vice presidential candidates and the allotments of favorable and unfavorable stories.[4]

Two major implications should follow from the relative degree of uniformity in the news during the broadcasting age. First, each news organization's credibility will be enhanced inasmuch as its news resembles the news of other news organizations. When news organizations agree about the definition of the news, a social consensus develops that the news faithfully represents an important reality. Further, when news organizations produce similar news products, people have a difficult time seeing bias in the news; they come to see the news media as fundamentally impartial when a variety of news outlets produce similar news. Agreement in news content, irrespective of the political leaning of a news organization, may lead people to see news as essentially unbiased. Further, not only may each news organization develop a credible reputation, but people may view the whole news sector as credible. Of course, this only makes sense if the news media are formally and economically independent from government. Uniformity in news when government controls the news media and/or the public believes that the government controls the news media will undermine the credibility of the press, as is likely the case in countries with heavy government control over the news media.[5]

Second, relative uniformity in the news may increase the impact of news on people's political opinions. Each successive news story will reinforce the message of the earlier encountered news stories. Using Zaller's (1992) terminology, when the news is uniform, a one-message state exists (Goidel, Shields, and Peffley 1997; Krosnick and Kinder 1990). Furthermore, the likelihood that a person with whom someone interacts will be exposed to the same news will be relatively high, assuming that they are exposed to news. Inasmuch as personal communications transmit news from one person to another, personal communications may reinforce the message that a person receives from direct news exposure.

## HIGH LEVELS OF HARD NEWS

The relatively high level of hard news reporting of the golden age of broadcasting may also affect public opinion. A continual stream of hard news may signal to a person that affairs of government and politics are important. We may hypothesize that when the news media produce a relatively high level of hard news, news about government and politics, that a societal norm may develop in which governmental affairs is considered an important aspect of life.[6]

While no direct evidence on this point exists, the large literature on the agenda-setting effects of the mass media is consistent with this idea. The unit of analysis of most agenda-setting research is the issue area, for instance, crime, race, abortion, and other issues. That research finds that as levels of news coverage of issue areas rise or fall, the issue correspondingly rises or falls on the public's agenda, measured by how many people cite the issue as important or how the issue ranks compared to other issues in terms of importance. In her review of that literature, Graber (2004) states that "the mere fact that a story has received prominent media attention signals that it is important and therefore potentially worthy of consideration when making political judgments" and "the finding that many people equate news coverage with significance has lead to the heavily research 'agenda-setting hypothesis.'" (549).

We can draw on and refine this agenda-setting literature. First, where the agenda-setting literature only looks at the issue or public affairs component of the public's agenda, if we consider the public's agenda to be those items of interest or importance to the public more broadly, then we can also identify a nongovernmental or private component to the public's agenda. It should follow then that if the public takes cues from the news agenda to inform their own agendas, then we can hypothesize that as the news media grant relatively more attention to nonpolitical as opposed to political concerns the public's agenda will adjust accordingly.

Data required to test this hypothesis directly do not exist, but we can offer an indirect test. The news media presents the public with higher levels of political news during presidential election years than midterm election years, one of the important distinctions in Campbell's (1960) classic high-stimulus, low-stimulus model of surge and decline. We would then expect that levels of political interest will be higher in presidential than midterm election years. To take this as an indirect test of this hypothesis we have to assume that interest in politics is related to the culture norm that politics and governmental affairs is important.

Using the pooled 1952–2000 ANES data, I regressed the three-point scale of interest in the election and the four-point scale on interest in public affairs on a dummy variable for midterm elections, controlling for a battery of demographics, including strength of party identification.[7] With these massive controls, results indicate that interest in the election and public affairs is lower in midterm than presidential elections (elections: $b = -0.17$, $t = -15.38$, $p = .000$; public affairs: $b = -0.05$, $t = -3.37$, $p = .000$). These results, which are consistent with the hypothesis, however, offer a far from definitive test. Other factors besides news coverage distinguish midterm and presidential elections. Yet these results points in the same direction as this hypothesis, and thus are suggestive of the hypothesized relationship between news content and the importance that one attaches to government and public affairs.

Returning to the implications of the news media assigning a large part of the news hole to hard news, we may hypothesize that even if people do not pay much personal attention to hard news, they may adopt the societal norm that what the government does is important. In other words, a high volume of hard news may prime people to take government and politics seriously, even if they do not attend much to the details of government, politics, issues, and/ or individual news stories. When issues of importance arise, a public primed to think that government and public affairs is important may be more likely to attend to those issues. Even if people do not learn much detail about those issues, they may use these issues in evaluating their political leaders. When the public is not primed to think that government and public affairs is important, even when issues of consequence arise, the public may disregard the issue and/ or may not employ the issue to evaluate its leaders.[8]

## A LARGE AUDIENCE FOR NEWS

The relatively large audience for news during the golden age also has implications for news media impact on public opinion. For news to affect a person's opinion, that person must be exposed to news, either directly or indirectly (e.g., through contact with people who are exposed and who communicate something about the news to the nonexposed person) (Bartels 1993, Bennett 2002a, Cappella 2001). The large audience for news during the broadcasting age increased the likelihood of both direct and indirect news exposure.

News media effects during the broadcasting age operate at both the individual and aggregate levels. At the individual level, the large news audience meant that a large number of people were directly exposed to news reports. Plus, the probability that people who do not pay attention to news will interact with someone who does increases as the audience for news grows.[9] Thus as the audience for news expands in size, the likelihood that people will be exposed to news increases either because of direct exposure or indirectly through contact with people who are directly exposed to news.

Thus each individual's probability of news exposure increases as audience size grows. News exposure is the minimal condition for news to affect a person's political opinions and attitudes. Cumulated across people, as audience size grows, the number of people whose opinions may change due to the higher likelihood of news exposure, either direct or indirect, also increases. Through this process, the aggregate effect of news on opinion may also increase.

HIGH NEWS MEDIA CREDIBILITY

Above I suggested that uniformity in news may lead to the public viewing the news media as credible. Independent of this effect, the relatively high level of credibility of news organizations during the broadcasting age may also lead to increased impact of news on public opinion. Source credibility is an important mediating factor for communications effects (e.g., Miller and Krosnick 2000). When the recipient views the message source as credible, the likelihood of communication effects rises. The public trusted the news media at relatively high levels during the broadcasting age. This high level of trust or credibility should lead to comparatively strong news impacts on public opinion during the golden age.[10]

NEWS TONE

The last ingredient of the signaling theory refers to the signal itself, an aspect of the content of the news. Here the focus is on one attribute of news with relevance to the issue of presidential support, tonality. Page, Shapiro, and Dempsey (1987, 24) identify five necessary conditions for communication to change public opinion—(1) the message is received, (2) it is understood, (3) it is relevant to the object or topic being evaluated, (4) it is discrepant with past beliefs, and (5) it is credible. Thus far, the argument is that during the broadcasting age, many people receive the message (news) (condition 1). Because of the high level of hard news, such news is relevant to evaluating the president (condition 3), and the public viewed the news media as a credible source (condition 5). It is not clear whether people understand the news in terms of the details of public policy or governmental performance. In fact, one may argue that the high level of hard news reporting may have been overwhelming to many (see Zaller 2003 on this point).

But people may understand the meaning of the tone of the news. It may not always be difficult for a person to judge that a news story conveys good versus bad news. For instance, when a news story points out that a policy is working well, that the president made the correct decision, that the president won in Congress, that unemployment declined, and the like, people may easily understand or perceive that this is good news for the president. Similarly many types of bad news, such as worsening economic conditions and defeats on Capitol Hill, may be easily seen as bad news for the president. Thus, many people much of the time may have a relatively easy time judging a story as either good or bad news for the president, whether it reflects well or poorly on the president. Inasmuch as events are the stuff of news and those events are relatively clear and unambiguous, people may not have much trouble interpreting those events. And inasmuch as people hold the president in some way responsible or accountable for the turn in events, their interpretation of these events (news) may affect their evaluations of the president.

As argued throughout, presidential news during the broadcasting age was generally positive toward the president, especially when compared to presidential news during the new media age.[11] Positive news, then, should lead to public approval of the president and a stream of positive news should reinforce public approval of the president. Part of the power of a steady stream of positive news about the president comes not from each individual news story (signal) itself, but the repetition of these stories (signals) that point in the same direction.

Despite the preponderance of good news on the president during the broadcasting age, not all news was positive. Bad things happened—the economy was not always in good shape, presidents lost on votes in Congress, the Vietnam War dragged on, among other things. In the system being described here, negative news about the president stands in sharp contrast to the relatively steady diet of positive news. Ironically, the impact of negative news about the president on recipients is likely to be strong, even though most news about the president during this age was positive. Negative news about the president, being somewhat unexpected, becomes highly noticeable.

Research on negativity effects argues that negative news should have greater impact on public opinion than positive news (Lau 1985).[12] Lau suggests two reasons. First, negative news stands out from a world that is generally portrayed in positive terms, a "figure-ground" effect. Second, a survival orientation, in which people are more strongly motivated to avoid costs than to realize gains, leads people to take notice of negative news and events that may be costly to them. Both processes may be operative in the context of presidential evaluations, although the "figure-ground" perspective may have important implications for news reporting in the new media age.[13]

Other attributes of the presidential news system during the broadcasting age may have heightened the effect of negative presidential news on public opinion. Relative uniformity in news meant that when one news organization began to report negative and critical news, others would also do so. To average people, the uniformity in news suggests a consensus about presidential performance in office. The high level of hard news during the broadcasting age reinforced the importance of negative news in evaluating the president, and the large audience for news increased the chances that a person would encounter negative news about the president. Finally, the high level of trust in the media meant that people took the change in news tone seriously.

Despite the fact that news in the broadcasting age was basically positive toward the president, when news turned negative, it could undermine and gravely threaten a president. Arguably, two presidents at the height of the golden age, Lyndon Johnson and Richard Nixon, were driven from office in part because negative news undermined their support with the mass public. Importantly, the news turned negative when events and presidential decisions led journalists and other opinion elites to revise their assessment of the president's job performance. The lingering war in Vietnam, coupled with domestic discontent about the war, altered judgments about Johnson's leadership. The Watergate scandals and a deteriorating economy caused a shift in news tone about Nixon. Notably, in both instances, the shift in news tone and public opinion took a considerable period of time because of basic trust toward the presidency and its incumbents.

## The Signaling Theory and the Age of New Media

The irony of the age of new media is that, in spite of negativity being the norm for news reporting about the president, news media effects may be weaker on public opinion than they were during the golden age of broadcasting. In the new media age, the news media pose a weaker challenge to presidents. First, news reporting is less uniform in the new media age. Rather than a few elite news organizations defining the news, many more news media outlets exist, presenting the public with a variety of news. For instance, people so inclined could turn to news from outlets with a decided political slant, like the *Washington Times*, Fox Cable News, and talk radio, which mostly represent the political right. The internet also provides an alternative source of information and opinion about the president, from sites such as the Drudge Report to chat rooms, even if one does not want to consider such outlets to be news. The variety of programs, such as *Crossfire* and others, in which pundits of the left and right verbally spar with each other, exposes people (who care to tune in) to different perspectives on the president. Even soft news programs (Baum 2003a, 2003b), which present mostly entertainment and celebrity news, may expose people to important news stories, such as major international events, from time to time.

On such broadcasts, viewers may encounter a news frame far different from the traditional network report.

Thus, during the new media age, the news is less uniform than was the case during the broadcasting age. The decline in uniformity may weaken the impact of any single news story or news outlet on the public at large, although selection effects (Barker 2002) may increase the impact of such news and information on the viewer or reader, even if the tendency is for such news and information to merely reinforce preexisting attitudes.[14]

Second, the decline in hard news reporting may also weaken the impact of news on public opinion. As hypothesized above, a high level of hard news coverage may convey to the public that government and public affairs are important. The drop in level of hard news coverage may lead to erosion in people's estimation of the importance and/or relevance of government and public affairs to their lives. The survival reaction to negative news (Lau 1985) may abate as people come to view government and public affairs as less consequential aspects of life. In other words, as hard news coverage declines, people view government as a less important component of their life. When negative news is reported, the potential or estimated costs of the bad news to a person's life declines compared to during the broadcasting age. Thus people will react less strongly to negative news when there is less hard news coverage than when the level of hard news coverage is higher.

Third, the decline in the size of the news audience may also weaken the impact of news on public opinion. As audience size recedes, the probability that a person will be directly exposed to news reduces, and nonnews watchers may be less likely to interact with someone who watches the news simply because there are fewer news watchers. Because people tend to travel within relatively homogenous social networks, it is quite likely that a nonnews watcher will interact with other nonnews watchers. The public may bifurcate into two types of social networks, those composed of mainly nonnews watchers and those composed mainly of news watchers, which may impede the flow of political information and news.[15]

Fourth, the decline in trust toward the news media may further erode the impact of the news on people's opinions because the news media loses its source credibility.[16] Many people view the news media's tendency to criticize political leaders as a form of news media "partisanship," in which criticism and negativity serve the needs of news organizations and journalists rather than being rooted in deteriorating conditions, bad decisions, or the public interest. People may have come to view criticism, negativity, sensationalism, and the like, as stunts to promote sales or to further the speaking fees of celebrity journalists (Fallows 1996). They may also view the criticism of the news media as part of a power game between politicians and journalists. This perception of media "partisanship" may weaken the credibility of the news media with the public.

Finally, the combination of negative news and perceptions of media partisanship may undermine the "figure-ground" contrast effect of negative news. During the broadcasting age, negative news was the figure to the background of positive news. And negative news was less common than positive news, heightening the contrast effects of negative news. Further, during the broadcasting age, negative news was rooted in events and presidential decisions. The credibility of the press and the public's perception that the press impartially reported the news and only turned negative when events warranted, accented the contrast between the negative news figure and the positive news background.

The degree of contrast between figure and background in part measures the strength of the news signal to the public. Several factors in the new media age weakened the negative news signal to the public. One, negative news became the background because of its high level compared to positive news. Two, media "partisanship" makes it difficult for people to distinguish "truly bad news" from "media inspired bad news." "Truly bad news" can be defined as news on events and decisions that pose real world costs on people's lives and/or their estimation of political leadership. Deterioration in economic conditions, mounting battle deaths, successful terrorist attacks, and reports of rising crime, come to mind as examples of "truly bad news." "Media inspired bad news" is news that many people may believe does not hold such implications for their lives, news that the media report with a negative cast because it serves the particularistic needs of the news media, for example, their profits or their power position in society.

When the negative news is a combination of "truly bad news" and "media inspired bad news," many people, especially those who are less sophisticated about politics and possess less knowledge, may have a relatively hard time distinguishing one form of bad news from the other. In other words, the negative news signal may be noisy, mixing both types of bad news. Thus the impact of "truly bad news" on public opinion may be weaker in the context of the presidential news system of the new media age compared to the broadcasting age.

The factors identified here—decreasing news uniformity, declines in hard news coverage, the shrinking audience for news, the diminished trust in the news media, and the high level of negative news—help account for the lesser impact of negative news on public thinking about the president in the new media age compared to the golden age of presidential television. One of the great ironies of the new media age is that despite the higher quotient of negative news compared to the broadcasting age, negative news may have less implications for presidents than it did during the broadcasting age. But just as the new media age lessens the damage that bad news can do to a president, the structure of the presidential news system in the new media age may also limit the president's ability to lead the broad mass public, the subject of the next two sections.

## The Implications of the New Media Age II: Presidential Leadership of Public Opinion

In a recent book, George Edwards (2003) confronts the conventional view that presidents can easily lead public opinion. Instead, he argues that most presidential campaigns to alter public thinking on issues of the day fall "on deaf ears." Edwards lists a number of factors that he argues limit the president's ability to lead public opinion. We may add to Edwards account the changes in the structure of the presidential news system. The same factors that lead to weaker news effects on public opinion in the new media age also heightened the barriers to presidential leadership of public opinion writ broadly.

Presidents can attempt to lead public opinion by speaking to the public directly. National addresses broadcast on prime time can reach the largest audience, but network resistance to giving presidents unrestricted access to the airwaves (Foote 1990), viewer fatigue, and the declining audience for presidential speeches (Baum and Kernell 1999) all limit presidential reliance on major addresses to reach and lead the public. To reach the nation's citizenry, presidential communications must become news. The news media become an indispensable avenue for communicating with the mass public. As a consequence, the structural changes in the presidential news system become especially important in understanding the lessening ability of the president to lead the public.

The decline in hard news coverage lessens the president's ability to get his message across to the public. First, the public receives less information about presidential activities as news coverage of the president declines. A story about a presidential decision or action may have attracted several days of coverage during the broadcasting age. In the new media age that same story may stay in the news for a shorter period of time. And inasmuch as people come to view government and policies as being of less importance as the level of hard news coverage ebbs, people may also come to see what the president does as less important. And when the president is viewed as less important, people may pay less attention to what he does. This should further weaken presidential leadership effects on the mass public.

In response to the decline in hard news coverage and the increasing likelihood that both the media and the public's attention will be diverted to something else, some presidents in the age of new media have followed Ronald Reagan's strategy of organizing daily presidential public activities around a central theme or "message of the day" or "week" (DiClerico 1993).[17] Tighter control of journalist access to White House, administration, and other personnel is also consistent with the idea of presenting a uniform message to journalists in an attempt to focus their attention and keep them from covering a different story. In effect, news management becomes a more important element of the president's leadership strategy in the new media age.

The smaller audience for news erects another barrier to presidential leadership. A smaller audience for news affects the potential for presidential leadership of public opinion through two routes. First, fewer people are exposed to news about the president and the president's message contained in news reports. Second, there are fewer people with whom to interact who have been exposed to news. Thus the decline in hard news coverage and the shrinking news audience hold major implications for presidential leadership.

George Edwards (2003) focuses on presidential attempts to alter public thinking about policies and issues. Policy conversion is difficult under the most propitious of circumstances. Presidents may be more successful in affecting the public agenda, the issues and problems that the public deems most important. A small literature has unearthed relatively robust presidential effects on the public agenda (Cohen 1995, 1997; Hill 1998; Lawrence 2004). However, indications exist that due to the effects noted above, presidents may be less able to move the public agenda during the new media age than during the golden age.

The Cohen-Hill-Lawrence approach looks at the impact of presidential rhetoric in the State of the Union Address on the public's most important problem. Generally, their results find that as presidents increase the amount of attention to an issue in the address, the percentage of people who cite that issue as important also grows. Young and Perkins (2005), in an imaginative test, contend that the Cohen-Hill-Lawrence approach fails to take into account the decreasing size of the audience for presidential speeches (or news), as well as the impact of the diffusion of television in the 1950s and 1960s, which boosted the size of the speech audience in those years. Comparing presidential policy utterances with the size of the television and cable television audience, Young and Perkins find that presidents seemed only able to move the public agenda during the golden age of television, when the audience for presidential speeches and news was large. In both the era before television's widespread diffusion and in the era of the new media, when many had access to cable television and thus could watch something other than a presidential speech, presidential leadership effects on the public's agenda appear negligible. This provides some empirical evidence that the structural changes associated with the age of new media have dampened the president's ability to alter the public agenda, presumably the aspect of public opinion most amenable to presidential leadership effects.[18]

## The Implications of the New Media Age III:
## A New Style of "Going Public" for a New Media Age

Because of the decreasing ability of the president to lead the broad mass public, the new media age has also affected the style of presidential leadership, a third implication. Presidential public leadership is always a combination of seeking and mobilizing the support of narrow groups and the broad mass public. As the ability of presidents to lead the broad mass public has dwindled, they look more and more to narrower groups, such as special interests and their partisan bases. Kernell's (1993) "going public" model is the most accepted understanding of presidential leadership and behavior in the modern era. That model is used as a basis to understand the nature of presidential leadership style in the new media age.

### "Going Public": The Traditional View

According to Kernell, as the institutional pluralism of the mid-twentieth-century Congress gave way to individual pluralism, presidents found it increasingly difficult to build coalitions within Congress. Under institutional pluralism, a president needed only to bargain with a relatively small number of committee chairs and party leaders to forge a coalition large enough to win acceptance of his policy initiative. Because they could deliver blocs of votes (the rank-and-file membership of their committees) for policies that they supported, committee chairs often were critical in building winning coalitions behind a policy. Moreover, as committee chairs earned those posts through seniority, they tended to be relatively insulated from national opinion tides that would on occasion sweep from office members representing more competitive districts. Thus the members to whom presidents turned most often for votes in Congress were among the least attuned to public pressures. Public support under such conditions did not always help a president in his dealings with Congress.

Unlike institutional pluralism, with its centralization of power in Congress, individual pluralism produced a more decentralized Congress. Committee reforms in the 1970s expanded the number of congressional power centers, while also diminishing the power of full committee chairs. With this dispersion of power, building a support coalition became a more difficult task. To construct a winning coalition presidents had to negotiate with a larger number of legislators, each with their own agenda, constituents, and career ambitions to satisfy. Presidents needed a less taxing method of building coalitions in Congress. "Going public" became a favored approach.

Kernell defines "going public" as "a strategy whereby a president promotes himself and his policies in Washington by appealing to the public for support" (1993, 2). Generating public support, from Kernell's perspective, is instrumental to building a support coalition in Congress for the president's policies,[19] although presidents might also receive a personal payoff from increased levels of public support—an increased likelihood of being reelected, for instance.

Kernell identifies several types of "going public" activities, such as delivering major presidential addresses to the nation on prime-time television broadcasts, offering minor addresses to narrower and more select audiences, traveling around the nation and the globe, and appearing in public (which usually entails speaking to an audience). For my purposes here, going public activities can be categorized into two sets, those aimed at the nation (e.g., major prime time presidential addresses, international travel) and those aimed at select audiences and groups (e.g., minor speeches and domestic travel).

Kernell argues that presidents rely on major addresses less than other forms of going public because addressing the nation too frequently will induce a counterreaction among citizens, causing many to lose interest in what the president has to say (93).[20] However, major addresses are potentially the most effective form of going public, in part because of their drama, and if used sparingly, their ability to focus the public's attention (1993, 93). Finally, major speeches may be a cost-effective method of applying public pressure on Congress, as such speeches theoretically tap constituents throughout the nation, in every congressional district. Despite these limitations, Kernell finds increases in major speech activity from the 1950s into the 1980s (92–98; also Ragsdale 1998, 159–67).

Owing to the limitations in the number of major speeches a president may make, presidents turn to minor speeches and other public activities geared at more select and narrower audiences. Kernell argues that minor presidential speeches are especially suited for building coalitions in an individualized pluralism setting, which requires building temporary coalitions among diverse constituencies issue by issue (1993, 98). Coalition building under individualized pluralism entails a mix of major and minor going public activities, with the choice of going "major-national" or "minor-narrow" a function of the issue, how often the president has already gone national, and the alignment of groups and public opinion on the issue, among other factors.

There are important implications to going "national" versus going "narrow." Since the public at-large tends to be moderate compared to interest groups and other population segments, going "national" will pull a president toward a moderate stance in comparison to going "narrow," which will pull him toward a more extreme position. There are two reasons why "going national" versus "going narrow" will pull or make a president appear more or less extreme.

One, presidents might be responsive to the policy preference of the target group, as presidents adjust their public stance to more closely match the group that they are trying to mobilize, the message-tailoring hypothesis (Goggin 1984, Doherty and Anderson 2003). Two, a selection process could be at work, which does not involve any position adjustment, but merely reflects the presidential choice of a "moderate" versus an "extreme" policy. When presidents go narrow (national), it is because they have selected a somewhat more extreme (moderate) position on a policy or issue. Whether going "national" versus going "narrow" indicates presidential responsiveness to a targeted audience or merely reflects the position that he has selected on an issue, the more a president goes "narrow" relative to going "national," the more politically extreme the president will look.

## A Model of Presidential Going Public Strategies

This section formalizes the above argument about presidential "going public" behavior to account for the dynamic influence of the new media age on such presidential behavior. I begin with the assumption that presidents want to maximize the odds that Congress will enact their policy proposals. "Going public" is one resource that presidents can employ to motivate congressional enactment of their policy proposals (Canes-Wrone 2001). From this perspective, "going public" is a leadership style aimed at mobilizing the public or a segment of the public in support of the president's policy proposals and initiatives.

Presidents can select from two mutually exclusive "going public" types. They can "go national," that is, activate or mobilize the mass public or they can "go narrow," that is, activate selective publics or interest groups.[21] Going "national" and going "narrow" are mutually exclusive options because "national" and "narrow" constituencies prefer different policies on the issue at hand.[22] Furthermore, the narrow constituency always holds a more extreme policy preference than the national constituency.[23] When a president goes "national," he must express support for the preference of the national constituency; thus, he cannot express support for the preference of the narrow constituency. If the president tries to go both "national" and "narrow" by expressing support to the national constituency for its policy preference and by doing the same for the narrow constituency, he will undermine his credibility and perhaps the support of either or both groups. As members of the two constituencies lose confidence that the president truly supports their policy preference, the president's ability to activate or mobilize either constituency declines. Competitors to the president also possess an incentive to inform both constituencies of the president's "two-faced" approach. Thus, presidents must either to go "national" or go "narrow."

Presidents will select the going public strategy that has the greater probability of affecting congressional behavior. The probability of impact on congressional behavior is in part a function of the relative receptivity of members of Congress to either type of group, which is a function of the relative impact that either constituency has on members' reelection. Normally, one might assume that members of Congress will be more responsive to the national constituency, which is composed of voters, as opposed to narrow constituencies. But narrow constituencies may form an important voting block within the members' district, presenting the member with a winning vote margin against a challenger. Further, narrow constituencies may possess resources, like campaign contributions, important to the member's reelection efforts.[24]

Second, the probability that the president will select a "national" or "narrow" going public strategy depends on the president's ability to activate either constituency. With the rise of the new media age, the president's ability to activate national opinion declined relative to that probability during the broadcasting age.[25]

Above, I argued and reviewed evidence that the president's ability to activate the national constituency, that is, public opinion, declined during the new media age. The audience for news and presidential speeches is smaller, and there is less news about the president; also, Young and Perkins (2005) find that presidents are less able to affect the public's agenda in the new media age. Influencing the public's agenda is similar to activating opinion, as used here. Hence in the new media age presidents should be marginally more likely to opt to go "narrow" than "national" compared to during the broadcasting age. Moreover, as narrow constituencies, by definition, always hold more extreme policy preferences than national constituencies, by going "narrow" more often, presidents are also more likely to espouse extreme policy positions. In the new media age, presidents will be more extreme in policy terms than in the golden age.

This model presents us with two hypotheses. One, presidents will "go narrow" relatively more in the new media age than the broadcasting age. Two, presidential policy positions will be relatively more extreme in the new media age than the broadcasting age.

## Existing Evidence on the New Going Public Hypotheses

Some empirical support exists for the first hypothesis that the mix of going national versus going narrow has shifted during the new media age. Kernell (1993, 92–93) notes a decline in the number of major speeches from the Reagan to G. H. W. Bush administration in the first three years of a president's term, while the number of minor speeches continued to rise. Ragsdale's data (1998, 169, 173–84) indicates a continuation of these trends into the second Clinton term. Maltese (2003, 14–18) too argues that confronted with the barriers of reaching the public in the new media age, presidents have increased some types of public activities, such as travel around the nation, designed to attracted the attention of targeted constituencies. And organizationally, White House resources dedicated to interest group relations increased with the creation and enhancement of the Office of Public Liaison (see for instance Pika 1991, 1993).

From another perspective, Patterson (2002, 35–39) argues that since the late 1970s the political parties have become increasingly attuned to special interest groups and that the public increasingly came to feel that interest groups controlled the parties. "Dozens of small- and medium-sized policies, everything from school uniforms to prescription drugs for the elderly, were the currency of presidential politics," (Patterson 2002, 38), a description that sounds quite similar to what one would expect in the age of new media. Patterson, however, does not trace this change to the new media, instead linking it to the political mobilization of interest groups and to a postindustrial environment, which spurred such developments. Still, it is noteworthy that Patterson dates these developments just as the new media age was beginning to take hold. In all likelihood, several factors, perhaps including the rise of the new media, account for the growing sensitivity of the political system to interest groups.[26]

In a multivariate empirical assessment, Powell (1999) reports that the increase in cable penetration, which I have used as an indicator of the rise of the new media system, correlates positively to an increase in the yearly number of presidential speeches from 1960 through 1994, although cable penetration seems not to affect the number of non-DC speeches. Powell uses a relatively liberal definition of presidential speeches, which includes any spoken presidential statement of 150 words or more (156). Thus, his speech measure includes major speeches into the total, and therefore, does not test the current hypothesis, that the mix of presidential going public activities changed with the rise of the new media era. The next section presents such a test.

## Testing the New Media, Going Public Hypothesis

This revised going public perspective suggests that the rise of the new media age affected the mix of presidential going public activities, as well as the president's policy position location. Presidents in the new media age will be marginally more likely to target narrow constituencies as opposed to a national constituency than they were wont to do during the earlier broadcasting age. Presidents can target and mobilize narrow constituencies through several activities, including delivering minor speeches intended and crafted directly for narrow constituencies, as well as making appeals to narrow constituencies in their major speeches. By marginally shifting their going public style to one that emphasizes narrow to national constituencies, presidents will also become relatively more extreme in their expressed policy positions.

TEST 1: THE MIX OF PUBLIC ACTIVITIES

The first test looks at presidential public activities to compare the use of minor to major presidential public activities, with the assumption that minor activities are narrowly focused, while major activities are more nationally focused. Using Ragsdale's (1998, 169–84) data on presidential public activities, I create a ratio of major to minor presidential speeches with the formula: major discretionary speeches per year divided by the sum of the total presidential appearance and minor speeches per year from 1946 through 1997.[27]

Figure 9.1 displays the ratio of major to minor speeches. Clearly, major speeches comprise but a small fraction of minor speeches. Rarely do they amount to as much as 10 percent of the number of minor presidential speeches. The trend line shows a generally downward slope in this ratio across the entire period, but also a steep drop-off beginning in the mid 1970s. Across the entire period the ratio averages 3.7 percent. (To ease interpretation, the ratio is rescaled to 0–100 by multiplying the original variables by 100.) The average from 1946–75 equals 5.4 percent, but is only 1.3 percent for 1976–97. Removing

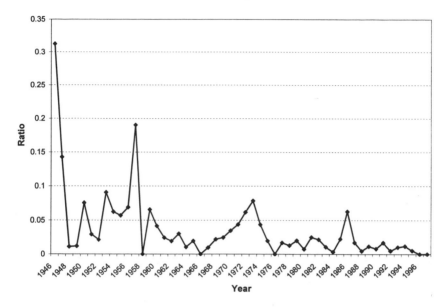

Figure 9.1  Ratio of major to minor presidential speeches, 1946–97. Source: Ragsdale (1998).

the years with pronounced spikes (1946, 1947, and 1957) reduces the 1946–75 average to 3.6 percent.

Our main hypothesis suggests that the rise of the new media system had something to do with this decline in major speeches relative to minor presidential speeches. To test this hypothesis, I again use the percentage of households that subscribe to cable television as the indicator of the new media age. To guard against spuriousness, the analysis also employs a number of control variables. These include the percentage of households with broadcast television; dummy variables for the first year of a presidential term, presidential reelection years, and lame duck years; and the percentage of people who do not mention either economic or foreign policy issues as the most important problem in the last poll reading before the president's State of the Union Address. Finally, because of the very high values for 1946, 1947, and 1957, I create a dummy variable coded "1" for those years, "0" otherwise to control for their outlier status.

The hypotheses for these control variables suggests that as television penetration grows, the mix of going public will lean in the "national" as opposed to the "narrow" direction, the opposite of the new media age. With the arrival of broadcast television, presidents possess access to a large audience for their major announcements. As such we should expect presidents marginally to increase their use of major speeches. During presidential first years, presidents should hypothetically emphasize national political issues over narrow ones, in

Table 9.1
Impact of new media context on ratio of major to minor presidential speeches, 1946–97

| | Model 1 | | Model 2 | | Model 3 | | Model 4 | | Model 5 | |
|---|---|---|---|---|---|---|---|---|---|---|
| | b | p* | b | p* | b | p* | b | p* | b | p* |
| Spike | 16.95 | .00 | 18.01 | .00 | 18.08 | .00 | 17.02 | .00 | 17.02 | .00 |
| First year | .04 | .49 | xxxx | | xxxx | | xxxx | | xxxx | |
| Reelection | −.67 | .28 | xxxx | | xxxx | | xxxx | | xxxx | |
| Lame duck | −.72 | .32 | xxxx | | xxxx | | xxxx | | xxxx | |
| Most important Problem | .02 | .25 | xxxx | | xxxx | | xxxx | | xxxx | |
| TV pct | −.02 | .18 | xxxx | | xxxx | | xxxx | | xxxx | |
| CATV pct | −.04 | .03 | −.04 | .01 | −.04 | .22 | .01 | .43 | .01 | .45 |
| Polarization | xxxx | | xxxx | | −2.23 | .88 | xxxx | | .07 | .50 |
| Time | xxxx | | xxxx | | xxxx | | −.09 | .10 | −.09 | .10 |
| Constant | 4.23 | .01 | 3.51 | .00 | 4.74 | .55 | 4.96 | .00 | 4.92 | .53 |
| $R^2$/adj. $R^2$ | .75 | .71 | .74 | .73 | .74 | .72 | .75 | .74 | .75 | .73 |
| N | 52 | | 52 | | 52 | | 52 | | 52 | |
| Q lag1 | .06 | .80 | .10 | .75 | .09 | .77 | .11 | .74 | .11 | .74 |
| Q lag 5 | 1.90 | .86 | 1.20 | .94 | 1.22 | .94 | 2.02 | .85 | 2.02 | .85 |
| Q lag 10 | 5.97 | .82 | 4.77 | .91 | 4.87 | .90 | 6.12 | .81 | 6.12 | .81 |

Source: See text for details.
* One-tailed tests of statistical significance.

part because they came into office on those issues. During lame duck years, feeling less pressure from interest groups and public opinion, presidents may feel freer to attend to the larger issues that affect society. Reelection years, however, may lead presidents in either direction, emphasizing national issues to reach the median voter, but perhaps emphasizing narrow issues to attract narrow constituencies into his reelection coalition.[28] Finally, presidents should be responsive to the public mood. When national concerns are important to a larger segment of the population, presidents will increasingly address those concerns and embark on a national going public strategy. In contrast, when national concerns, here the economy and foreign affairs, wane in importance, presidents shift their emphasis to narrow constituencies.

Table 9.1 presents OLS results of the impact of these variables on the ratio. The appendix to this chapter, which appears on the webpage for this book, presents details of the time series diagnostics of the ratio.[29] Only two of the variables in this full estimation reach statistical significance, the spike term and the cable penetrations variable. Results indicate 17 percent more major to minor speeches during the three spike years than the nonspike years. Turning to the key variable of interest, each 1-percentage-point increase in households with cable reduces the major to minor speech ratio by 0.04 percent. Comparing precable years to years of maximum penetration of cable (about 70 percent), produces a reduction in the ratio of 2.8 percent (70 * 0.04 = 2.8). Although this increment may appear modest, it is about one-half the standard deviation for the entire period (5.3), and slightly larger than the standard deviation of the series without the three spike years (2.3). This finding is consistent with our guiding hypothesis.

However, there are major caveats to this finding of cable's impact on the national/narrow mix in presidential speechmaking. During the time period under study other trends were also transpiring, such as the increase in political polarization or the decline in mass political participation. These trends may steer presidents away from major speeches and toward minor ones. For instance, the decline in mass political participation and engagement may heighten the barrier to the president's successful mobilization of the mass public. Plus, as participation declines, the impact of mass opinion relative to interest groups on Congress may also lessen.

Increasing party polarization may also incline a president toward a "narrow" going public strategy too, as presidents find it appealing to activate interest groups already aligned with their own party in Congress or even just their party base. Party polarization also may have altered the internal structure of Congress, centralizing power in the key party posts, such as the Speaker in the House and the majority and minority leaders in both chambers. During this recent period of party polarization in Congress, the parties in both chambers seemed to have built more elaborate governing structures. And congressional rank-and-file member support for the parties, such as on roll call votes, has risen as well. In such a system, a president's legislative strategy would emphasize working with his party in Congress. Broad-based appeals to the mass public, intended to exert pressure across a wide swath of the membership, will decline in effectiveness as members of Congress feel increasing pressures from their party leaders to conform to the party line. This is not meant to suggest that presidential appeals to the broad mass public always will be ineffective, just that they will be less effective and less often effective than if the parties were less polarized.

This presents alternative hypotheses to account for the decline in the ratio of major to minor speeches. One research strategy when presented with rival hypotheses is to enter indicators of each into a multivariate framework. Such an approach may not be possible here due to the high correlation between the cable television variable and measures of these other trends: cable measures correlates with a measure of party polarization in Congress at 0.93 (p = .000) and a simple time counter at 0.94 (p = .000), and party polarization and time correlate at 0.86 (p = .000).[30] With such high correlations, multicollinearity among these variables will be present, making it impossible statistically to disentangle the separate effects of each of these variables.

As expected, none of these three variables proves statistically significant when two or more are entered in the model. Table 9.1 provides several alternative specifications employing these variables. All suggest that same finding: when entered alone, the time counter, party polarization, and the cable measure are all statistically significant predictors with comparable summary statistics, such as the $R^2$. Plus, estimations that include two or all three of these variables produce an $R^2$ no better than using only one of them. This indicates no added explanatory power by adding one of these variables when one is already present.

Thus we cannot disentangle the effects of the new media, party polarization, or some other trend (denoted with the time counter) on the ratio of major to minor speeches. Chapter 4 noted the possible reinforcing effects of the new media age and party polarization on each other. Following that lead, I created an interaction variable by multiplying the cable and the party polarization variables. This interaction variable here failed to reach statistical significance in any estimation, either with the cable and party polarization variables as controls (the accepted method for detecting interaction effects) or without.

Hence we face ambiguous findings. The rise of the new media may affect presidential leadership strategies as the revised "going public" model indicates, but we cannot distinguish the effects of the new media on presidential behavior from that of the party context in Congress or other trends. The next section employs a second indicator of presidential behavior to test the revised "going public" hypothesis. But that indicator too has it problems.

TEST 2: THE MIX OF POLICY MENTIONS

The second test compares the number of narrow versus national policy appeals that presidents make in their State of the Union Addresses. The State of the Union Address is not ideally suited for our purposes for several reasons. First, the primary target audience is the entire mass public, not narrow constituencies, as is the case for minor speeches and most domestic public appearances. Second, the address is more an indicator of the president's agenda, the policies that he aims to work on, than an indicator of public activity toward groups. Plus, as an indicator of the agenda, factors other than those associated with the new media age context may influence presidential agenda choice, for instance, the ongoing needs of government.

Yet the mix of narrow and national policy appeals in the president's address should tap into the strategic considerations associated with the revised "going public" hypothesis. First, although the president certainly views the broad mass public as the primary target of the address, presidents craft their addresses with multiple targets in mind, including members of Congress and special or narrow constituencies (Cohen 1997, Light 1999). Thus the address presents an opportunity for presidents to mobilize these special publics. Second, although the address provides the most visible setting for presenting the president's agenda, the selection of which agenda items to pursue and to be mentioned in the address should reflect to some degree the strategic factors identified in the revised "going public" hypothesis, such as the relative ability to mobilize the

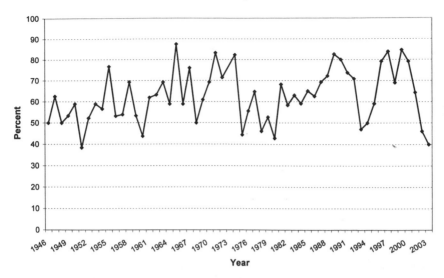

Figure 9.2 Percentage of "narrow" policy mentions in the State of the Union Address, 1946–2003. Source: Data obtained from Adam Lawrence. See Lawrence (2004) for details on the data. The plot is the percentage of policy mentions that do not refer to either economic or foreign policy in the president's State of the Union Address.

mass public and narrow constituencies. Third, inasmuch as the mass public tunes into the address, presidents may feel a pull to emphasize national as opposed to narrow policy appeals. In this sense, the address offers a hard test of the revised "going public" hypothesis, as national concerns may to some degree trump narrow concerns. But fourth, over the years the audience for the president's State of the Union Address has shrunk (e.g., Baum and Kernell 1999), which may offset the pull on the president to stress national versus narrow policies. Thus, even if the address pulls the president toward national over narrow concerns, over time, as the audience for the address has dwindled, the strength of that pull should also diminish.

Figure 9.2 plots "narrow" policies mentions as a percentage of all policy mentions in the president's State of the Union Address from 1946 through 2003.[31] National policy appeals are those that refer to economic and foreign policy. Narrow policies constitute the remainder. The plots suggest no trend with time; in fact, the percent of narrow mentions plummets after 2000.[32] This is in spite of 9/11 and the rise of terrorism and foreign policy on the nation's agenda.

Table 9.2 presents the regression results using the same variables as above, but with some minor modifications.[33] First, the spike variable is no longer employed. Second, experimentation found that percentage change in cable television had greater impact on the percentage of narrow policy appeals than the percentage of households with cable television (the levels form of the vari-

Table 9.2
Impact of new media on percentage of narrow policy mentions in the State of the Union Address, 1946–2003

| | Model 1 | | Model 2 | | Model 3 | | Model 4 | | Model 5 | | Model 6 | | Model 7 | |
|---|---|---|---|---|---|---|---|---|---|---|---|---|---|---|
| | b | p* | b | p* | b | p* | b | p* | b | p* | b | p* | b | p* |
| First year | 3.60 | .17 | 2.59 | .25 | 2.29 | .27 | xxxx | | xxxx | | xxxx | | xxxx | |
| Reelection | -2.63 | .28 | -3.52 | .21 | -2.94 | .25 | xxxx | | xxxx | | xxxx | | xxxx | |
| Lame duck | .82 | .45 | -.48 | .47 | -1.71 | .39 | xxxx | | xxxx | | xxxx | | xxxx | |
| Most important problem | .24 | .05 | .33 | .00 | .28 | .00 | .29 | .00 | .29 | .00 | .33 | .00 | .33 | .00 |
| TV pct | .12 | .03 | .05 | .23 | .25 | .05 | .18 | .04 | xxxx | | xxxx | | xxxx | |
| CATV pct-levels | -.04 | .31 | -.09 | .14 | .21 | .25 | xxxx | | xxxx | | xxxx | | xxxx | |
| CATV pct-changes | xxxx | | 2.97 | .02 | 3.56 | .01 | 3.93 | .00 | 2.87 | .01 | 3.06 | .00 | 3.41 | .01 |
| Polarization | xxxx | | xxxx | | 57.79 | .16 | 70.88 | .10 | xxxx | | -11.61 | .26 | xxxx | |
| Time | xxxx | | xxxx | | -1.02 | .07 | -.71 | .05 | xxxx | | xxxx | | -.09 | .21 |
| Constant | 44.33 | .00 | 44.65 | .00 | 16.13 | .30 | 8.22 | .38 | 48.33 | .00 | 54.13 | .00 | 49.03 | .00 |
| R²/adj. R² | .24 | .15 | .30 | .20 | .34 | .21 | .31 | .24 | .26 | .23 | .27 | .22 | .27 | .23 |
| N | 57 | | 56 | | 56 | | 56 | | 56 | | 56 | | 56 | |
| Q lag1 | .51 | .48 | .04 | .85 | .00 | .94 | .06 | .80 | .05 | .82 | .00 | .97 | .00 | .98 |
| Q lag 5 | 5.55 | .35 | 2.81 | .73 | 2.34 | .80 | 3.04 | .69 | 3.09 | .69 | 3.24 | .66 | 2.97 | .70 |
| Q lag 10 | 9.13 | .52 | 5.22 | .88 | 5.94 | .82 | 5.41 | .86 | 5.96 | .82 | 5.26 | .85 | 5.15 | .88 |

*Source:* Data obtained from Adam Lawrence. See Lawrence (2004) for details on the data.
* One-tailed tests of statistical significance.

able). The change in cable penetration has another nice property. It is not as strongly related to time as the levels form of the variable.[34]

Turning to the results, compare model 1 and model 2 on table 9.2. Model 1 includes the controls for first year, reelection year, lame duck year, the most important problem variable, the percentage of households with broadcast television, and the percentage of households with cable television. Model 2 contains each of those variables, but adds the percentage change in cable variable. The change in cable variable is highly significant (b = 2.97, p = 0.02). The addition of this variable boosts the $R^2$ from 0.24 for Model 1 to 0.30 for Model 2, a difference that an F test indicates is statistically significant. Adding the change in cable variable to the estimation increases the amount of variance that we can explain.

Model 2 on table 9.2 finds two significant variables, the most important problem and the percentage change in cable. None of the other variables is significant. The percentage of narrow mentions in the State of the Union Address appears responsive to public sentiment. As the public's agenda veers toward national concerns, so does the president's agenda in the State of the Union Address. Each 1 percent change from national to narrow concerns in the public's agenda moves the president's agenda in the same directions by about 0.33 percent.

Each 1 percent increase in households with cable alters the presidential ratio nearly 3 percent. Change in the percentage of households with cable varies from 0 to 4.6, with a mean change of 1.2 percent across the whole series and 1.7 percent once cable was introduced. A year of maximum change in cable penetration will increase the percentage of narrow appeals by nearly 14 percent. For years of average change in cable access the effect will be slightly higher than 3.5 percent (3 * 1.2). In the years since cable's introduction, the impact is on average 5 percent (3 * 1.7).

Again, these results may be threatened by the same trends identified above. To check on this possibility, model 3 adds both the time counter and the party polarization variable to those already used in model 2, a saturated model using all variables. These results indicate that public sentiment retains its influence and that the percentage of homes with broadcast television may also affect the president's agenda mix. The time counter falls just short of conventional levels of significance (p = 0.07), but the party polarization variable does not reach statistical significance.

Most critically, the change in cable variable maintains its statistical significance and even seems to slightly improve in impact. In this saturated model, each 1 percent change in cable leads to a corresponding 3.6 percent change in the president's agenda. Models 4 through 7 on table 9.2 present alternative combinations of the cable change variable, the time counter, and the party polarization variable, but without the statistically insignificant control variables. In all of these estimations, change in cable remains significant, with effects that vary from about 3 percent to 4 percent. Party polarization never attains statistical significance, while the time counter sometimes reaches significance levels. I also experimented with a change in party polarization variable. Never did that variable attain significance or wipe out the effects of the change in cable variable (results not shown). Despite these various estimations, change in cable television maintains its effects on the mix of narrow to national policy appeals in the president's State of the Union Address.

## Conclusions

This chapter focused on three implications of the new media age on the presidential news system—the impact of news on the mass public's evaluations of the president, the ability of the president to lead public opinion, and the affect of the new media age on presidential leadership style. A signaling theory of news was offered to account for the puzzle that motivated this study, the seeming lack of impact of news on presidential evaluations in the new media age compared to the age of broadcasting. Paralleling the declining impact of news on how people rate the president is the diminished presidential ability to lead the public in the new media age. Responding to this decline in their leadership fortunes, presidents have altered their public leadership style. Compared to the broadcasting age, presidents in the new media age increased the attention that they pay to narrow constituencies, while marginally decreasing the attention they would give to leading the broad mass public.

The next and final chapter of this book discusses the broader implications of this research—the implications of the new media age on the democratic linkage role of the news media and the quality of presidential leadership and democracy in this new media age.

# CHAPTER 10

# Conclusions

## The New Media, the Presidency, and American Politics

This study began with a puzzle: over the past several decades, news about the president has become increasingly negative and critical, yet news does not appear to affect public evaluations of the president as strongly as it did a generation ago. The example of Bill Clinton in 1998 illustrates this puzzle. In the face of a major public scandal that led to a congressional impeachment trial, events that produced reams of bad press for the president, Clinton's polls remained high and even marginally rose.

This study found the concept of the *presidential news system* useful in addressing this puzzle. The presidential news system is composed of the president, the news media, and the mass public and their interrelationships. Sometime in the late 1970s or early 1980s, this system underwent a transformation, evolving from the broadcasting age, or "golden age of television" of the 1950s through 1970s (Baum and Kernell 1999), into the age of new media of the late 1970s to the present.

Several important attributes distinguish the presidential news system of the broadcasting and new media ages. For instance, Davis and Owen (1998), Hamilton (2003), and Patterson (2000), among others, cite these changes: (1) increased competition among news organizations in the new media age; (2) greater economic pressures on news organizations; (3) the development of new communications media, like cable television and the internet; (4) the rise of soft news; and (5) the adaptation of older media into new form, such as talk radio. To understand the political implications of the evolution into the new media, however, requires looking beyond these factors, to changes in the relationships among the president, the public, and the mass media. For instance, two aspects of news reporting about the presidency also differentiate the broadcasting age from the new media age—the amount of presidential news has declined and presidential news is on average more critical of and negative toward the president than during the golden age. Moreover, the opinions and behavior of the mass public toward the news media have changed. The public consumes less news from the traditional news media than it once did, and public regard for the news media has deteriorated, although as Baum argues (2003a, 2003b), some people pick up news as a by-product of their consumption of entertainment and soft news programs.

In the new media age, to some degree, the mass public has splintered into special interest publics. One of those special publics is that group that Baum studies, those with low levels of interest in politics. Others with higher interest levels may gravitate to specialized broadcasts and media, such as PBS, the cable news networks, the internet, and talk radio, for news and political information. People can also now gravitate to ideologically compatible specialized media, where they receive what some may think is more propaganda than traditional, objective news and where their preexisting attitudes will be reinforced (Morris 2005). But many watch the major network evening news broadcasts, still the major news source for the largest number of Americans, although the size of this segment has fallen appreciably in recent decades. The expansion in media choice is one factor leading to the splintering of the mass public into specialized publics and the decline in size of the audience for hard news.

Not only have news consumption habits changed, but public attitudes toward the news media have also transformed. Once a highly regarded and trusted social institution, the news media is no longer viewed so positively by the public. The decline in trust in the media is in part a function of the general decline in trust in most major social and political institutions during the past thirty years or so. But changes in the news media have also affected media trust independent of the effect of this wider, secular change in trust. The decline in trust toward the news media appears steeper than for most other social and political institutions. Here evidence is circumstantial at best, but a case can be made that the retreat from hard news reporting and the rise of cynicism, criticism, negativity, scandal news, and the like have alienated the public from the news media to some degree (Patterson 2000). In other words, practices that characterize reporting in the age of new media have taken a toll on public regard for the news media.

Change within the presidential news system comes through two routes. First, exogenous factors may alter the behavior of any actor. Thus changes in federal regulations and the arrival of new technologies of communication, such as cable, affected the competitive position of news organizations. These factors had a hand in altering news reporting practices and styles, leading to the decline in presidential news at the same time that presidential news became increasingly negative and critical in tone. Similarly, secular changes in the mass public, the erosion of social capital, the decline in political and social participation, and the waning of institutional trust led to declines in public consumption of news and trust in the news media. The second route that produces change in the presidential news system occurs when change in one actor affects the behavior and attitudes of other actors. Thus the shrinkage in the audience for news redounded onto news organizations, affecting news reporting styles (Patterson 2000). Changes in news reporting styles also affected public consumption of and attitudes toward the news.

Presidents, the third actor in the system, also feel the effects of changes in the news media and the mass public. The diminished amount of presidential news, its critical tone, and the smaller audience for news all undermine the president's ability to lead the public. As a consequence, to some degree, presidents have turned away from the mass public and toward narrower, specialized publics as targets of their leadership efforts. In an age when the political parties are highly polarized, presidents target their party bases, perhaps the most important specialized public in the new media age. This presidential behavior, turning away from the broad mass public and toward special publics, reinforces the trend of splintering the public into select subsets. It may also buttress the political disengagement of the broad mass public from politics, as the public feels left out of political conversation. Furthermore, as presidents boost their relative attention to segments of the public, they take policy positions generally more in tune with those population segments, rather then with the mass public writ large. Thus public disengagement may grow even more, as many feel that the president is not attending to their needs and opinions.

The rise of the new media age has important implications for politics and the workings of the political system. Ironically, news has less impact on presidential evaluations that it once did. But the ability of the president to lead the mass public is also impaired, leading to changes in presidential leadership and governing styles. The next sections discuss the broader implications of the new media age on governance and democracy, starting with the democratic linkage role of the news media and then turning to the importance of presidential leadership for a modern society.

## The New Media Age and the Democratic Linkage Role of the News Media

To hold its political leaders accountable, the public needs information about the policies that officeholders implement, the consequences of those policies, and/or the behavior and performance of its leaders in office. An individual's personal experiences, as well as the experiences of people with whom an individual comes into contact, may provide a basis for evaluating governmental leaders. But personal experience provides people with only a narrow slice of relevant information about the activities and decisions of government policymakers and/or the consequences of those decisions. The news media are indispensable for learning about the fuller variety and range of leader activities and decisions, and the consequences of those decisions. As Brody (1991) wisely observes, most people vicariously participate in politics and government. The news media provides people not only with information, but a channel through which they can participate vicariously.

Not only do the news media increase the information available to individuals, but the news media may shift the evaluation standard that a person employs from egocentrism to sociotropism. Democratic theory variously views democracy from either a liberal, individualist or a communitarian perspective. The liberal, individualist perspective is consistent with the idea that individuals are egocentric and can judge their own best interests. News may provide individuals with information necessary to judge whether government officials have pursued and are pursuing the individual's best interests.

But news may also inform people about the implications of government leaders' decisions on the wider polity, the nation, and other people, both similar to and different from the individual watching the news. Through such information, a person may employ a sociotropic standard to evaluate its government leaders, in effect acting in accord with a communitarian perspective on democracy. We cannot resolve the debate between liberal, individualist democracy and communitarian democracy here: the point, however, is that news may help individuals apply either egocentric or sociotropic standards in evaluating their leaders.

Understanding the importance of information for democratic accountability, the founders granted constitutional protections to the press. They reasoned that a free press provided the greatest likelihood that the public would receive reliable information about government, and not merely propaganda in support of the government, which they thought would be more likely if the press was government owned or controlled.

The role of the news media as a democratic linkage institution resides in the character of the public and the quality of the information that the news media imparts to the public. The changes in the presidential news system in the age of new media documented in this book have compromised this linkage function of the news media. For example, the substitution of soft news for hard news and the decline of news reporting about the president raise the issue of whether the current news system produces enough news for the public.

Obviously, this is a thorny question without an easy or agreed on answer: How much hard news is enough? When relevant events occur, do they get reported? Is providing more hard news, as occurred during the golden age, necessarily better from a public accountability standard? Rather than trying to settle such questions, perhaps a more useful standard is one in which the amount of news is enough to signal to the public that it should take public affairs with some degree of seriousness. In developing the signaling theory of media effects, I remarked that declines in the quantity of hard news may signal to the public that government and public affairs are not as important to their lives as was once the case, that people can feel free to ignore what government does without consequence, because they feel that government only trivially touches or affects their lives. Although lacking data on the point, it may be the case that the decline of hard news and the rise of soft news, features, and "news that you can use" (Patterson 2000) has undermined this connection between the public and its government.

Perhaps as consequential for the linkage role of the news media is the tone with which it reports on affairs of state. Sycophantically cheerleading every governmental action is no better than cynically criticizing every action of government. Both paint a false picture of government and help instill either a naïve trust or cynical disdain for government and its leaders. Although objectivity in news reporting is impossible, the standards of the golden age of reporting had its benefits for a public bent on holding its leaders accountable.

During the golden age of broadcasting, the press generally viewed governmental leaders as deserving of respect, as long as events and the state of the nation warranted such respect. When events deteriorated, the press did not hesitate to inform the public of souring conditions. The sharp contrast between generally supportive news about government, which was the norm and was expected, with critical news, which was unexpected, meant that bad news caught the public's attention. In the current climate, when the public expects reporters to be cynical, bad news lacks the attention-focusing ability because it is so common. Ironically, in a climate in which bad, critical, and/or cynical news is the norm, politicians may be able to ride out any storms that blow their way, knowing that the public is not paying much attention to the bad news, and even if the public is attentive, it is heavily discounting the bad news. Thus the decline in hard news, the impact of that decline on the seriousness with which the public views government, and the negative tone of the news in the current age undermines the value of the news for holding political leaders accountable.

## Presidential Leadership and the Quality of American Democracy in the Age of New Media

At least since the presidency of Franklin Roosevelt, if not earlier, presidential leadership has been a vital element of the American political system. Usually when we think of presidential leadership, among the first thoughts that come to mind is presidential promotion of policies to deal with the nation's problems. Closely related are the ideas that presidents set the agenda for both Congress and the public and that presidential activity is required before the public and Congress will address pressing and important national problems and issues. Obviously, such a view is highly president-centric and is far from a realistic portrait of the workings of our political system, as Charles Jones (1994) reminds us. Congress can and does act on important issues, even when the president is not highly involved. Presidential involvement in the legislative policymaking process does not guarantee that Congress will enact the president's preferred policy solution. The president-centric version of American politics lacks veracity. But it is also clearly the case that during the past seventy-odd years presidents have taken a more active role in the policymaking process, often playing a leading role.

Presidential leadership has important consequences for the mass public, even if the president is unable to influence the public's preferences over policies, which according to Edwards (2003), is difficult for presidents to achieve.

Through presidential leadership, the public is brought into the political and policymaking process, which enhances the quality of citizenship. In this sense, the presidency has been an important democratizing agent for American politics. Changes in the presidential news system have degraded this aspect of the presidency to the detriment of our political system.

This perspective differs from those, such as Theodore Lowi (1985), who maintains that the presidency had become too democratic, personalistic, plebiscitary, or even demagogic in nature. Lowi's treatise is now two decades old and was written before the full force of the new media age became apparent. He writes more about the presidency of the golden age than the new media age. Still, Lowi is correct in reminding us that presidential leadership may not always benefit the political system. There can be too much presidential leadership, especially as it regards the mass public. The institution can become too personalized and the incumbent too dependent on public support.

In speaking of presidential leadership of the public, different scholars mean different things, in part because presidential public leadership is a complex and multifaceted phenomenon. Lowi, for instance, is concerned with presidents building support for themselves, an aspect that one finds also in Kernell's (1993) theory of going public. Such personalistic leadership may indeed corrode the political system, as it builds loyalties not for political structures or long-term interests, but for or against the person in office. In a unified executive some personalization of the office to the public is unavoidable. What matters is the degree of personalization. Lowi contends that this aspect of presidential public leadership had become dominant.

But presidential public leadership also has attributes that may be more beneficial for the political system. Through the president, the public engages in the political system and the policymaking process. The president may be the only actor in the political system capable of attracting or focusing public attention; the fact that the office is unitary also makes the presidency more intellectually accessible for the public.

George Washington understood this aspect of the presidency. Fearful that he was positioned to rouse public passions, but also understanding that part of the power of the presidency in government came from public support, Washington tried to steer the public to respect the institution. He did this through his actions in office, his public rectitude, and his restrained ambition. Andrew Jackson went one step further, pulling the public into the policy debate over the national bank. Jackson helped transform the public from passive spectators to voters who could affect the composition of government through their actions at the ballot box (Milkis and Nelson 1990, chaps. 3 and 5).

Presidential public leadership can affect democracy by enhancing public citizenship.[1] Through presidential public leadership, the public can be made an active participant in the political system. To be active citizens, the public must develop some knowledge of public affairs. That level need not be overly sophis-

ticated, but on major issues it should be discriminating enough to choose leaders. Presidential leadership can help politically educate the public in this way.
Presidential public leadership may also enhance democracy by giving voice to
the national interest, by helping the mass public express its concerns. Giving
voice to a national or public interest helps balance or counteract the voices of
special interest. Giving voice to a national interest also helps build a sense of
political community, again a counterweight to individualist impulses that so
often characterize American politics and culture. Looking at presidential public leadership from these other perspectives suggests its potential benefits for
democracy. This is not to suggest that presidents have provided such beneficial
leadership. Lowi would maintain that little such leadership has ever emanated
from modern presidents, as presidents followed a personalistic leadership style.

My point, however, is that in the age of new media, the presidency may not
be able to provide enough such leadership. Rather than being the voice of the
nation, presidents in the new media age appear more spokespeople for special
interests than they did in the golden age. The structure of the presidential
news system in the new media age in part accounts for this. When presidents
are less able to lead the public, they seek other ways to get Congress to act
favorably on their policies. With less opportunity or ability to lead the public
in the era of the new media, presidents instead seek the support of interest
groups, special publics, and their partisan base. In this process, the president
becomes less a spokesperson for the broad national interest and more a spokesperson of special interests. The public loses perhaps its most important ally or
voice in the political system as a result.

This marginal shift in presidential behavior, from the nation's leader to a
leader of interests or of a party, erects another barrier to public participation
in politics and may account in part for the public's increasing disengagement
from the political system in recent decades. As people disengage from politics
both psychologically and behaviorally, the quality of their citizenship erodes.
Disengagement also frays the linkages between the mass public and its political
leaders, and in the course, the fabric of democracy flags.

This is not meant to suggest that the rise of the new media age is the only
force acting on the president and pushing him in this direction. Party and
ideological polarization and changes in the nomination process, which have
made primaries, party activists, and campaign contributions increasingly important, have also pushed the president to seek support of narrower, as opposed
to broader, interests.[2] But factors associated with the new media age play their
part as well. Not only should we be wary of forces that produce an overly
democratic presidency, as Lowi warns, but we also need to be on the lookout
for factors that so weaken the public leadership side of the presidency, that
democracy itself is threatened.

# NOTES

1. Although much has been written about the Clinton scandals and impeachment by journalists and partisans, especially during the period of the events, a definitive history and analysis has yet to appear. Posner (1999) is useful from a legal perspective. Kaplan and Moran (2001) and Rozell and Wilcox (2000) provide academic perspectives on the effects of the scandal and impeachment. The studies in Denton and Holloway (2003) discuss the communications strategies that the Clinton administration used in responding to the many events and news stories on the scandal. A useful list of the dates of this and other major government scandals and corruption incidents can be found at http://users.commkey.net/fussichen/otdwgat.htm.

2. Lanoue and Emmert (1999), I. Morris (2001) and Rae and Campbell (2003) analyze why the Republicans in Congress continued with the impeachment in spite of the party's poor showing in the 1998 elections.

3. There were two votes. One was on the perjury charge, with the Senate voting not guilty by a 55 to 45 margin. On this vote ten Republicans voted not guilty. The second vote was on obstruction of justice, where the vote split 50–50 with five Republicans voting not guilty. Conviction requires a two-thirds vote.

4. For instance, the Center for Media and Public Affairs content analyzed network news during the scandal period. The center divided the scandal period into three phases. The first, from January 21 to April 30, 1998, spans the initial period of the scandal. During that phase Clinton received 44 percent negative news and 56 percent positive, according to the center, while Ken Starr received 26 percent positive and 74 percent negative. Phase 2 runs from July 27 through September, the period of the grand jury testimony. Clinton's news became increasingly negative, now with only 37 percent positive and 63 percent negative, but Ken Starr's press fell too, to 15 percent positive and 85 percent negative. Phase 3 is the congressional impeachment period, from November 19 through December 10. Clinton's news tone stabilized, with 33 percent positive and 67 percent negative, while Starr's rose to 31 percent positive and 69 percent positive. See the Center for Media and Public Affairs (2004, 5–6).

5. Literally hundreds of books have been written about Watergate. Genovese (1999) provides a useful, tempered academic perspective, while Lang and Lang (1983) focus on the roll of polls, public opinion, and news in their seminal study.

6. See figure 1.3 below. These data are also reported in Ragsdale (1997) and Cook and Ragsdale (1998).

7. But while the economy seemed on the upswing in 1998, which helped Clinton's polls according to Newman (2002), the economy was deteriorating in 1974 and 1975. Still, Newman (801) estimates that Watergate depressed Nixon's polls by over 16 percent even when controlling for the state of the economy and other factors. This is about 2.25 times as large of an impact on Nixon as the largest impact that Newman could find for the Lewinsky scandal on Clinton.

8. Like Watergate, hundreds of accounts of Iran-Contra have been written. A useful account includes Busby (1999).

9. However, Smyth and Taylor (2003) argue that most studies overstate the impact of Lewinsky and Watergate and understate the impact of economics on presidential approval. Their analysis finds no impact of the Lewinsky scandal on Clinton's polls once both inflation and unemployment are taken into account. They also find that Watergate only depressed Nixon's polls by 10 points. Notice that the 10-point difference in impact between Lewinsky and Watergate is the same difference that Newman estimates, even though Newman's analysis points to each scandal having a somewhat larger effect than Smyth and Taylor.

10. A large number of other studies exist beyond those discussed below, see Bennett (2002c), Denton and Holloway (2003), Heith (2000), Joslyn (2003), Kiousis (2003), Lawrence and Bennett (2001), Lind and Rarick (1999), Rozell and Wilcox (2000), Shah et al. (2002), and Yioutas and Segvic (2003). General analyses can be found in Pious (1999/2000) and Renshon (2002a, 2002b).

11. Pfiffner (2004, especially 119–39) is one important exception. Pfiffner, however, does not directly discuss these scandals in light of the public's reaction, focusing his attention on developing a standard by which to judge presidential character.

12. This is Lyn Ragsdale's data mentioned above.

13. More formally, Y (Approval) = 63.7 (4.0) − .40 (0.16) Negative News, $R^2$ = 0.13 F = 6.36 Prob. of F = 0.015 n = 44. Inspection of both series finds them to be stationary, thus we can proceed with linear regression. The Dickey-Fuller test statistics for the approval series is −3.64 and for the news tone series is −3.10. The critical value for the Dickey-Fuller test is −2.95.

14. I use Jimmy Carter as the cut point here. I tried various other cut points, and they all reveal the same relationship as reported in the text. The value of using 1976–77 as the cut point is that it allows a reasonable number of cases for statistical analysis in the second series, an important consideration given the small n for the entire series.

15. $R^2$= 0.08, equation F = 1.22, probability of F = 0.28.

16. Importantly, I have not controlled for other factors that we know affect presidential approval, like the state of the economy. But if we view news as a summary of events and conditions, then much of the impact of the economy may be represented in the news tone variable. Several studies find that economic news affects presidential approval (Erikson, MacKuen, and Stimson 2002; Nadeau et al. 1999; De Boef and Kellstedt 2004).

17. Bennett (2002c) argues that one reason that the Lewinsky scandal had so little effect on Clinton's polls was that few people paid much attention to the news about the scandal.

18. In contrast the audience for cable network news is minuscule and newspaper readership has also declined. For a variety of data on trends in news consumption based on ratings, see the web site, journalism.org, especially their annual reports, the "State of the News Media." A useful review of the decline in news consumption can be found in Wattenberg 2004.

19. This is Baum and Kernell's (1999) colorful term. Also see Rosen and Taylor (1992).

20. I use the term *new media era* differently from Davis and Owen (1998), who also speak of the new media. My use of the terms *new media era* or *age of new media* refers

to a property of the political system, one that relates to the structure of the news media and the relationship of that structure to political leaders and the mass public. Davis and Owen, instead, use the term *new media* to refer to types of media. To them, the new media are "mass communications forms with primarily nonpolitical origins that have acquired a political role" (7). To Davis and Owen, entertainment and economic values supersede public interest values in the new media, and the new media become political only when it pays to do so (7). Examples of new media to Davis and Owen include talk radio, television talk shows, television newsmagazines, tabloids (both print and broadcast), the internet, etc. (see 9–17).

My categorization also differs from West's (2001). West contends that there are two periods or news media eras since the golden age (or what he labels, the era of objective media)—an era of interpretive news and an era of fragmented news. He does not date when the fragmented news era begins, but implies that it appeared in strong force in the 1990s, with the flourishing of cable news networks, but more importantly because of the rise of alternative news media, such as the internet. I do not make such a firm distinction between the interpretive and fragmented news eras in this analysis. My "era of new media" sees strong continuities between the two, especially in how they differ from the golden age.

21. Not everyone agrees that Fox Cable News is always conservative, politically tilted, or biased. While its evening commentary programs may lean in that direction, several media critics find its straight news reporting to be relatively balanced. Thus says Neil Hickey (1998) in the *Columbia Journalism Review*: "A close monitoring of the channel over several weeks indicates that the news segments tend to be straightforward, with little hint of political subtext except for stories the news editors feel the 'mainstream' press has either downplayed or ignored." Howard Kurtz (2001), the media reporter for the *Washington Post* more recently made this judgment about Fox Cable News: Fox's "chat consistently tilts to the conservative side [and] may cast an unwarranted cloud on the news reporting, which tends to be straightforward." These assessments are based upon impressionistic evidence.

Journalism.org, the web site of the Project for Excellence in Journalism and which is funded by the Pew Charitable Trusts and affiliated with the Columbia Graduate School of Journalism, has been issuing annual reviews of the news media for the past several years. The project conducted a relatively extensive content analysis of news on the cable networks in 2004 with the following description of their sampling methods: "We . . . studied five sample days of each of the three cable news networks for sixteen hours each day, or 240 hours of programming. That provided us with a sense of the types of stories and the level of repetitiveness that appeared over the course of a cable news day. In addition . . . we selected three different types of programs from each of the three channels to study for twenty days to see how their choice and treatment of topics compared with other media studied the same days. The programs studied included one prime-time talk show, one daytime news show and the closest each news channel comes to producing a traditional evening newscast. That added up to 180 more hours of programming involving another 4,551 stories." Based on their content analysis, the project did detect some differences in news reporting among Fox, CNN, and MSNBC. While disclaiming that their study attempted to look at bias in the news, the project found that "Fox was measurably more one-sided than the other networks, and Fox journalists were more opinionated on the air. The news channel was also decidedly more positive in its coverage of the war in Iraq, while the others were largely neutral. At the same time, the story segments on the Fox programs studied did have more sources and shared more about them with audiences." As to reporting on the 2004 election, however, "the majority of stories on every network had no overwhelming tone. Here MSNBC stood out as being twice as likely to air candidate and issue stories with a positive tone as with a negative tone. CNN's coverage, on the other hand, was more likely to be negative. Fox was divided equally among positive and negative stories." For details see the project's web site, http://www.stateofthemedia.org/2005/index.asp.

NOTES TO CHAPTER 2

1. My notion of a presidential news system is neither entirely unique nor original. Leighley (2004, 8–9) employs a similar concept, and Zaller (1999) throughout discusses the interactions of politicians, journalists, and citizens. Moreover, Cook's (1998; also Cook and Ragsdale 1998) idea of governing with the news and Sparrow's (1999) idea of the news media as a political institution is closely related to the notion of a presidential news system, as is Grossman and Kumar's (1981) notion of transactions between the president and the press.

2. Presidents possess other uses for the news media. Through news, presidents can communicate efficiently to members of their administration, the bureaucracy, presidential allies, among others about such matters as presidential priorities, shifts in policy directions, etc. Such news coverage may be more effective in reaching these targets than other devices such as interoffice memos and official documents.

3. Graber (2001, 106–9) also cites four other characteristics that affect the selection of news stories. Like Groeling and Lichter (2004), she cites novelty and drama (or conflict), as well as proximity and stories likely to have strong impact on readers (viewers), which is similar to importance. Proximity, which refers to the geographic distance of the event to the reader or viewer's location, is of less relevance to presidential news, although many local news organizations will often try to find the local relevance or angle in a story about the president, and presidential travel to a locality will tend to generate generous amounts of local news coverage because it allows the local angle to be highlighted.

4. As Delli Carpini and Keeter point out, "The governor of one's own state was the only elected official other than the president and vice president whom 75 percent or more of constituents could name (1996, 74).

5. Presidents may also generate some bargaining leverage with journalists if they "negotiate the definition of news" (Cook and Ragsdale 1998) when they provide journalists with these services. Inasmuch as presidents make journalists dependent on the White House provision of news, presidents may be able to marginally affect the content of the news with the implied threat that the supply of news may dry up if journalists report stories not to the president's liking.

6. This is somewhat ironic given the volume of presidential news (see chapter 3). Barrett's findings raise the question of the content of presidential news stories.

7. The Pew News Interest Index is based on multiple surveys of the mass public conducted by the Pew Center for People and the Press (originally called the Times Mirror Center). In surveys dating since 1986, the public was asked how closely they

followed particular news stories. The King et al. research analyses responses to 413 news stories from 1986 through 1994. However, in an analysis of local television news that uses Nielsen rating, Just and Belt (2004) find higher ratings for stories that employ traditional news techniques, as opposed to tabloid styles, and for stories of important substantive content and issues.

8. Another important factor leading to relatively uniform news content was that journalists shared a common understanding of the nature of their profession, which led to them define newsworthiness in similar ways.

9. For instance, facing increased competitive pressures, many local broadcasters began to utilize market research in deciding what to air on their news broadcasts. In other words, consumer tastes entered formally into the decision about what was newsworthy. Inasmuch as consumers professed a preference for softer news over hard news, news organizations that relied on market research would likely replace some increment of hard news with softer news (see McManus 1994 and Underwood 1998 for more on this as it applies to local news providers).

10. I am not suggesting that regional newspapers offered as much hard and national news as television network broadcasts or national newspapers and magazines, like the *New York Times* or *Newsweek*, but that in the golden era the level of hard news reporting in regional newspapers was higher than it is now.

11. Pearson's r = 0.87, p = .000.

12. On other issues with the Vanderbilt Archives see Althaus et al. (2002).

13. The archives began in their operations in August 1968. Thus, 1969 is the first full year of operations.

14. The Pearson correlations across the three networks range from 0.88 to 0.93, all of which are significant at the 0.001 level or better.

15. The first journalistic use of the term that I can find is by *New York Times* columnist Tom Wicker in 1966.

16. Also see figure 1.5, which plots these data by year.

17. For instance, news coverage of the war in Iraq.

18. Baum and Kernell (1999) report similar ratings for major presidential addresses from the late 1960s to mid 1970s. Also see figure 7.1 below, which presents data that Nielsen Media Research provided to me on the ratings of the three networks from 1970 through 2004.

19. It is quite likely that presidential campaigns will stimulate interest in political news. Thus these figures may overstate the amount of news consumption compared to noncampaign periods. But still these types of data should tell us much about comparative use of television and newspapers as well as much about trends in their use over time.

20. We need to take these numbers with caution. People seem to inflate their news exposure, as they overreport turnout. Given that surveys indicate that some people consider programs like *Entertainment Tonight* and reality crime shows like *Cops* to be news, people may overstate their news consumption when all that they have done is watch an entertainment program. Similarly, newspaper reading may be inflated as sports readers glance at the news headlines about the campaign. Still, despite these sources of measurement error, assuming that such problems are relatively constant across years, we can track some trends. But it is quite likely that these numbers understate those who are

inattentive to either medium. Other data suggests that the percentage of the population that is inattentive to all forms of hard news has increased (Patterson 2000).

21. These are from polls taken in May 1972, April 1974, and June 1976. The text of the question reads: "How much trust and confidence do you have in the mass media—such as the newspapers, TV (television) and radio in general—when it comes to reporting the news fully, accurately, and fairly: A great deal, a fair amount, not very much, or none at all?"

22. There are many histories of the news media and the new media. Starr (2004) is just the most recent relevant study to this discussion. I also found Cable Center website, http://www.cablecenter.org, useful for facts and dates. The Cable Center is an independent nonprofit education organization formed to serve the public's interest in telecommunications.

23. Data on the audiences, profits, and costs of the three cable networks come from the Project for Excellence in Journalism, Annual Report on Journalism, from its website, journalism.org.

24. Chadwick (2006) provides the most comprehensible overview of the now extensive research on the intersection of the internet and politics. Although Chadwick spends considerable time discussing government and the internet, his review focuses mostly on the development of government web pages as they relate to the topic of e-government (177–203).

25. The PUST surveys were accessed from the Roper Center survey archive at the University of Connecticut, at their website, http://www.ropercenter.uconn.edu. We also need to be somewhat careful in using reports of computer and internet use from surveys. Tewksbury (2003) finds that survey respondents overreport their use of the internet for news.

26. The Pew data were downloaded from their "Usage over Time" spreadsheet, which compiles data from Pew surveys dating from March 2000 at http://www.pewinternet.org/trends.asp#adoption.

27. See the Pew "Usage over Time" spreadsheet noted above.

NOTES TO CHAPTER 3

1. See related market models for news, especially Hamilton (2003).

2. Media content is often characterized as being informative (news) or entertaining. Here nonpresidential news content may be either news that is not concerned with the president as well as entertainment. This simplification is useful for isolating the factors that affect the production of presidential news.

3. However, local and smaller news organizations have access to presidential news through the wire services such as the Associated Press, and news syndicates. Thus they also provide their readers with some presidential news. The marginal cost of adding a presidential news story to these news outfits might be small given that their subscription to these news services is a fixed cost to them. Importantly, these news organizations rarely produce presidential news in the sense of initiating the reporting on a story.

4. Shaw and Sparrow (1999) argue that political coverage in local or regional newspapers often differs from that of the major national media.

5. AP was established in 1848–49. By 1880, about 52 percent of morning and 24 percent of evening newspapers used some news from wire services (West 2001, 27).

6. On October 25, 1896, Ochs's slogan, "All the News That's Fit to Print," began appearing on the editorial page, moving to page 1 on February 10, 1897 (Source: http://www.nytco.com/company-timeline-1881.html).

7. *Time* magazine began publication on March 3, 1923, and NBC, the first radio network, began broadcasting nationally in November 1926.

8. Monitoring of other news organizations also served as a way of overseeing reporters and helped insure that reporters are not shirking on the job.

9. Although no one claims that Coolidge was as effective on radio as FDR, Coolidge appears to have employed the new device to some effect. Few of Coolidge's radio addresses focused on public policy issues and rarely did he use them to rally the public to pressure Congress. Coolidge's clerkship view of the office inhibited vigorous policy and legislative leadership. Yet Coolidge addressed the public on radio nearly every month, as well as gave regular press conferences, understanding the importance of indirect communication to the public for building his image. Rather than use the medium to drum up support for his policies, he used radio to personalize himself to the public, part of a larger image building campaign that included donning all manner of hats and costumes as he sought the Republican presidential nomination and election in 1924 (Cornwell 1966, 89–94; Ponder 1998, 119–24). In this regard, Coolidge appears quite successful. Noted for his lackluster traditional campaigning, through radio Coolidge became something of a public personality. He handily won the Republican nomination, beating back Hoover, and also won the 1924 election, which some observers trace in part to his skillful use of radio in transforming himself into something with "tangible meaning for millions," (Cornwell 1966, 92). Thus even before FDR's fabled fireside chats, we have evidence that radio helped personalize the president to the public (Ponder 1998, 109–26).

10. Patterson (2000) also argues that the rise of soft news in the traditional media repelled news viewers who wanted hard news. Presumably they could satisfy their news demand from other sources, like the 24/7 cable news networks and internet news sites.

11. In an intriguing analysis of public interest in different types of news stories, King et al. (1999) analyze the correlates of public interest from the Pew News Interest Index. Since the mid 1980s, the Pew Center for the People and the Press (formerly the Times Mirror Center) asked survey respondents how much they pay attention to selected news stories. King et al. analyze the aggregated interest ratings for the 413 stories for which Pew queried respondents from 1986 through 1994, but detected no significant effect on interest whether a story concerned government or not. In contrast, stories that covered personal pocketbook issues, natural disasters, and human interest stories did spark public interest. The public also expressed less interest in news stories about foreign nations.

12. For more details of the Project study see http://www.journalism.org/resources/research/reports/definitions/subjects.asp.

13. The n of stories ranges from 119 to 738 per year, with an average of 280.6 and a standard deviation of 186.2 stories per year.

14. Regressing the percentage of government news on a time counter (e. g., 1980 = 1, 1981 = 2, etc.) suggests that for each year there is a 0.9 percent decline in the percentage of news about government. Across the 19-year period, this amounts to an overall decline of about 17 percent, and this simple linear trend accounts for 48 percent of the variance in government news.

15. The two correlate at 0.86, p = .000.

16. A linear regression of the series on the time counter finds a 0.75 percent decrease in policy news for each successive year. Across the 19-year time span, this amounts to an overall decline of about 14 percent. Moreover, the linear regression accounts for a substantial amount of the variance in policy news ($R^2 = 0.41$).

17. A linear regression suggests that with each passing year, the amount of presidential news declines by about 0.34 percent. Over the 19-year period, this accumulates into an aggregate decline of about 6.5 percent.

18. Also, the first data point, 1980, Carter's last year in office, is one of the lower readings at 15 percent. If we remove that data point and regress the remaining 18 data points on the year counter, we now find that each additional year leads to a loss of 0.47 percent. Plus the $R^2$ increase from 0.17 to 0.29. There appears to be no uptick with George H. W. Bush's first year in office, 1989, perhaps because of his service as Reagan's vice president. Also, unlike Reagan and Clinton, Bush did not push a new agenda.

19. Patterson (2000, 2) explicitly recognizes the impact of cable television and the internet: "In response to the intensely competitive environment created by cable news and entertainment, news outlets have softened their coverage. Their news has also become increasingly critical in tone." But Patterson's focus is on the impact of news content on news audiences, rather than the causes of change in news content.

20. These data were downloaded from their website: http://www.policyagendas.org/

21. Linear time trend lines are also superimposed on figure 2.1. Although the Policy trend line suggests a slight decline over time (b = −0.14), the president trend line is flat (b = 0.05) and a paltry amount of the variance in presidential news is accounted for by time ($R^2 = 0.05$).

22. Smoller (1986; 1990) and Slattery et al. (2001) discuss presidential news on the evening network broadcasts up through the mid 1980s.

23. On other issues with the Vanderbilt Archives see Althaus et al. (2002). See Althaus et al. (2001) for a general discussion of issues in content analysis of electronically retrieved texts.

24. This is accomplished by regressing the number of presidential news stories per six months on a time counter.

25. The result is statistically significant (t = 2.88, p = 0.006). However, the $R^2$ drops from 0.25 to 0.16.


NOTES TO CHAPTER 4

1. Admittedly, the several national news organizations will produce a different level of presidential news at any time point. But they will respond similarly to systemic factors that affect news production. Thus their trends over time will be relatively similar even if their absolute levels of presidential news coverage differ. In other words, the fraction of network television news devoted to the president will likely be higher than for a major national newspaper like the *Times* at any one time point. But over time, the ebbs and flows of presidential news across the television network news and the *Times* are likely to be quite similar because they respond to many of the same systemic forces and adhere to the same definition of newsworthiness. Last, while this argument is pertinent for the modern era, scholars contend that great variability in news content exists across

newspapers in earlier times (e.g., Schudson 1978). Yet Cornwell justifies using the *Times* even in earlier periods, finding "a very close parallelism" (1959, 281) in presidential news coverage between the *Times* and the *Providence Journal*, although the level of presidential news tends to be higher for the *Times* than the *Journal*.

2. See Shaw and Sparrow (1999) on the differences in the political coverage of local and regional newspapers from the major national media. Thus it is important to distinguish between the national and local press, but they do find a broad similarity in political coverage of the national news media. But in a recent and thorough review of the literature on the mass media, Comstock and Scharrer (2005) suggest there is considerable competition across news media forms. They especially point to competition across newspapers. Newspaper competition with other newspapers has declined because of the consolidation of newspapers; now most localities possess only one major newspaper. Economic and technological factors, as well as mass behavior, have intensified the competition among news outlets across media forms. Newspapers "face a situation in which readership is declining" and feel fierce competition "from television, national newspapers, and the Internet" (87). This competition, they argue, should lead to both convergence in news coverage and to strategies among news providers to differentiate their news product from their competitors (88). Comstock and Scharrer also argue that local and regional media emulate the national news coverage of the national and elite press (180).

3. And even if we wanted to trace levels of presidential news on television, the primary source of news for the largest segment of the public, we would be stymied by the fact that the Vanderbilt Television Archives only began collecting such data in 1968, nearly two decades after television began broadcasting. Thus we are forced to rely on printed sources to recover levels of presidential news over a long time frame. The *New York Times* serves this purpose better than any other newspaper.

4. On the quality of different databases, see Althaus et al., 2001.

5. The ProQuest system retains facsimile copies of every page of the *New York Times*. This completeness overcomes many of the issues that Althaus et al. (2001) identify in using electronic databases, such as Lexis-Nexis, whose content may differ from the actual newspapers, or in using abstracts, which may vary over time. Subsequently ProQuest has made similar databases available for the *Wall Street Journal*, the *Chicago Tribune*, and the *Los Angeles Times*. Unfortunately, subscriptions to these other newspapers databases are quite expensive and few universities currently subscribe. Thus I was unable to create comparable series for these other newspapers. An interesting future research project would be to compare historical trends in news coverage across these newspapers.

6. Searching headlines or lead paragraphs would miss many stories in which the president was a prominent actor.

7. Part of the Reagan treatment involved an "issue or message of the day." Covington et al. (1993) find some success of this media management strategy by Reagan during the 1980 presidential election campaign.

8. Using this dummy variable increases the model fit by improving the equation $R^2$, but has little impact on the other variables in the analysis. Thus it matters little substantively whether the spike dummies are included in the statistical model or not.

9. Even though such words might appear multiple times within each item, the search will count each item only once.

10. The number of presidential news stories and the count of total items correlates at −0.38, p < .000.

11. They correlate at 0.93, p < .00.

12. The specific correlations between the *New York Times* series for these years and the other series are: Big Three Index r = 0.59, p < .000; ABC r = 0.59, p < .000; CBS r = 0.49, p < .000; NBC r = 0.63, p < .000.

13. Although from its inception in 1851, the *New York Times* had embarked on a news style that emphasized objectivity and restraint in reporting compared to the other mass circulation newspapers in New York at the time, by the 1890s, the *Times* had fallen on hard times, with the smallest circulation of the eight major dailies in New York. Ochs revitalized the newspaper, cutting its price from three cents to one and proclaiming on its front page that it would print "All the News that's Fit to Print," an obvious jibe at its yellow journalist competitors, but also a sign of its ambitions. As a result, its circulation grew in short order from about 25,000 in the mid 1890s to 100,000 by the early 1900s. It is during this period that the *Times* was turned around and emerged as the leading newspaper in the United States. On the history of the *New York Times*, see Diamond (1994) and Tifft (1999).

14. Theodore Roosevelt took the first presidential trip outside of the United States as president in 1906 to Panama. The State Department list of presidential travel abroad can be obtained from http://www.state.gov/r/pa/ho/trvl/pres/.

15. Appendix 4B on the webpage details the construction of the presidential public activity index and details.

16. In other words, this is a threshold model in which a threshold must be reached before a variable is expected to have effects. For a good discussion of threshold models and when they may be appropriate, see Pierson (2004, 83–86).

17. The first radio broadcast was in 1922. In 1926 only 17 percent of households owned radios, which grew to 24 percent by 1927 and 33 percent by 1928. CBS was organized shortly after NBC, in 1927. Cable was available as early as 1965. By 1980, however, only about 20 percent of households had cable, which grew to 25 percent by 1981 and to almost 30 percent by 1982. In 1950, 9 percent of households owned televisions, which grew to 20 percent by 1951, a much faster adoption rate than either radio or cable.

18. In statistical terms, we will control for these other factors to guard against spuriousness.

19. From the *Historical Statistics of the United States* and OMB's webpage, http://www.whitehouse.gov/omb/budget/fy2004/, in particular, table 1 1—Summary of Receipts, Outlays, and Surpluses or Deficits (-): 1789–2008, to locate the government expenditure data.

20. Unemployment data are not available that far back in time, although historically unemployment often covaries strongly with economic growth.

21. The spikes in the amount of presidential news for these years present statistical estimation issues, which we can think of as outliers. Outliers may become especially important data points. One method of dealing with outliers is to drop them from the analysis, arguing that they are not of the same class of observations as the other cases. Dropping cases from time series disrupts the time series and makes it difficult to perform some statistical operations, like diagnosing nonstationarity issues. Thus I employ the spike variable to keep these cases in the analysis and to guard against the potentially

large impact that the presence of these spikes might have on the analysis. Although not shown, use of the spike variable in the analysis has no impact on the statistical performance of the substantive variables of interest here. All that the spike variable does is increase the overall model fit of the estimation, the $R^2$.

22. Also, diagnostics revealed that the presidential news variable has an AR(2) structure, that is, values of presidential news at one and two lags affect current values of presidential news. This confirms the hypothesis of organizational routine effects on presidential news coverage. That the effects are temporary, as the AR(2) structure implies, also attests to the ability of news organizations to respond to their news environment. See details in appendix 4E on the webpage.

23. A technical discussion of time series analysis is presented in appendix 4E on the webpage.

24. Alternative specifications of these insignificant variables produced similarly insignificant results. For instance, it may be the case that wars vary in their impact on presidential news, with some wars having stronger effects on presidential news coverage than others, perhaps a function of greater or lesser presidential involvement and the geographic distance of the war from the United States. To test this hypothesis I created dummy variables for each war. Results indicated that none of the individual war dummies significantly affected presidential news across this 1897–1998 time span.

Also, the analysis experimented with multiple versions of the television and radio variables. Only when the time counter was removed did the radio variables expressed in levels (e.g., the percentage of households with radio) have a significant impact. These radio penetration variables however are highly correlated with the time counter (r = 0.90), making it impossible to separate their individual effects. Moreover, the time counter seems the more predictive and stronger variable than any versions of the radio variable. In no case did any version of the television variables display any significant impact on presidential news.

25. We can estimate how long these lagged effects persist with the formula: T(time units) = 1 / ( 1 − b(lag)) = n years. Substituting 0.55 for b(lag1) into the equation produces 2.22 years, and substituting 0.22 for b(lag 2) produces 1.28. In other words, lag one effects persist for slightly more than two years, while lag two effects last for little more than one year.

26. Again, we can estimate how long these lagged effects last. The one year lag effects last for about one and one-half years (1 / 1 − 0.37 = 1.58), while the two year lag effects last for about one and one-third years ( 1 / 1 − 0.75 = 1.33).

NOTES TO CHAPTER 5

1. We must keep in mind, though, that the decline looks pronounced only when comparing news coverage of the last several decades with news coverage at the height of the broadcasting era. When compared to earlier eras, presidential news coverage during the new media age looks healthy, comparable to levels of the mid twentieth century and much higher than earlier time periods.

2. "The First 100 Days: How Bush Versus Clinton Faired in the Press." Available at http://www.journalism.org/resources/research/reports/100days/default.asp

3. See the Center for Media and Public Affairs, Media Monitor, July–August 2004, 3, downloaded from http://www.cmpa.com/Mediamon/documents/julaug04.pdf. Also see Farnsworth and Lichter (2003) who present a somewhat more detailed analysis of the center's data, but only for presidents Reagan, Clinton, and G. W. Bush.

4. In a personal communication (December 4, 2001), Professor Ragsdale explained the data collection procedures and coding rules to me: The data are "based on the number of presidential stories recorded in the *New York Times* as taken from the indexes and then a search of the stories to determine if they were positive, negative, or neutral. I initially used the Grossman/Kumar data as the base, but actually rechecked and revised it. Positive stories included those stories in which there was a report of the White House position on a story without examining other positions critical of the White House; a presidential success on Capitol Hill (passage of presidential legislation, upholding of veto, or approval of nominees); accomplishments in international affairs; accomplishments in domestic politics, including dealings with governors; and increase in presidential approval; and happy family stories. Negative stories were those which featured critics of the White House; concentrated on internal divisiveness in the WH; discussed a failed decision or failure of the president to get what he wanted from Capitol Hill, a head of state, other national, state, local politician; a decline in popularity; a confrontation with the press itself; stories about errant family members or president's own problems."

5. A regression of negative news on a time counter (1949 = 1) is strongly statistically significant, and suggests that each year that the series progresses the president will receive about a half a percentage point more negative news. The regression equation (standard errors in parentheses) is y = 10.10 (2.93) Constant + 0.54 (.11) Counter; $R^2$ = 0.35. A similar regression for positive news finds a near mirror result. Each additional year subtracts about 0.4 percentage points of positive news. The resulting equation is y = 50.41 (2.83) Constant − 0.39 (.11) Counter; $R^2$ = 0.23.

6. One irony is that as the amount of presidential news declined, even if the news on the president turned increasingly negative, typical news readers and viewers might not encounter an absolute increase in the number of negative news stories. This raises the obvious question of whether it is the tonality mix of news stories or the absolute number of negative news stories that affect public evaluations of the president. I attempted to test this with the Ragsdale data but the correlation between the number of negative news stories and the percentage of negative stories is 0.97 (p = .00), making such an analysis impossible.

7. Reiter and Stam (2002) report that public support for war declines as war prolongs.

8. There are several limitations to the analysis that should be noted. First, annual dummies to account for war obviously induce a degree of measurement error. What should one do if the war took place during only part of a year or in the case of the Gulf War, if it did not last for very long, only a few months? Ideally, we want data in more refined time units, such as months. But Professor Ragsdale was only able to provide me with annual data on the tone of presidential news in the *New York Times*, which limits the analysis to annual time units. Further, using annual unit provides us with only 44 cases for analysis, but in some estimates, there are as many as 12 independent variables. We must be cautious in interpreting the results of this analysis due to these analytic constraints.

9. I also experimented with economic perceptions data, in particular the Consumer Sentiment and Consumer Expectations series from the Survey of Consumers of the University of Michigan. The consumer sentiment series, however, only begins in 1951, while the expectations series begins the next year, 1952. This represents a significant loss of cases, considering that we only have 44 for the negative news series to begin with. Analysis with the economic perceptions variables found that they had no impact on negative news. Thus, they are dropped from further discussion.

10. The small literature on presidential honeymoons suggests that they may be less congenial to presidents than commonly thought. See Mannheim (1979), Lammers (1981), and Hughes (1995).

11. This is similar to Bennett's (1990) indexing hypothesis.

12. I also experimented with several measures of presidential success in Congress under the hypothesis that presidential victories in Congress will lead to positive news and losses will results in negative news. Rivers and Rose (1985) and Brace and Hinckley (1992) find that presidential victories in Congress help boost public approval levels. From Ragsdale (1998) I used three measures of presidential success, Total House and Senate Concurrence with the President, House Concurrence, and Senate Concurrence (390–91). None of these were found to affect news tone. Moreover, these congressional concurrence scores only begin with 1953, which results in the loss of several cases. Thus, like the economic perceptions variables, these are dropped from further discussion.

13. I have rescaled four variables to ease their interpretation. Negative news and the percentage of households with television and cable television are scaled from 0 to 100. The Party Polarization score, as presented by the authors, ranges from 0 to 1. To make it comparable in scale to the percentage variables, I multiply it by 100. This has important mathematical implications later on, when I create an interaction term between cable and party polarization by multiplying the two together. This shift in scale for these four variables from 0–1 to 0–100 has no impact otherwise on interpretation of these variables.

14. Appendix 5B on the webpage discusses the time series properties of the negative news variable in more detail and establishes that it is stationary, and thus, despite its association with time, should not be differenced. Although time series diagnostics indicated that the presidential news series is AR(1), estimates of the multivariate analysis found the AR(1) term to be insignificant. Thus an OLS was performed and the residuals were found to be white noise. Hence the OLS results are reported unless otherwise noted. For the reduced form estimation, the AR(1) term nearly reaches statistical significance (b = 0.29, p = 0.08). If the AR(1) model is used instead of OLS for the reduced form model, the only changes in the findings are that the Gulf War and Iran-Contra variables become insignificant. All other results remain with essentially the same impact as the OLS model produces. The Portmanteau Q test for the reduced form OLS model also indicates white noise in the residuals.

15. The correlation between cable television and time is 0.90 (p = .000) and party polarization and time is 0.88 (p = .000).

16. This correlation, r = 0.59, p =.000.

17. Statisticians call this problem multicollinearity. With these three variables all correlating with time, a natural reaction is to difference the three series to remove this time covariation as well as to remove the temporal trend. However, as appendix 5B

presents, the negative news series is stationary, thus differencing is not only not called for but should not be done.

18. There is no statistical solution to multicollinearity other than collecting more data, something we are unable to do. Even if we were able to collect a longer series on negativity in presidential news, for instance, extending to 2000, it is unlikely to change matters much because polarization has continued to grow, while cable penetration has slightly increased its presence in American households. Until one of these abates, that is, the new media evolve into another form or the degree of party polarization recedes, these two sets of variables will continue to be highly correlated and thus present us with this multicollinearity issue.

19. This may derive from professional norms, political power motives, but also may be a marketing strategy in which they try to distinguish their news product from other news products.

20. Brody (1991; also Zaller 1992) contends that whether opinion leaders support the president or not determines if an event turns into a rally behind the president or not. The process described here has much in common with Brody's perspective.

21. By relatively extreme, here I mean those political leaders in authoritative posts, like members of Congress, but who are decidedly conservative or liberal. My use of the term *extreme* is not meant to connote extremists who fall outside of the established confines of the two parties or the major, established institutions of American society and politics.

22. Moderate politicians may follow suit and shift to the extremes also, as a way to compete with the growing influence of extreme politicians and to fend off attacks from challengers who are relatively politically extreme. Inasmuch as moderates are vulnerable to challenges from extremists, the ranks of moderates will dwindle and those of extremists will swell. On the replacement of moderates with extremists as a source of increasing party polarization see Fleisher and Bond (2004).

23. It has a t statistic of 2.24 and a p value of 0.02,

24. The formula for the F test is $F = \{(R_u^2 - R_r^2)/q\} / \{(1 - R_u^2)/(n - k)\}$; where the subscripts u and r stand for unrestricted and restricted, in this case restricted includes the interaction term and unrestricted does not; q = number of restrictions, in this case 1; n = number of cases; k = number of variables in the unrestricted model. With $R_u^2 = 0.892$; $R_r^2 = 0.875$, q = 1, n = 44, k = 10, we get a significant $F (1, 34)$ of 5.31, p = 0.03.

25. 13 percent of the total variance remains $(1 - 0.87 = 0.13)$; 2/13 = 15 percent.

26. The calculations require that we plug into the regression equation specific values. Quite common among interaction effects is that we only see their impact when both variables take on high values. Consider these three simulations, where all of the dummy variables are set at "0," as is the constant, but time is set at its mean, 22, and agenda is also set at its mean, 118. When cable penetration and party polarization are at their minimum values (0 for cable and 0.452 for party polarization), a president will receive 26.6 percent negative news. Setting both at their means (cable = 17, party polarization at 0.588) produces only 26.9 percent negative news. But when both are set near their maximums (cable = 60 and party polarization = 0.750), presidents will receive 36.9 percent negative news. See Friedrich (1982) for a good explanation of estimating and interpreting interaction terms.

NOTES TO CHAPTER 6

1. See Patterson (2000, 23–28) for a detailed discussion of trends in soft news and his codebook. The news outlets include the *New York Times, Washington Post, USA Today,* ABC, NBC, *Newsweek,* and *Time,* among major national news organizations, as well as twenty-six local-regional papers (e.g., *Omaha World Herald, Buffalo News, Knoxville News Sentinel*).

2. Patterson's coding rules for variable 36, Negative-Positive News Frame are: "This code is designed to pick up whether the story is thought on the whole to be in the good news or bad news category. In some instances it might be helpful to ask yourself the following questions: If about a newsmaker, and you were his or her press secretary, would you consider this a favorable or unfavorable story? If about an institution (e.g. Congress), does this reflect favorably or unfavorably on the institution? If about a development (e.g., a social trend, event, or incident), is this a good or bad thing for society" (Patterson 2000, 25).

3. For nonpresidential news we find: clearly positive—11.6 percent; more positive than negative—13.9 percent; neutral/balanced—20.7; more negative than positive—18.7; and clearly negative—35.1 percent. Despite some differences in the negativity of presidential and nonpresidential news, combining the two negativity categories produces nearly identical percentages, presidential news, 52.3 percent and nonpresidential news, 53.8 percent. Furthermore, the correlation between type of news (presidential and nonpresidential) with negativity is an insignificant and tiny −0.02 (p = 0.23).

4. The equation is (regression coefficient, standard errors in parentheses): Negative News = −8.51 (Constant) + 0.64 (.29) Counter + 18.79 (5.11) Scandal; $R^2$ = 0.59, Adjusted $R^2$ = 0.54.

5. Furthermore, this simple, two-variable model accounts for nearly 60 percent of the variance in negative news from 1980–98.

6. Collective terms "reflect categorical modes of thought, such as social groupings (for example, crowd, humanity), task groups (army, Congress), and geographical entities (country, republic)" (Patterson 2000, 4–5).

7. Presidential news stories with a human interest angle existed long before the new media age. Theodore Roosevelt was perhaps the first president to understand that such news stories could build public support for and/or identification with the president. He often offered to reporters his large and rambunctious family as the topic of human interest news stories (E. Morris 2001). The point here is not that human interest stories about the presidency were invented during the age of new media. Rather the point is that their incidence and frequency have increased in the new media age compared to other times.

8. With the possible lone exception of Grover Cleveland, who fathered an illegitimate child, had the mother interred into a mental facility, but then continued to financially support his offspring. Republicans in the 1884 campaign used the slogan, "Ma, Ma, where's my Pa?" against Cleveland, the slogan hinting at Cleveland's scandal. After Cleveland won the election, the Democrats added the refrain, "Gone to the White House, ha ha ha!" (Welch 1988).

9. A factor analysis of these six variables produces three factors, but four variables (soft news, human interest, sensationalism, and nonpolicy news load together on the same factor with factor scores ranging from 0.39 to 0.65). Scandal also loads strongly

on this same factor (0.22), although it loads slightly more strongly on a separate factor (0.35). "News you can use" loads separately on a third factor (0.18).

10. An ordered probit analysis produces essentially the same substantive results, but as regression is more common and more intuitive, I present the regression results.

11. Unfortunately Patterson does not report any results of tests of intercoder reliability or the like.

12. Some 20 stories or 2 percent were not classified and appear as missing data, lowering our n to 930.

13. Patterson also codes stories for whether their style is descriptive or interpretive, which is highly related to whether a story is straight news or analytic. The chi-square between straight-analytic news and descriptive-interpretive is 532.38 (p = .000). Given the high correlation between the two, we are unable to use both simultaneously in a multivariate model.

14. Unfortunately, Patterson's code book does not describe fully what is meant by a call for action and whether such a call is policy related.

15. The analysis in chapter 5 also suggests that larger presidential agendas may increase negativity in presidential news, but the agenda size series (Binder 2002) ends in 1996. In analyses not reported here, I also entered this variable, but found that it did not significantly affect the news tone of individual presidential news stories. As the loss of 1997 and 1998 also means the loss of a considerable number of cases, results here report on the full 1980–98 period without the use of the agenda size variable. None of the other variables seemed affected by the inclusion or exclusion of the agenda size variable.

16. Groeling and Kernell (1998) also find that news organizations are more likely to report on poll results when presidential approval has been falling, rather than staying stable or rising, an indication of journalistic willingness to take on the president when he is weak.

17. See Brace and Hinckley (1992) and Gronke and Brehm (2002) for a list of events and how they are coded.

18. Moreover, adding the presidential scandal variable in an equation with the two scandal period variables the $R^2$ rises to 0.08.

19. I used an F test to make this assessment.

20. Surprisingly, there is no correlation between policy content and whether a story cites an action.

21. However, it might also be the case that with the trend toward the new media age style of reporting that journalists are just less likely to write stories about action and are more likely to write stories that do not refer to action or that call for an action.

22. When these new dependent variables were dichotomous, probit was employed. Table 6.3 denotes whether probit or regression is used.

## Notes to Chapter 7

1. Remember, this point holds for the traditional media, like newspapers and network television. If we consider the rise of the 24/7 cable news channels, such as CNN and Fox News, as well as the internet, and even talk radio, then there might actually be more news in the new media age than during the broadcast age,

2. On the general point of the decline in news attention in the mass public, see Putnam (2000), Mindich (2005), and Wattenberg (2004).

3. A similar argument can be made with regard to other news technologies, such as the internet and VCRs. I focus on cable's effects, rather than the internet and VCRs, because the internet comes late in the transformation into the new media age and VCRs are closely associated with cable use.

4. One case in point is ABC's *Nightline*. After two decades of anchoring the late night news program, Ted Koppel retired in 2005. The show's format was revamped after he stepped down from the anchor spot. The show's new format included a higher dose of soft news, and its hard news coverage was scaled back in both quantity and depth of coverage. Some critics charged that hard news stories had become more superficial than during the Koppel regime. Yet the program's ratings rose after Koppel's departure and the institution of the changes in content. Some—for instance, network executives and the program's producers—attributed the ratings rise to these content changes. See Kurtz (2006).

5. This market research is rarely made public for obvious competitive and proprietary reasons; thus at best we can only infer from changes in news programming the results of such research.

6. Patterson gave survey respondents this choice, reflecting differences between hard and soft news: "What type of news do you generally like? News that sticks mainly to stories about major events and issues affecting the community and the country; or news that focuses on specific incidents such as a crime, fire or accident?" (Question SN-14a).

7. Patterson reports that hard news consumers think more negatively about the news than soft news consumers on list of characteristics (7–8).

8. Prior also finds that those who prefer entertainment to news and have access to cable and/or the internet also vote at lower rates than those who prefer entertainment but lack cable and internet access.

9. Here I am referring to the average person. News junkies, those who crave news, may be better informed and consume higher amounts of news in the new environment, due to cable TV and the internet, than they did a generation ago, before these communication media existed. However, this group is likely to be a small fraction of the public. Most people receive the bulk of their news from the traditional news media, especially the evening network news broadcasts, which, despite their ratings declines, are still the most common source for news for the largest number of Americans.

10. I want to thank Jo LaVerde of Nielsen Media Research who made these data available to me. West reports similar television news ratings data that span the years from 1952 through 1999 (2001, 132). His data point to slightly higher viewer totals, although the shape of his trend and that on figure 7.1 are similar.

11. In the ANES 1948–2000 cumulative file these are questions vcf0724 (television), vcf0725 (radio), vcf0726 (magazines), and vcf0727 (newspapers).

12. See variable vcf0728 in the ANES 1948–2000 cumulative file. ANES did not ask respondents about television use in 1988 or magazine use in 2000.

13. On the substitutability of news media see Neuman (1991) and Althaus and Tewksbury (2000).

14. All correlations are significant at the .000 level because of the very large n's. The specific correlations are: between TV with radio (0.09), magazines (0.13), and

newspapers (0.21); the correlations between radio with magazines (0.15) and newspapers (0.17), while the correlations between magazines and newspapers is 0.29.

15. Here I rely on figures from the *Statistical Abstract of the United States*, various years (Series 910: Utilization of Selected Media in 2000, 567). Mayer (1993, 601) reports different figures from Gallup surveys, which ask people if they have a television set in their home. In the Gallup figures, about 45 percent claimed to own a television set in late summer 1952. By August 1956, the figure hit 80 percent and reached 97 percent by January 1966. Gallup ceased asking people the home television question in 1966.

16. I tested this more formally by regressing the number of hours spent watching television from the GSS series on year. The results find a small negative relationship between year and television watching (b = −0.003, SE = 0.002, t = −1.77, p = 0.08, Equation F = 3.15), but given the massive n (26,016) this is hardly a substantively significant result.

17. The literature on the audience and effects of talk radio has exploded recently. See Barker (1998a, 1998b, 1999, 2002), Barker and Knight (2000), Bennett (2002a, 2002b), Bolce and De Maio (1996); Cappella (2001); Davis and Owen (1998); Hall and Cappella (2002); Hofstetter (1998); Hofstetter and Barker (1999); Hofstetter and Donovan (1994); Hofstetter and Gianos (1997); Hollander (1997); Jones (1998, 2002); Owen (1997); Page (1996b); Pfau, Cho, and Chong (2001); Pfau and Kendall (1997); Pfau and Moy (1998); and Yanovitzky and Cappella (2001).

18. Last, since 1960 ANES has also asked about the frequency of radio listening about the campaign with this question: "Did you listen to any speeches or discussions about the campaign on the radio? If Yes: Would you say you listened to a good many, several, or just one or two?" Here I scored "a good many" a "3," "several" a "2," one or two a "1," and "none" a "0." Again, radio shows a use pattern that differs from the other media. Although never relied on much, radio use deteriorates very slightly from 1960 (0.9) through 1984 (0.84). Then it use plummets in 1988 (0.5), but shortly afterward, we see a rebound in radio use through to 2000 (0.73). The rebound in radio use in the 1990s is probably a function of the rise of talk radio, as noted above.

19. It is important to reiterate that the new media is about more than the diffusion of cable television. But the creation and marketing of cable television was among the first developments associated with the rise of the new media age. Other aspects of the new media age, like the internet, come relatively late. And while talk radio did emerge early on in the new media age, and helped give that age its shape, early talk radio did not have the mainstream appeal of cable television, and thus did not have the degree of impact on the presidential news system of cable television. Thus, as noted before, the spread of cable television should be read as an indicator of the maturing of the new media age.

20. This point also needs clarification. There is some suggestion that the strength of party identification and turnout have been on the upswing, at least in recent years. But beginning in the mid to late 1960s, strength of party identification and turnout rates displayed a notable decline. On these trends see Bartels (2000).

21. Some interesting factors, like political trust, are not used in this initial analysis because they are absent from most of the early surveys. Inclusion of political trust, while it depresses the available n and constricts the time span, does not affect the substantive findings reported below.

22. One complication with this analysis is that the relationship between some variables and news consumption may have changed over the decades. For instance, due to the civil rights and women's movements, we might expect increases in political interest and participation among minorities and women. To test this "changing relationship" hypothesis, I divided the surveys in five decades, 1952–60, 1962–70, 1972–80, 1982–90, 1992–2000, creating a dummy variable for each of these five time periods. I then created interactions terms between the demographics and attitudinal variables and entered these interactions in the estimations. This was a long and complex process because of the large number of variables. Although in several instances these time-period interactions showed that the relationship between factors grew stronger or weaker (e.g., age), and others showed a sign reversal (blacks from negative to positive), none of the time period relationships affected the overall performance of the model, and more importantly, none affected the relationship between cable television and use of the four news media. Because the models without the time-period interactions are simpler to comprehend, I only report results without the time-period interactions. I will supply interested readers with copies of the analysis with the time period variables on request.

23. Another analysis looked at the impact of cable's aggregate spread on the extent of newspaper reading and television news viewing using the ANES variables that ask how many days a week the respondent engaged in those activities. However, ANES only asked these questions since 1984, which severely truncates the variance on the cable variables and misses the period of cable's most rapid growth, the late 1970s and early 1980s. Using a battery of controls, such as those reported above, results indicate that the aggregate spread of cable television did depress both of these forms of news attention. Based on these results, from 1984 to 2000 the average number of days that a person watched television news dropped by about one-half day per week and the average person read a newspaper approximate 0.8 fewer days in 2000 than 1984. However, when controls for a time counter are applied, these effects are erased, a function of the exceedingly high intercorrelation between time and cable diffusion across this shortened time frame. Details of this analysis may be obtained from the author on request.

24. There is one crucial difference between my analysis and Baum and Kernell's other than my addition of the media trust variable. Baum and Kernell look at whether or not a respondent watched the presidential debate. In 1996 ANES asked about whether the respondent viewed each debate. In the 2000, the ANES only asked whether or not the respondent watched a debate between George Bush and Al Gore. VAR 001644: "Did you watch a televised presidential debate between Al Gore and George W. Bush?" In an attempt to replicate Baum and Kernell's debate analysis, I found that this variable did not discriminate well among respondents. Sixty-nine percent of respondents claimed to have watched "a debate," but from this question we cannot tell which debate or how much of the debates a person watched.

25. Neither type of news consumption seems to affect media trust. However, when newspaper reading is eliminated from the media instrument equation, the $R^2$'s fall from 0.20 to 0.19, which an F test finds is a statistically significant. Elimination of the television watching variable from that instrument equation seems to have little impact. OLS finds that media trust affects television watching, but the effect of media trust on television watching is much stronger with the 2SLS (b = 0.90, p = 0.03) results than OLS (b= 0.18, p = 0.07).

Notes to Chapter 8

1. Obviously, trust and confidence toward the news media are different concepts, although they are likely strongly related. I use both terms interchangeably.

2. The three-point scale ranges from 1 to 3. The GSS question is: "I am going to name some institutions in this country. As far as the people running these institutions are concerned, would you say you have a great deal of confidence, only some confidence, or hardly any confidence at all in them? TV, Press." The eleven institutions are banks and financial institutions, business, Congress, the courts and legal system, the executive branch, the government, medicine, the military, organized labor, organized religion, the scientific community, schools and the education system, and the Supreme Court. GSS only began including the banks and financial institutions item in 1976; confidence in the other ten institutions, along with the press and television, were posed to respondents dating to 1972. The coding here assigns "1" to hardly any confidence, "2" to some confidence and "3" to a great deal of confidence.

3. This 2000 confidence score for the eleven major institutions actually represents a rise compared to 1998, when the average score across institutions stood at 1.90, a drop of 0.27 since 1976. Confidence for the press and television stood at 1.66 and 1.71 in 1998, about the same as for 2000.

4. A related literature finds that exposure to this new, more critical and cynical journalism also depresses trust toward political institutions (Cappella and Jamieson 1997, Moy and Pfau 2000, Moy and Scheufele 2000, D. Jones 2004). Others find little effect of news exposure on political cynicism, but that heavy exposure to entertainment programming appears to increase political cynicism (Norris 2000 and Aarts and Semetko 2003).

5. Cook, Gronke, and Rattliff (2000) prefer the mean score approach because it retains all the information from the question. They also report a 1966 figure for the Harris survey, but I could not locate it in the Roper archive, although it has been reported elsewhere. It is slightly higher than the 1972 Harris reading, but like 1972, is lower than the 1974 reading.

6. The GSS question reads: "I am going to name some institutions in this country. As far as the people running these institutions are concerned, would you say you have a great deal of confidence (1) , only some confidence (0), or hardly any confidence at all in them (−1)?" Codes for each response are in the parentheses. The index ranges from −11 to 11.

Notes to Chapter 9

1. As discussed throughout this book, when noting that the amount of hard news or presidential news declined, the reference is to the traditional, major news media, such as the broadcast networks and national newspapers (e.g., the *New York Times*). The rise of cable television, with its 24/7 news networks, and the internet may have increased the availability of news about the president.

2. Much of what follows, although based on the analyses of the previous chapters and other research, is at times speculative. Although I present the elements of the theory

in authoritative tones, much presented here are also hypotheses to be tested and an agenda for future research.

3. Neuman creates an index of news coverage for each issue area that combines the coverage from each of the sources because, as he argues, the great similarity of news coverage across providers allows him to do so. In creating this index, he does not include CBS, because data on CBS only begin with 1972, the year that the Vanderbilt Television Archives began their data collection, and thus does not cover as long a time frame as for the printed media in his study.

4. In contrast, in their study of the 1992 campaign, well into the new media age, Shaw and Sparrow (1999) find that while regional newspapers do rely on the elite press to set their news agenda, regional newspapers also show some discretion in what they publish.

5. Press credibility may also be undermined if the public believes that an economic elite controls the press and uses it for its own economic and/or political ends.

6. People, however, may not pay much attention to any single news story, a continual barrage of news may prove confusing to some, and a barrage of news stories about a multitude of topics may limit one's attention to any one news story or topic as news organizations turn their attention to the next story. Thus single news stories in an environment of high levels of hard news may not affect most people very much.

7. In all I used twenty-three control variables besides strength of party identification: age, female, black, Hispanic, education, urban residence, suburban residence, south, income, professional, clerical, skilled worker, laborer, farmer, homemaker, unemployed, union member, Protestant, Catholic, Jew, church attendance, parent born in the United States, social class identification, and an annual time counter, the last to pick up the secular decline in political interest.

8. A corollary is that as hard news coverage declines, the relative importance of personal versus sociotropic perceptions in evaluating the president and in voting may shift, with sociotropic reasoning declining in importance and personal reasoning rising in importance. This is because exposure to the news media is a major source of developing a sociotropic perspective (Mutz 1992, 1994). If media content changes, deemphasizing hard news, then information that people use to construct a sociotropic understanding of the world may be sparser, making it harder to view the world in sociotropic terms.

9. This indirect path assumes that as the amount of hard news increases, people are more likely to talk to other people about news stories because of the agenda-setting effects of news. However, the multitude of hard news stories may limit the agenda-setting impact of any one news story or topic, as stories and topics compete for public attention. It is likely then that only when a story or topic receives a certain amount of news coverage will it produce agenda setting effects (Erbring, Goldenberg, and Miller 1980). It is an empirical question as to how much coverage is required for agenda setting effects to take hold. Following from the point that a heavy diet of hard news primes the public to think that public affairs is important, it may also be the case that the coverage threshold to affect the public agenda is lower when the public is primed to think that governmental affairs is important.

10. Here "trust" and "credibility" are used somewhat interchangeably, although they differ subtly. One cannot view a source as credible if one lacks trust in that source.

11. Given the generally positive tone of news during this era, it is little wonder that many scholars argue that news essentially supports authorities in power (see for instance, W. L. Bennett, 2002).

12. I refine this point below.

13. We need to distinguish negative effects in communications from positivity effects for political leaders. Edwards (1983), for instance, argues that a positivity bias exists with respect to the presidency (also Lau et al. 1979, on positivity bias toward leaders in general).

14. That news during the new media age tends to be negative and is also less uniform may seem contradictory. Think of tone as having a central tendency and variance. During the broadcasting age, the central tendency of news was to be positive toward the president and there was little variance. In the new media age, the central tendency was negative, but with greater variance.

15. A spiral of silence (Noelle-Neumann 1984) mechanism may also operate in heterogeneous groups composed of both news watchers and non–news watchers. Especially when news watchers are in the minority, they may refrain from bringing up politics and government as a topic to discuss because of disinterest of non–news watchers, who make up the majority in the group. Non–news watchers may steer the conversation to other topics that a larger number of group members may feel more comfortable discussing.

16. In a recent paper Tsfati (2003) demonstrates that when people were skeptical of the news media, they also rejected the media's definition of the climate of opinion.

17. Covington et al. (1993) find that the message of the day strategy affected Reagan's news coverage in the 1980 presidential election campaign as Reagan and his campaign intended.

18. One also wonders if similar patterns hold for the impact of presidential speeches on approval.

19. Kernell claims that "in going public, the ultimate object of the president's designs is not the American voter, but fellow politicians in Washington." (1993, xiii).

20. The networks have also become increasingly resistant to numerous presidential addresses that preempt their prime-time programming (Foote 1990).

21. Canes-Wrone (2001) argues that by going public a president activates public opinion and that presidents are strategic in activating public opinion. They may stay "private" because of their position, the status quo, the position of the median member of Congress, and the median member of the mass public. When the public is closer to Congress than the president and the president prefers the status quo to Congress's position, the president may stay private instead of going public.

22. When national opinion and group opinion agree about a policy, a consensus exists. Presidents need not go public nor even have to bargain with members of Congress much as agreement exists over the form that the policy should take.

23. This assumption is based on the large literature that finds that the politically active and members of interest groups tend to be more politically extreme (e.g., either/or more liberal and conservative) than the public at large, which tends to be moderate on most issues.

24. See, for instance, Denzau and Munger (1986) on the comparative importance of "unorganized" and "organized" interests on legislators. Unorganized roughly parallels my use of the term *national* and organized parallels *narrow*.

25. Notice in this model that presidential preferences play no role here, which is not a realistic assumption. We would not expect presidents to try to activate either national or narrow constituencies when presidents prefer not to alter the status quo on the policy in question or when the president holds a minority preferred preference on the issue. We could add such an element into the model, whereby the president goes "national" or "narrow" depending on which group holds preferences closer to the president's. Adding such a term would complicate the model, but does not affect the dynamic element of interest here, the impact of the new media on presidential going public activity. For simplicity's sake, the model does not include such an element, noting that the basic model can accommodate presidential preferences.

26. Campaign finances reforms of the 1970s, which led to the expansion in PACs, and the growing political polarization in the political system, may be other relevant factors for politician's abandoning a median voter strategy. See Jacobs and Shapiro (2000).

27. In 1958, 1966, 1976, 1996, and 1997, presidents made no major discretionary speeches. Non-DC and DC appearances comes from tables 4-7 (minor speeches), 4-8 (DC appearances), 4-9 (non-DC appearances), and 4-1 (major speeches) in Ragsdale (1998). I exclude State of the Union and Inaugural addresses, which are nondiscretionary, from major addresses.

28. Political appearances are not included in minor speeches because my interest is more with governing than running for reelection. Political appearances display a sawtoothed pattern, spiking in the fourth year of the presidential term (Kernell 1993, Ragsdale 1998, Powell 1999).

29. Dickey-Fuller tests indicate the ratio series is stationary, which allows us to analyze the ratio variable in levels form. However, diagnostics also detected an AR1 process, but when estimating multivariate models using the ARIMA command in STATA, the AR1 term does not maintain statistical significance. Moreover, the substantive results of AR1 and OLS are quite similar, all of which suggests using the less restrictive OLS instead of the AR1 estimation model. See the appendix to this chapter on the webpage for details on the time series properties of this ratio variable.

30. The party polarization measure is the difference in the DW-NOMINATE score of the two party medians.

31. I thank Adam Lawrence for providing me with these data. See Lawrence (2004). Nonnarrow, national policy mentions is the combination of economic and foreign policy mentions; the rest are narrow. Lawrence only classified appeals into three types, economic, foreign, or domestic.

32. The correction between the percent "narrow" and a time counter is only 0.26 (p = 0.04).

33. Time series diagnostics, presented in the appendix to this chapter, which is located on the webpage for this book, indicate that the series is stationary. Like the ratio variable used in table 9.1, diagnostics also indicated a potential AR1 process. But again, when estimating the multivariate models, the AR1 term, which is essentially the first order lag of the dependent variable, was no longer significant. With similar substantive results, I opted to use the less restrictive OLS estimation. Details can be obtained from the author.

34. After detecting this effect, I re-estimated the models on table 9.1 using the percent change form of the cable variable, but this change variable never proved statistically significant.

NOTES TO CHAPTER 10

1. For a thoughtful treatment on citizenship for modern democracy, see Schudson (1998).

2. Jacobs and Shapiro (2000) review these and other factors that lessen politicians' responsiveness to the broad middle, the median voter.

# BIBLIOGRAPHY

Aarts, Kees, and Holli A. Semetko. 2003. "The Divided Electorate: Media Use and Political Involvement." *Journal of Politics* 65 (August): 759–84.

Adams, Edward A. 1995. "Chain Growth and Merger Waves: A Macroeconomic Historical Perspective on Press Consolidation." *Journalism and Mass Communication Quarterly* 72 (summer): 376–89.

Allen, Craig. 1993. *Eisenhower and the Mass Media: Peace, Prosperity, and Prime-time TV.* Chapel Hill: University of North Carolina Press.

Althaus, Scott L., Jill A. Edy, and Patricia F. Phalen. 2001. "Using Substitutes for Full-Text News Stories in Content Analysis: Which Text Is Best?" *American Journal of Political Science* 45 (July):707–24.

———. 2002. "Using the Vanderbilt Television Abstracts to Track Broadcast News Content: Possibilities and Pitfalls." *Journal of Broadcasting and Electronic Media* 46 (September): 180–200.

Althaus, Scott L., and David Tewksbury. 2000. "Patterns of Internet and Traditional Media Use in a Networked Community." *Political Communication* 17, no. 1: 21–45.

Altheide, David L. 1982. "Three-In-One News: Network Coverage of Iran." *Journalism Quarterly* 59 (autumn): 482–86.

Andolina, Molly W., and Clyde Wilcox. 2000. "Public Opinion: The Paradoxes of Clinton's Popularity." In *The Clinton Scandal and the Future of American Politics*, ed. Mark J. Rozell and Clyde Wilcox. Washington, DC: Georgetown University Press, 171–94.

Baldasty, Gerald J. 1992. *The Commercialization of the News in the Nineteenth Century.* Madison: University of Wisconsin Press.

Balke, Nathan S., and Robert J. Gordon. 1989. "The Estimation of Prewar Gross National Product: Methodology and New Evidence." *Journal of Political Economy* 97 (February): 38–92.

Balutis, Alan P. 1976. "Congress, the President, and the Press." *Journalism Quarterly* 59 (autumn): 505–9.

———. 1977. "The Presidency and the Press: The Expanding Public Image." *Presidential Studies Quarterly* 7 (fall): 244–51.

Barker, David C. 1998a. "The Talk Radio Community: Nontraditional Social Networks and Political Participation." *Social Science Quarterly* 79 (June): 261–72.

———. 1998b. "Rush to Action: Political Talk Radio and Health Care (Un) Reform." *Political Communication* 15, no. 1: 83–97.

———. 1999. "Rushed Decisions: Political Talk Radio and Vote Choice, 1994–1996." *Journal of Politics* 61 (May): 527–39.

———. 2002. *Rushed to Judgment: Talk Radio, Persuasion, and American Political Behavior.* New York: Columbia University Press.

Barker, David, and Kathleen Knight. 2000. "Political Talk Radio and Public Opinion." *Public Opinion Quarterly* 64 (summer): 149–70.

Barnhurst, Kevin G., and Diana Mutz. 1997. "American Journalism and the Decline in Event-Centered Reporting." *Journal of Communication* 47 (autumn): 27–53.

Barnhurst, Kevin G., and John Nerone. 2001. *The Form of News: A History.* New York: Guilford Press.

Barnouw, Erik, David Lieberman, Patricia Aufderheide, Richard M. Cohen, and Mark C. Miller. 1997. *Conglomerates and the Media.* New York: New Press.

Barrett, Andrew W. 2003. "If He Speaks and the Press Doesn't Report It, Does the President Make A Sound?" Paper prepared for delivery at the annual meeting of the American Political Science Association, Philadelphia, PA.

Bartels, Larry M. 1993. "Messages Received: The Political Impact of Media Exposure." *The American Political Science Review* 87 (June): 267–85.

———. 2000. "Partisanship and Voting Behavior, 1952–1996." *American Journal of Political Science* 44 (January): 35–50.

Baum, Matthew A. 2002. "Sex, Lies, and War: How Soft News Brings Foreign Policy to the Attentive Public." *American Political Science Review* 96 (March): 91–110.

———. 2003a. *Soft News Goes to War: Public Opinion and American Foreign Policy in the New Media Age.* Princeton, NJ: Princeton University Press.

———. 2003b. "Soft News and Political Knowledge: Evidence of Absence or Absence of Evidence?" *Political Communication* 20 (April/June): 173–90.

Baum, Matthew A., and Samuel Kernell. 1999. "Has Cable Ended the Golden Age of Television?" *American Political Science Review* 93 (March): 99–114.

Becker, Lee, Wilson Lowrey, Dane Claussen, and William Anderson. 2000. "Why Does the Beat Go On?" *Newspaper Research Journal* 21 (fall): 2–16.

Becker, Samuel L. 1961. "Presidential Power: The Influence of Broadcasting." *Quarterly Journal of Speech* 47 (February): 10–18.

Bennett, Stephen Earl. 1998. "Young Americans' Indifference to Media Coverage of Public Affairs." *PS: Political Science and Politics* 31 (September): 535–41.

———. 2002a. "Americans' Exposure to Political Talk Radio and Their Knowledge of Public Affairs." *Journal of Broadcasting and Electronic Media* 46 (March): 72–86.

———. 2002b. "Predicting Americans' Exposure to Political Talk Radio in 1996, 1998, and 2000." *Harvard International Journal of Press/Politics* 7 (winter): 9–22.

———. 2002c. "Another Lesson about Public Opinion during the Clinton-Lewinsky Scandal." *Presidential Studies Quarterly* 32 (June): 276–92.

Bennett, Stephen Earl, Staci L. Rhine, and Richard S. Flickinger. 1998. "Assessing Americans' Opinions About the News Media's Fairness in 1996 and 1998." *Political Communication* 18 (April): 163–83.

Bennett, Stephen Earl, Staci L. Rhine, Richard S. Flickinger, and Linda L. M. Bennett. 1999. "'Video Malaise' Revisited: Political Trust in the Media and Government." *Harvard International Journal of Press/Politics* 4, no. 4: 8–23.

Bennett, W. Lance. 1990. "Toward a Theory of Press-State Relations in the United States." *Journal of Communication* 40 (spring): 103–25.

———. 2002. *News: The Politics of Illusion.* 5th ed. New York: Longman.

Bennett, W. Lance, and David L. Paletz, eds. 1994. *Taken By Storm: The Media, Public Opinion, and U.S. Foreign Policy in the Gulf War.* Chicago: University of Chicago Press.

Bimber, Bruce. 2003. *Information and American Democracy: Technology in the Evolution of Political Power.* New York: Cambridge University Press.

Binder, Sarah. 2002. *Stalemate: Causes and Consequences of Legislative Gridlock.* Washington, DC: Brookings.

Blumler, Jay G., and Dennis Kavanagh. 1999. "The Third Age of Political Communication: Influences and Features." *Political Communication* 16 (July): 209–30.

Bolce, Louis, and Gerald De Maio. 1996. "Dial-in Democracy: Talk Radio and the 1994 Election." *Political Science Quarterly* 111 (fall): 457–81.

Brace, Paul, and Barbara Hinckley. 1992. *Follow the Leader: Opinion Polls and the Modern Presidents.* New York: Basic Books.

Brody, Richard. 1991. *Assessing the President: The Media, Elite Opinion, and Public Support.* Stanford: Stanford University Press.

Busby, Robert. 1999. *Reagan and the Iran-Contra Affair: The Politics of Presidential Recovery.* New York: St. Martin's Press.

Campbell, Angus. 1960. "Surge and Decline: A Study of Electoral Change." *Public Opinion Quarterly* 24 (autumn): 397–418.

Canes-Wrone, Brandice. 2001. "A Theory of Presidents' Public Agenda Setting." *Journal of Theoretical Politics* 13 (April): 183–208.

Cappella, Joseph N. 2001. "The Effects of Political Talk Radio on Political Attitude Formation: Exposure versus Knowledge." *Political Communication* 18 (October): 369–94.

Cappella, Joseph N., and Kathleen Hall Jamieson. 1997. *Spiral of Cynicism: The Press and the Public Good.* Oxford: Oxford University Press.

Cappella, Joseph N., Joseph Turow, and Kathleen Hall Jamieson. 1996. *Call-in Talk Radio: Background, Content, Audiences, Portrayal in the Mainstream Media.* Philadelphia, PA: Annenberg Public Policy Center, University of Pennsylvania.

Center for Media and Public Affairs. 2004. "The Book on Bill Clinton." *Media Monitor* 18 (July/August): 1–9, accessed at http://www.cmpa.com/Mediamon/documents/julaug04.pdf.

Chadwick, Andrew. 2006. *Internet Politics: States, Citizens, and New Communications Technologies.* New York: Oxford University Press.

Chanley, Virginia A., Thomas J. Rudolph, and Wendy M. Rahn. 2000. "The Origins and Consequences of Public Trust in Government: A Time Series Analysis." *Public Opinion Quarterly* 64 (fall): 239–56.

Citrin, Jack, and Donald Philip Green. 1986. "Presidential Leadership and the Resurgence of Trust in Government." *British Journal of Political Science* 16 (October): 431–53.

Clayman, Steven E., Marc N. Elliott, John Heritage, and Laurie L. McDonald. 2006. "Historical Trends in Questioning Presidents, 1953–2000." *Presidential Studies Quarterly* 36 (December): 561–83.

Clayman, Steven E., and John Heritage. 2002. "Questioning Presidents: Journalistic Deference and Adversarialness in the Press Conferences of U. S. Presidents Eisenhower and Reagan." *Journal of Communication* 52 (December): 749–75.

Cohen, Jeffrey E. 1995. "Presidential Rhetoric and the Public Agenda." *American Journal of Political Science* 39 (February): 87–107.

———. 1997. *Presidential Responsiveness and Public Policy Making: The Public and the Policies that Presidents Make.* Ann Arbor: University of Michigan Press.

———. 1999a. "The Polls: Favorability Ratings of Presidents." *Presidential Studies Quarterly* 29 (September): 690–96.

Cohen, Jeffrey E. 1999b. "The Polls: The Dynamics of Presidential Favorability, 1991–1998." *Presidential Studies Quarterly* 29 (December): 896–902.

———. 2000. "The Polls: The Components of Presidential Favorability." *Presidential Studies Quarterly* 30 (March): 169–77.

———. 2004. "If the News Is So Bad, Why Are Presidential Polls So High? Presidents, the News Media, and the Mass Public in an Era of New Media." *Presidential Studies Quarterly* 34 (September): 493–515.

Comstock, George, and Erica Scharrer. 2005. *The Psychology of Media and Politics*. Burlington, MA: Elsevier.

Conley, Patricia Heidotting. 2001. *Presidential Mandates: How Elections Shape the National Agenda*. Chicago: University of Chicago Press.

Cook, Timothy E. 1998. *Governing with the News: The News Media as a Political Institution*. Chicago: University of Chicago Press.

Cook, Timothy E., and Paul Gronke. 2001. "Dimensions of Institutional Trust: Is Public Confidence in the Media Distinct from Other Institutions?" Paper presented at the Annual Meeting of the Midwest Political Science Association, Chicago, IL.

———. 2002. "Disdaining the Media in the Post 9/11 World." Paper prepared for delivery at the annual meeting of the American Political Science Association, Boston MA.

Cook, Timothy, Paul Gronke, and John Rattliff. 2000. "Disdaining the Media: The American Public's Changing Attitudes toward the News." Paper prepared for delivery at the annual meeting of the American Political Science Association, Washington, DC.

Cook, Timothy E., and Lyn Ragsdale. 1998. "The President and the Press: Negotiating Newsworthiness in the White House." In *The Presidency and the Political System*, ed. Michael Nelson. 5th ed. Washington, DC: CQ Press, 323–57.

Cornwell, Elmer E., Jr. 1959. "Presidential News: The Expanding Public Image." *Journalism Quarterly* 36 (summer): 275–83.

———. 1966. *Presidential Leadership of Public Opinion*. Bloomington, IN: Indiana University Press.

Covington, Cary R., Kent Kroeger, Glenn Richardson, and J. David Woodard. 1993. "Shaping a Candidate's Image in the Press: Ronald Reagan and the 1980 Presidential Election." *Political Research Quarterly* 46 (December): 783–98.

Craig, Douglas B. 2000. *Fireside Politics: Radio and Political Culture in the United States, 1920–1940*. Baltimore, MD: Johns Hopkins University Press.

Cronin, Thomas E., and Michael A. Genovese. 1998. *The Paradoxes of the American Presidency*. New York: Oxford University Press.

Crouse, Timothy. 1973. *The Boys on the Bus*. New York: Random House.

Dautrich, Kenneth, and Thomas H. Hartley. 1999. *How the News Media Fail American Voters: Consequences and Remedies*. New York: Columbia University Press.

Davis, Richard. 1998. *The Web of Politics*. New York: Oxford University Press.

Davis, Richard, and Diana Owen. 1998. *New Media and American Politics*. New York: Oxford University Press.

Deakin, James. 1968. *Lyndon Johnson's Credibility Gap*. Washington, DC: Public Affairs Press.

Dean, Wally, and Lee Ann Brady. 2002. "After 9/11 Has Anything Changed?" *Columbia Journalism Review* 41 (November/December): 94–95.

De Boef, Suzanna, and Paul Kellstedt. 2004. "The Political (and Economic) Origins of Consumer Confidence." *American Journal of Political Science* 48 (October): 633–49.

Delli Carpini, Michael X, and Scott Keeter. 1996. *What Americans Know about Politics and Why It Matters.* New Haven, CT: Yale University Press.

Denton, Robert E., Jr., and Rachel L. Holloway, eds. 2003. *Images, Scandal, and Communication Strategies of the Clinton Presidency.* Westport, CT: Praeger.

Denzau, Arthur T., and Michael C. Munger. 1986. "Legislators and Interest Groups: How Unorganized Interests Get Represented." *American Political Science Review* 80 (March): 89–106.

Diamond, Edwin. 1994. *Behind the Times: Inside the New York Times.* New York: Villard.

DiClerico, Robert E. 1993. "The Role of Media in Heightened Expectations and Diminished Leadership Capacity." in *The Presidency Reconsidered*, ed. R. W. Waterman. Itasca, IL: F. E. Peacock, 115–43.

Doherty, Brendan, and Melissa Anderson. 2003. "Presidential Message Tailoring: Courting Latino Voters in the 2000 Presidential Advertising Campaign." Paper presented at the annual meeting of the American Political Science Association, Philadelphia, PA, September 2003.

Dorfman, Lori, Helen Halpin Schauffler, John Wilkerson, and Judith Feinson. 1996. "Local Television News Coverage of President Clinton's Introduction of the Health Security Act." *JAMA: Journal of the American Medical Association* 275 (April 17): 1201–5.

Downs, Anthony. 1957. *An Economic Theory of Democracy.* New York: Harper.

Druckman, James N. 2003. "The Power of Television Images: The First Kennedy-Nixon Debate Revisited." *Journal of Politics* 65 (May): 559–71.

Edelman, Murray. 1964. *The Symbolic Uses of Politics.* Urbana, IL: University of Illinois Press.

———. 1971. *Politics as Symbolic Action; Mass Arousal and Quiescence.* Chicago: Markham.

Edwards, George C. III. 1983. *The Public Presidency: The Pursuit of Popular Support.* New York: St. Martin's Press.

———. 1997. "Aligning Tests with Theory: Presidential Approval as a Source of Influence in Congress." *Congress and the Presidency* 24 (fall): 113–30.

———. 2000. "Building Coalitions." *Presidential Studies Quarterly* 30 (March): 47–78.

———. 2003. *On Deaf Ears: The Limits of the Bully Pulpit.* New Haven, CT: Yale University Press.

Ender, Walter. 2004. *Applied Econometric Times Series.* 2d ed. New York: John Wiley.

Erbring, Lutz, Edie N. Goldenberg, and Arthur H. Miller. 1980. "Front-Page News and Real-World Cues: A New Look at Agenda-Setting by the Media." *American Journal of Political Science* 24 (February): 16–49.

Erikson, Robert S., Michael MacKuen, and James A. Stimson. 2002. *The Macropolity.* Cambridge, MA: Cambridge University Press.

Eshbaugh-Soha, Matthew. 2003. "Presidential Press Conferences over Time." *American Journal of Political Science* 47 (April): 348–53.

Esser, Frank. 1999. "Tabloidization of News: A Comparative Analysis of Anglo-American and German Press Journalism." *European Journal of Communication* 14 (September): 291–324.

Fallows, James M. 1996. *Breaking the News: How the Media Undermine American Democracy.* New York: Pantheon Books.

Farnsworth, Stephen J., and S. Robert Lichter. 2003. "New Presidents and Network News: Covering the First Year in Office of Ronald Reagan, Bill Clinton and George W. Bush." Paper presented at the annual meeting of the American Political Science Association Philadelphia Marriott Hotel, Philadelphia, PA.

———. 2004. "Increasing Candidate-Centered Televised Discourse: Evaluating Local News Coverage of Campaign 2000." *Harvard International Journal of Press/Politics* 9 (spring): 76–93.

———. 2006. *The Mediated Presidency: Television News and Presidential Government.* Lanham, MD: Rowman and Littlefield.

Feder, Don. 1997. "The Trouble with Network News." *The American Enterprise* 8 (September/October): 44–45.

Fishman, Mark. 1980. *Manufacturing the News.* Austin: University of Texas Press.

Fleisher, Richard, and Jon R. Bond. 2004. "The Shrinking Middle in the U. S. Congress." *British Journal of Political Science* 34 (July): 429–51.

Foote, Joe S. 1990. *Television Access and Presidential Power: The Networks, the Presidency, and the "Loyal Opposition".* New York: Praeger.

Foote, Joe S., and Michael E. Steele. 1986. "Degree of Conformity in Lead Stories in Early Evening Network TV Newscasts." *Journalism Quarterly* 63 (spring): 19–23.

Fowler, J. S., and S. W. Showalter. 1974. "Evening Network News Selection: A Confirmation of News Judgment." *Journalism Quarterly* 51 (winter): 712–15.

Friedrich, Robert J. 1982. "In Defense of Multiplicative Terms in Multiple Regression Equations." *American Journal of Political Science* 26 (November): 797–833.

Gaines, Brian J., and Brian D. Roberts. 2005. "Hawks, Bears, and Pundits: Explaining Presidential Approval Rally Effects." Paper presented at the Midwest Political Science Association, Chicago, IL, April 7–10, 2005.

Gans, Herbert J. 1979. *Deciding What's News: A Study of CBS Evening News, NBC Nightly News, Newsweek, and Time.* New York: Vintage.

Genovese, Michael A. 1999. *The Watergate Crisis.* Westport, CT: Greenwood Press.

Gilbert, Robert E. 1981. "Television and Presidential Power." *Journal of Social, Political, and Economic Studies* 6, no. 1: 75–93.

———. 1989. "President versus Congress: The Struggle for Public Attention." *Congress and the President* 16, no. 1: 91–102.

Gillespie, Mark, 2004. "Media Credibility Reaches Lowest Point in Three Decades." Gallup Tuesday Press Briefing, September, 23, 2004, 12.

Ginsberg , Benjamin, and Robert Weissberg. 1978. "Elections and the Mobilization of Popular Support." *American Journal of Political Science* 22 (February): 31–55.

Glynn, Kevin. 2000. *Tabloid Culture: Trash, Taste, Popular Power, and the Transformation of American Television.* Durham, NC: Duke University Press.

Goggin, Malcolm L.1984. "The Ideological Content of Presidential Communications: The Message-Tailoring Hypothesis Revisited." *American Politics Quarterly* 12 (July): 361–84.

Goidel, Robert K., Todd G. Shields, and Mark Peffley. 1997. "Priming Theory and RAS Models: Toward an Integrated Perspective on Media Influence." *American Politics Quarterly* 25 (July): 287–318.

Graber, Doris A. 1974. "Press Coverage and Voter Reaction in the 1968 Presidential Election." *Political Science Quarterly* 89 (March): 68–100.

———. 2001. *Processing Politics: Learning from Television in the Internet Age.* Chicago: University of Chicago Press.

———. 2002. *Mass Media and American Politics.* 6th ed. Washington, DC: CQ Press.

———. 2004. "Mediated Politics and Citizenship in the Twenty-first Century." *Annual Review of Psychology* 55 (November): 545–71.

Granato, Jim, Ronald Inglehart, and David Leblang. 1996. "The Effect of Cultural Values on Economic Development: Theory, Hypotheses, and Some Empirical Tests." *American Journal of Political Science* 40 (August): 607–31.

Greene, Stephen. 2001. "The Role of Character Assessment in Presidential Approval." *American Politics Research* 29 (March): 196–210.

Greenstein, Fred I. 1988. "Nine Presidents in Search of a Modern Presidency." In *Leadership in the Modern Presidency,* ed. Fred I. Greenstein. Cambridge, MA: Harvard University Press, 296–352.

Groeling, Tim, and Samuel Kernell. 1998. "Is Network News Coverage of the President Biased?" *Journal of Politics* 60, no. 4: 1063–87.

Groeling, Tim, and Robert Lichter. 2004. "Circling the Firing Squad: A Six Year Examination of Partisan Support and Discord in the Evening News." Paper presented at the American Political Science Association Meeting, Chicago, September 2, 2004.

Gronke, Paul, and John Brehm. 2002. "History, Heterogeneity, and Presidential Approval: A Modified ARCH Approach." *Electoral Studies* 21 (September): 425–52.

Grossman, Michael Baruch, and Martha Joynt Kumar. 1981. *Portraying the President: The White House and the News Media.* Baltimore: Johns Hopkins University Press.

Hager, Gregory L., and Terry Sullivan. 1994. "President-Centered and Presidency-Centered Explanations of Presidential Public Activity." *American Journal of Political Science* 38 (November): 1079–1103.

Hall, Alice, and Joseph N. Cappella. 2002. "The Impact of Political Talk Radio Exposure on Attributions about the Outcome of the 1996 U.S. Presidential Election." *Journal of Communication* 52 (June): 332–49.

Hamilton, James D. 1994. *Times Series Analysis.* Princeton, NJ: Princeton University Press.

Hamilton, James T. 2003. *All the News that's Fit to Sell: How the Market Transforms Information into News.* Princeton, NJ: Princeton University Press.

Hansen, John Mark, and Steven J. Rosenstone. 1993. *Mobilization, Participation, and Democracy in America.* Englewood Cliffs, NJ: Prentice-Hall.

Hansen, Wendy L., and Neil J. Mitchell. 2000. "Disaggregating and Explaining Corporate Political Activity: Domestic and Foreign Corporations in National Politics." *American Political Science Review* 94 (December): 891–903.

Hart, Roderick P. 2000. *Campaign Talk: Why Elections are Good for Us.* Princeton, N.J.: Princeton University Press.

Heckman, James J. 1976. "The Common Structure of Statistical Models of Truncation, Sample Selection and Limited Dependent Variables and a Sample Estimator for Such Models." *Annals of Economic and Social Measurement* 5, no. 4: 475–92.

Heith, Diane J. 2000. "The Polls: Polling for a Defense: The White House Public Opinion Apparatus and the Clinton Impeachment." *Presidential Studies Quarterly* 30 (December): 783–90.

Hertsgaard, Mark. 1989. *On Bended Knee: The Press and the Reagan Presidency.* Rev. ed. New York: Schocken Books.

Hess, Stephen. 1994. "The Decline and Fall of Congressional News." In *Congress, the Press, and the Public,* ed. Thomas Mann and Norman Ornstein. Washington, DC: Brookings and American Enterprise Institute: 141–56.

———. 2000. "Federalism and News: Media to Government: Drop Dead." *Brookings Review* 18 (winter): 28–31.

Hetherington, Marc J. 2001. "Resurgent Mass Partisanship: The Role of Elite Polarization." *American Political Science Review* 95 (September): 619–31.

Hibbing, John, and Elizabeth Theiss-Morse. 1995. *Congress as Public Enemy.* New York: Cambridge University Press.

———, eds. 2001. *What Is It about Government that Americans Dislike?* New York: Cambridge University Press.

———. 2002. *Stealth Democracy: Americans' Beliefs about How Government Should Work.* New York: Cambridge University Press.

Hickey, Neil. 1998. "Ten Mistakes That Led to the Great CNN/Time Fiasco." *Columbia Journalism Review* 37 (September/October): 26–29.

Highton, Bejamin. 2002. "Bill Clinton, Newt Gingrich, and the 1998 House Elections." *Public Opinion Quarterly* 66 (spring): 1–17.

Hill, Kim Quaile. 1998. "The Policy Agendas of the President and the Mass Public: A Research Validation and Extension." *American Journal of Political Science* 42 (October): 1328–34.

Hofstetter, C. Richard. 1998. "Political Talk Radio, Situational Involvement, and Political Mobilization." *Social Science Quarterly* 79 (June): 273–86.

Hofstetter, C. Richard, and David Barker. 1999. "Information, Misinformation, and Political Talk Radio." *Political Research Quarterly* 52 (June): 353–69.

Hofstetter, C. Richard, and Mark C. Donovan. 1994. "Political Talk Radio: A Stereotype Reconsidered." *Political Research Quarterly* 47 (June): 467–79.

Hofstetter, C. Richard, and Christopher L. Gianos. 1997. "Political Talk Radio: Actions Speak Louder than Words." *Journal of Broadcasting and Electronic Media* 41 (fall): 501–15.

Hollander, Barry A. 1997. "Fuel to the Fire: Talk Radio and the Gamson Hypothesis." *Political Communication* 14, no. 3: 355–70.

Huddy, Leonie, Nadia Khatib, and Theresa Capelos. 2002. "The Polls-Trends: Reactions to the Terrorist Attacks of September 11, 2001." *Public Opinion Quarterly* 66 (fall): 418–50.

Hughes, William J. 1995. "The 'Not-so-genial' Conspiracy: The *New York Times* and Six Presidential 'Honeymoons,' 1953–1993." *Journalism and Mass Communication Quarterly* 72 (winter): 841–50.

Iyengar, Shanto, and Donald Kinder. 1987. *News that Matters.* Chicago: University of Chicago Press.

Jacobs, Lawrence R., and Robert Y. Shapiro. 2000. *Politicians Don't Pander: Political Manipulation and the Loss of Democratic Responsiveness.* Chicago: University of Chicago Press.

Jacobson, Gary C. 1999. "Impeachment Politics in 1998 Congressional Elections." *Political Science Quarterly* 114 (spring): 31–52.

Jones, Charles O. 1994. *The Presidency in a Separated System*. Washington, DC: Brookings.

Jones, David A. 1998. "Political Talk Radio: The Limbaugh Effect on Primary Voters." *Political Communication* 15, no. 3: 367–81.

———. 2002. "The Polarizing Effect of New Media Messages." *International Journal of Public Opinion Research* 14 (summer): 158–74.

———. 2004. "Why Americans Don't Trust the Media: A Preliminary Analysis." *Harvard International Journal of Press/Politics* 9, no. 2: 60–75.

Jones, Jeffrey M. 2004. "Does the State of the Union Affect Presidential Popularity?" Accessed at http://209.157.64.200/focus/f-news/1056757/posts, January 14, 2004.

Joslyn, Mark B. 2003. "Framing the Lewinsky Affair: Third-Person Judgments by Scandal Frame." *Political Psychology* 24 (December): 829–45.

Just, Marion, and Todd Belt. 2004. "The Local News Story: Is Quality a Choice?" Paper presented at the annual meeting of the American Political Science Association, Chicago, IL, September 2, 2004.

Kagay, Michael R. 1999. "Presidential Address: Public Opinion and Polling During Presidential Scandal and Impeachment." *Public Opinion Quarterly* 63 (autumn): 449–63.

Kaniss, Phyllis. 1991. *Making Local News*. Chicago: University of Chicago Press.

Kaplan, Leonard V., and Beverly I. Moran, eds. 2001. *Aftermath: The Clinton Impeachment and the Presidency in the Age of Political Spectacle*. New York: New York University Press.

Kerbel, Matthew Robert. 1999. *Remote and Controlled: Media Politics in a Cynical Age*. 2d ed. Boulder, CO: Westview Press.

Kernell, Samuel C. 1993. *Going Public: New Strategies of Presidential Leadership*. 2d ed. Washington, DC: CQ Press.

Kernell, Samuel, and Gary C. Jacobson. 1987. "Congress and the President as News in the Nineteenth Century." *Journal of Politics* 49 (November): 1016–35.

King, David, Andrew J. Cooley, and Julie Curtis. 1999. "Interesting News: Politics and the Attributes of Popular News Stories." Manuscript, John F. Kennedy School of Government, Harvard University, January 11, 1999, downloaded on December 30, 2004 from http://www.ksg.harvard.edu/prg/king/news.pdf.

Kiousis, Spiro. 2003. "Job Approval and Favorability: The Impact of Media Attention to the Monica Lewinsky Scandal on Public Opinion of President Bill Clinton." *Mass Communication and Society* 6 (November): 435–51.

Krause, George A., and Jeffrey E. Cohen. 2000. "Opportunity and Constraint and the Development of the Institutional Presidency: The Issuance of Executive Orders, 1939–1996." *Journal of Politics* 62 (February): 88–114.

Krosnick, Jon A., and Laura A. Brannon. 1993a. "The Impact of the Gulf War on the Ingredients of Presidential Evaluations: Multidimensional Effects of Political Involvement." *American Political Science Review* 87 (December): 963–75.

———. 1993b. "The Media and the Foundations of Presidential Support: George Bush and the Persian Gulf Conflict." *Journal of Social Issues* 49 (winter): 167–82.

Krosnick, Jon A., and Donald R. Kinder. 1990. "Altering the Foundations of Support for the President through Priming." *American Political Science Review* 84 (June): 497–512.

Kulkarni, Rajendra G., Roger R. Stough, and Kingsley E. Haynes. 1999. "Towards an Information Entropy Model of Job Approval Rating: The Clinton Presidency." *Entropy* 1 (September): 37–49.

Kumar, Martha Joynt. 1997. "The White House Beat at the Century Mark." *Harvard International Journal of Press/Politics* 2 (summer): 10–30.

Kurtz, Howard. 1998. *Spin Cycle: Inside the Clinton Propaganda Machine.* New York: The Free Press.

———. 2001. "Doing Something Right; Fox News Sees Ratings Soar, Critics Sore." *Washington Post*, February 5, 2001, C.01.

———. 2006. "Basking in the Shadow of Ted Koppel: New 'Nightline' Draws Viewers, and Media Criticism." *Washington Post*, March 2, 2006, C1.

Lammers, William W. 1981. "Presidential Press Conference Schedules: Who Hides and When?" *Political Science Quarterly* 96 (summer): 261–78.

———. 1982. "Presidential Attention-Focusing Activities." In *The President and the Public*, ed. Doris Graber. Philadelphia: Institute for the Study of Human Affairs, 145–71.

Lang, Gladys Engel, and Kurt Lang. 1983. *The Battle for Public Opinion: The President, the Press, and the Polls during Watergate.* New York: Columbia University Press.

Lanoue, David J. 1988. *From Camelot to the Teflon President: Economics and Presidential Popularity since 1960.* New York: Greenwood Press.

Lanoue, David J., and Craig F. Emmert. 1999. "Voting in the Glare of the Spotlight: Representatives' Votes on the Impeachment of President Clinton." *Polity* 32 (winter): 253–69.

Lau, Richard R. 1985. "Two Explanations for Negativity Effects in Political Behavior." *American Journal of Political Science* 29 (February): 119–38.

Lau, Richard R, David O. Sears, and Richard Centers. 1979. "The 'Positivity Bias' in Evaluations of Public Figures: Evidence Against Instrument Artifacts." *Public Opinion Quarterly* 43 (fall): 347–58.

Lawrence, Adam B. 2004. "Does It Matter What the Presidents Say? The Influence of Presidential Rhetoric on the Public Agenda, 1946–2003." Ph. D. Diss., University of Pittsburgh.

Lawrence, Regina G., and W. Lance Bennett. 2001. "Rethinking Media Politics and Public Opinion: Reactions to the Clinton-Lewinsky Scandal." *Political Science Quarterly* 116 (fall): 425–46.

Leighley, Jan E. 2004. *Mass Media and Politics: A Social Science Perspective.* Boston: Houghton-Mifflin.

Lemert, James B. 1974. "Content Duplication by the Networks in Competing Evening Newscasts." *Journalism Quarterly* 51 (summer): 238–44.

Liebovich, Louis W. 2003. *Richard Nixon, Watergate, and the Press: A Historical Retrospective.* Westport, CT: Praeger.

Light, Paul C. 1999. *The President's Agenda: Domestic Policy Choice from Kennedy to Clinton.* Baltimore, MD: Johns Hopkins University Press.

Lind, Rebecca Ann, and David L Rarick. 1999. "Viewer Sensitivity to Ethical Issues in TV Coverage of the Clinton-Flowers Scandal." *Political Communication* 16 (April/June): 169–81.

Lowi, Theodore J. 1985. *The Personal President: Power Invested, Promise Unfulfilled.* Ithaca, NY: Cornell University Press.

Lynch, G. Patrick. 1999. "Presidential Elections and the Economy, 1872 to 1996: The Times They Are A'changin or the Song Remains the Same?" *Political Research Quarterly* 52 (December): 825–44.

———. 2002. "Midterm Elections and Economic Fluctuations: The Response of Voters over Time." *Legislative Studies Quarterly* 27 (May): 265–94.

Maltese, John Anthony. 1992. *Spin Control: The White House Office of Communications and the Management of Presidential News.* Chapel Hill: University of North Carolina Press.

———. 2003. "The President and the News Media." In *Media Power and Media Politics*, ed. Mark Rozell. Lanham, MD: Rowman and Littlefield, 1–24.

Mannheim, Jarol B. 1979. "The Honeymoon's Over: The News Conference and the Development of Presidential Style." *Journal of Politics* 41 (February): 55–74.

Mayer, William G. 1993. "Poll Trends: Trends in Media Use." *Public Opinion Quarterly* 57 (winter): 593–611.

Mazur, Allan. 1987. "Putting Radon on the Public Risk Agenda." *Science, Technology, and Human Values* 12 (summer/fall): 86–93.

McCartney, James. 1997. "News Life." *American Journalism Review* 19 (June): 19–25.

McCleary, Richard, and Richard A. Hay, Jr. 1980. *Applied Time Series Analysis for the Social Sciences.* Beverly Hills, CA: Sage.

McManus, John H. 1994. *Market-Driven Journalism: Let the Citizen Beware?* Thousand Oaks, CA: Sage Publications.

Milkis, Sidney M., and Michael Nelson. 1990. *The American Presidency: Origins and Development, 1776–1990.* Washington, DC: CQ Press.

Miller, Arthur H. 1999. "Sex, Politics, and Public Opinion: What Political Scientists Really Learned from the Clinton-Lewinsky Scandal." *PS: Political Science and Politics* 32 (December): 721–29.

Miller, Joanne M., and Jon A. Krosnick. 2000. "News Media Impact on the Ingredients of Presidential Evaluation: Politically Knowledgeable Citizens Are Guided By a Trusted Source." *American Journal of Political Science* 44 (April): 295–309.

Mindich, David T. Z. 1998. *Just the Facts: How "Objectivity" Came to Define American Journalism.* New York: New York University Press.

———. 2005. *Tuned Out: Why Americans Under 40 Don't Follow the News.* New York: Oxford University Press.

Miroff, Bruce. 1982. "Monopolizing the Public Space: The President As a Problem for Democratic Politics." In *Rethinking the Presidency*, ed. Thomas Cronin. Boston: Little, Brown, 218–32.

Morris, Edmund. 2001. *Theodore Rex.* New York: Random House.

Morris, Irwin. 2001. *Votes, Money, and the Clinton Impeachment.* Boulder, CO: Westview Press.

Morris, Jonathan S. 2005. "The Fox News Factor." *Harvard International Journal of Press/Politics* 10 (summer): 56–79.

Moy, Patricia, and Michael Pfau. 2000. *With Malice toward All? The Media and Public Confidence in Democratic Institutions.* Westport, CT: Praeger.

Moy, Patricia, Edith Manosevitch, Keith Stamm, and Kate Dunsmore. 2005. "Linking Dimensions of Internet Use and Civic Engagement." *Journalism and Mass Communication Quarterly* 82 (autumn): 571–86.

Moy, Patricia, and Dietram A Scheufele. 2000. "Media Effects on Political and Social Trust." *Journalism and Mass Communication Quarterly* 77 (winter): 744–59.

Mueller, John E. 1994. *Public Opinion in the Gulf War.* Chicago: University of Chicago Press.

Mutz, Diana C. 1992. "Mass Media and the Depoliticization of Personal Experiences." *American Journal of Political Science* 36 (May): 483–508.

———. 1994. "Contextualizing Personal Experience: The Role of the Mass Media." *Journal of Politics* 56 (August): 689–714.

Nadeau, Richard, Richard G. Niemi, David P. Fan, and Timothy Amato. 1999. "Elite Economic Forecasts, Economic News, Mass Economic Judgments, and Presidential Approval." *Journal of Politics* 61 (February): 109–35.

Neiva, Elizabeth MacIver. 1996. "Chain Building: The Consolidation of the American Newspaper Industry, 1953–1980." *Business History Review* 70 (spring): 1–41.

Neuman, W. Russell. 1990. "The Threshold of Public Attention." *Public Opinion Quarterly* 54, no. 2: 159–76.

———. 1991. *The Future of the Mass Audience.* New York: Cambridge University Press.

Newman, Brian. 2002. "Bill Clinton's Approval Ratings: The More Things Change, the More They Stay the same." *Political Research Quarterly* 55 (December): 781–804.

———. 2003. "Integrity and Presidential Approval, 1980–2000." *Public Opinion Quarterly* 67 (fall):335–67.

Noelle-Neumann, Elisabeth. 1984. *The Spiral of Silence: Public Opinion, Our Social Skin.* Chicago: University of Chicago Press.

Norris, Pippa. 2000. *A Virtuous Circle: Political Communications in Postindustrial Societies.* New York: Cambridge University Press.

Ostrom, Charles W., Jr., and Dennis M. Simon. 1985. "Promise and Performance: A Dynamic Model of Presidential Popularity."*American Political Science Review* 79 (June): 334–58.

———. 1989. "The Man in the Teflon Suit? The Environmental Connection, Political Drama, and Popular Support in the Reagan Presidency." *Public Opinion Quarterly* 53 (autumn): 353–87.

Owen, Diana. 1997. "Talk Radio and Evaluations of President Clinton." *Political Communication* 14, no. 3: 333–54.

Page, Benjamin I. 1996a. *Who Deliberates? Mass Media in Modern Democracy.* Chicago: University of Chicago Press.

———. 1996b. "Populistic Deliberation and Talk Radio." *Journal of Communication* 46 (spring): 33–54.

Page, Benjamin I., and Robert Y. Shapiro. 1992. *The Rational Public: Fifty Years of Trends in Americans' Policy Preferences.* Chicago: University of Chicago Press.

Page, Benjamin I., Robert Y. Shapiro, and Glenn R. Dempsey. 1987. "What Moves Public Opinion?" *American Political Science Review* 81 (March): 23–44.

Paletz, David L., and Robert M. Entman. 1980. "Presidents, Power, and the Press." *Presidential Studies Quarterly* 10 (summer): 416–26.

Patterson, Thomas E. 1994. *Out of Order.* New York: Vintage.

———. 2000. "Doing Well and Doing Good: How Soft News and Critical Journalism are Shrinking the News Audience and Weakening Democracy—And What News Outlets Can Do About It." Joan Shorenstein Center for Press, Politics, and Public Policy, John F. Kennedy School of Government, Harvard University.

———. 2002. *The Vanishing Voter: Public Involvement in an Age of Uncertainty.* New York: Knopf.

Pfau, Michael, Jaeho Cho, and Kirsten Chong. 2001. "Communication Forms in U.S. Presidential Campaigns: Influences on Candidate Perceptions and the Democratic Process." *Harvard International Journal of Press/Politics* 6 (fall): 88–105.

Pfau, Michael, and Kathleen E. Kendall. 1997. "Influence of Communication during the Distant Phase of the 1996 Republican Presidential Primary." *Journal of Communication* 47(autumn): 6–26.

Pfau, Michael, and Patricia Moy. 1998. "The Influence of Political Talk Radio on Confidence in Democratic Institutions." *Journalism and Mass Communication Quarterly* 75, no. 4: 730–45.

Pfiffner, James P. 2004. *The Character Factor: How We Judge America's Presidents.* College Station, TX: Texas A&M University Press.

Pierson, Paul. 2004. *Politics in Time: History, Institutions, and Social Analysis.* Princeton, NJ: Princeton University Press.

Pika, Joseph A. 1991. "Opening Doors for Kindred Souls: The White House Office of Public Liaison." In *Interest Group Politics*, ed. Allan J. Cigler and Burdett A. Loomis. 3d ed. Washington, DC: CQ Press, 277–98.

———. 1993. "Reaching Out to Organized Interests: Public Liaison in the Modern White House." In *The Presidency Reconsidered*, ed. Richard W. Waterman. Itasca, IL: F. E. Peacock, 45–168.

Pious, Richard M. 1999/2000. "The Paradox of Clinton Winning and the Presidency Losing." *Political Science Quarterly* 114 (winter): 569–84.

Ponder, Stephen. 1998. *Managing the Press: Origins of the Media Presidency, 1897–1933.* New York: St. Martin's.

Poole, Keith T., and Howard Rosenthal. 1996. *Congress: A Political-Economic History of Roll Call Voting.* New York: Oxford University Press.

Popkin, Samuel. 1998. "When the People Decline to Be Spun." *New York Times*, November 10, 1998, A29.

Posner, Richard A. 1999. *An Affair of State: The Investigation, Impeachment, and Trial of President Clinton.* Cambridge, MA: Harvard University Press.

Powell, Richard J. 1999. "'Going Public' Revisited: Presidential Speechmaking and the Bargaining Setting in Congress." *Congress and the Presidency* 26 (fall):153–70.

Price, Vincent, and John Zaller. 1993. "Who Gets the News? Alternative Measures of News Reception and Their Implications for Research." *Public Opinion Quarterly* 57 (summer): 133–64.

Prior, Markus. 2003. "Any Good News in Soft News? The Impact of Soft News Preference on Political Knowledge." *Political Communication* 20 (April/June): 173–90.

———. 2005. "News vs. Entertainment: How Increasing Media Choice Widens Gaps in Political Knowledge and Turnout." *American Journal of Political Science* 49 (July): 577–92.

Project for Excellence in Journalism. 1998. "Changing Definitions of News." Available at http://www.journalism.org/resources/research/reports/definitions/subjects.asp (Journalism.org, March 6, 1998).

———. 2004. "The State of the News Media 2004: An Annual Report on American Journalism." Available at http://www.stateofthenewsmedia.org. (Journalism.org).

———. 2005. "The State of the News Media 2004: An Annual Report on American Journalism." Available at http://www.stateofthemedia.org/2005/index.asp.(Journalism.org).

Putnam, Robert D. 2000. *Bowling Alone: The Collapse and Revival of American Community*. New York: Simon and Schuster.

Rae, Nicol C., and Colton C. Campbell. 2003. *Impeaching Clinton: Partisan Strife on Capitol Hill*. Lawrence: University Press of Kansas.

Ragsdale, Lyn. 1997. "Disconnected Politics: Public Opinion and Presidents." In *Understanding Public Opinion*, ed. Barbara Norrander and Clyde Wilcox. Washington, DC: CQ Press, 229–51.

———. 1998. *Vital Statistics on the Presidency: Washington to Clinton*. Washington, DC: CQ Press.

Rainie, Lee, Michael Cornfield, and John Horrigan. 2005. *The Internet and Campaign 2004*. Pew Internet and American Life Project, The Pew Research Center for the People and the Press, March 6, 2005. Available at http://www.pewinternet.org.

Reese, S. D., and Lucig Danielian. 1989. "Intermedia Influence and the Drug Issue: Converging on Cocaine." In *Communication Campaigns about Drugs*, ed. Pamela Shoemaker. Hillsdale, NJ: Erlbaum, 29–46.

Reiter, Dan, and Allan C. Stam. 2002. *Democracies at War*. Princeton, NJ: Princeton University Press.

Renshon, Stanley. 1998. "President Clinton's Troubles and Ours. Address to the Academy of Leadership, December 7, 1998. (Full text of the address is available at http://www.academy.umd.edu/publications/presidential_leadership/renshon.htm).

———. 2002a. "The Polls: The Public's Response to the Clinton Scandal, Part 1: Inconsistent Theories, Contradictory Evidence." *Presidential Studies Quarterly* 32 (March): 169–84.

———. 2002b. "The Polls: The Public's Response to the Clinton Scandal, Part 2: Diverse Explanations, Clearer Consequences." *Presidential Studies Quarterly* (June): 412–27.

Riffe, Daniel, Brenda Ellis, Momo K. Rogers, Roger L. Van Ommeren, and Kieran Woodman. 1986. "Gatekeeping and the Network News Mix." *Journalism Quarterly* 63 (summer): 315–21.

Rivers, Douglas, and Nancy L. Rose. 1985. "Passing the President's Program: Public Opinion and Presidential Influence in Congress." *American Journal of Political Science* 29 (May): 183–96.

Robinson, Michael J., and Andrew Kohut. 1988. "Believability and the Press." *Public Opinion Quarterly* 52 (summer):174–89.

Rogers, Everett M. 2003. *Diffusion of Innovations*. 5th ed. New York: Free Press.

Rosen, Jay and Paul Taylor. 1992. *The New News v. The Old News: The Press and Politics in the 1990s*. New York: Twentieth Century Fund Press.

Rozell, Mark J. 1995. "The Limits of White House Image Control." *Political Science Quarterly* 108 (fall): 453–80.

———. 1995. "Presidential Image-Makers on the Limits of Spin Control." *Presidential Studies Quarterly* 25 (winter): 67–90.

Rozell, Mark J., and Clyde Wilcox, eds. 2000. *The Clinton Scandal and the Future of American Government.* Washington, DC: Georgetown University Press.

Ryfe, David Michael. 1999. "'Betwixt and Between': Woodrow Wilson's Press Conferences and the Transition toward the Modern Presidency." *Political Communication* 16 (January–March): 77–94.

Sabato, Larry J. 1991. *Feeding Frenzy: How Attack Journalism Has Transformed Politics.* New York: Free Press.

Schiller, Dan. 1981. *Objectivity and the News: The Public and the Rise of Commercial Journalism.* Philadelphia: University of Pennsylvania Press

Schudson, Michael. 1978. *Discovering the News: A Social History of American Newspapers.* New York: Basic Books.

———. 1998. *The Good Citizen: A History of American Civic Life.* New York: Martin Kessler Books.

Shah, Dhavan V., Mark D. Watts, David Domke, and David P. Fan. 2002. "News Framing and the Cueing of Issue Regimes: Explaining Clinton's Public Approval in Spite of Scandal." *Public Opinion Quarterly* 66 (fall): 339–70.

Shaw, Daron R., and Bartholomew H. Sparrow. 1999. "From the Inner Ring Out: News Congruence, Cue-Taking, and Campaign Coverage." *Political Research Quarterly* 52 (June): 323–51.

Shoemaker, Pamela, and Stephen Reese. 1996. *Mediating the Message: Theories of Influence on Mass Media Content.* 2d ed. New York: Pearson.

Slattery, Karen, Mark Doremus, and Linda Marcus. 2001. "Shifts in Public Affairs Reporting on the Network Evening News: A Move Toward the Sensational." *Journal of Broadcasting and Electronic Media* 45 (spring): 290–312.

Smoller, Fred T. 1986. "The Six O'Clock Presidency: Patterns of Network News Coverage of the President." *Presidential Studies Quarterly* 16, no. 1: 31–49.

———. 1990. *The Six O'Clock Presidency: A Theory of Presidential Press Relations in the Age of Television.* New York: Praeger.

Smyth, D. J., and S. W. Taylor. 2003. "Presidential Popularity: What Matters Most, Macroeconomics or Scandals?" *Applied Economics Letters* 10 (July):585–88.

Sparrow, Bartholomew H. 1999. *Uncertain Guardians: The News Media as a Political Institution.* Baltimore, MD: Johns Hopkins University Press.

Starr, Paul. 2004. *The Creation of the Media: Political Origins of Modern Communications.* New York: Basic Books.

Stempel, Guido H. III. 1985. "Gatekeeping: The Mix of Topics and the Selection of Stories." *Journalism Quarterly* 62 (winter): 791–815.

Sundquist, James L. 1968. *Politics and Policy: The Eisenhower, Kennedy, and Johnson Years.* Washington, DC: Brookings.

Tewksbury, David. 2003. "What Do Americans Really Want to Know? Tracking the Behavior of News Readers on the Internet." *Journal of Communication* 53 (December): 694–710.

Tidmarch, Charles M., and John J. Pitney. 1985. "Covering Congress." *Polity* 17 (spring): 463–83.

Tifft, Susan E. 1999. *The Trust: The Private and Powerful Family behind the New York Times.* Boston: Little, Brown.

Tsfati, Yariv. 2003. "Media Skepticism and Climate of Opinion Perception." *International Journal of Public Opinion Research* 15, no. 1: 65–82.

Tuchman, Gaye. 1973. "Making News by Doing Work: Routinizing the Unexpected." *American Journal of Sociology* 78, no. 1: 110–31.

Underwood, Doug. 1998. "Market Research and the Audience for Political News." In *The Politics of News: The News of Politics*, ed. Doris Graber, Denis McQuail, and Pippa Norris. Washington, DC: CQ Press, 171–92.

Verba, Sidney, and Norman Nie. 1972. *Participation in America: Political Democracy and Social Equality.* New York: Harper and Row.

Waterman, Richard W., Robert Wright, and Gilbert St. Clair. 1999. *The Image-Is-Everything Presidency: Dilemmas in American Leadership.* Boulder, CO: Westview Press.

Wattenberg, Martin P. 2004. "The Changing Presidential Media Environment." *Presidential Studies Quarterly* 34 (September): 557–72.

Welch, Reed L. 2000. "Is Anybody Watching? The Audience for Televised Presidential Addresses." *Congress and the Presidency* 27 (spring): 41–58.

Welch, Richard E. 1988. *The Presidencies of Grover Cleveland.* Lawrence: University Press of Kansas.

West, Darrell M. 1991. "Television and Presidential Popularity in America." *British Journal of Political Science* 21 (April): 199–214.

———. 2001. *The Rise and Fall of the Media Establishment.* Boston: Bedford/St. Martin's.

White, Graham J. 1979. *FDR and the Press.* Chicago: University of Chicago Press.

Wicker, Tom. 1966. "In the Nation: The Heel of Achilles Johnson." *New York Times*, November 6, 1966, E11.

Williams, Andrew Paul, and John C. Tedesco, eds. 2006. *The Internet Election: Perspectives on the Web in Campaign 2004.* Lanham, MD: Rowman and Littlefield.

Winfield, Betty Houchin. 1990. *FDR and the News Media.* Urbana, IL: University of Illinois Press.

Yanovitzky, Itzhak, and Joseph N. Cappella. 2001. "Effect of Call-In Political Talk Radio Shows on Their Audiences: Evidence from a Multi-Wave Panel Analysis." *International Journal of Public Opinion Research* 13 (winter): 377–97.

Yioutas, Julie, and Ivana Segvic. 2003. "Revisiting the Clinton/Lewinsky Scandal: The Convergence of Agenda Setting and Framing." *Journalism and Mass Communication Quarterly* 80 (autumn): 567–83.

Young, Gary, and William B. Perkins. 2005. "Presidential Rhetoric, the Public Agenda, the End of the Golden Age of Television." *Journal of Politics* 67 (November): 1190–1205.

Zaller, John R. 1992. *The Nature and Origins of Mass Opinion.* Cambridge, MA: Cambridge University Press.

———. 1998a. "Monica Lewinsky's Contribution to Political Science." *PS: Political Science and Politics* 33 (June): 182–89.

———. 1998b. "The Rule of Product Substitution in Presidential Campaign News." *Annals of the American Academy of Political and Social Science* 560 (November): 111–28.

———. 1999. *A Theory of Media Politics: How the Interests of Politicians, Journalists, and Citizens Shape the News.* Manuscript draft.

———. 2003. "A New Standard of News Quality: Burglar Alarms for the Monitorial Citizen." *Political Communication* 20 (April–June): 109–30.

Zeidenstein, Harvey G. 1983. "White House Perceptions of News Media Bias." *Presidential Studies Quarterly* 13 (summer): 345–56.